Time Perception and the Sense of Sight in Islamic Traditions

CHRONOI

Zeit, Zeitempfinden, Zeitordnungen

Time, Time Awareness, Time Management

Edited by
Eva Cancik-Kirschbaum, Christoph Markschies and
Hermann Parzinger

on behalf of the Einstein Center Chronoi

Volume 25

Time Perception and the Sense of Sight in Islamic Traditions

Edited by
Hannelies Koloska

DE GRUYTER

ISSN 2701-1453
ISBN 978-3-11-224002-1
ISBN 978-3-11-224003-8 (PDF)
ISBN 978-3-11-224004-5 (EPUB)
DOI https://doi.org/10.1515/9783112240038

Library of Congress Control Number: 2026934615

Bibliographic information published by the Deutsche Nationalbibliothek
The Deutsche Nationalbibliothek lists this publication in the Deutsche Nationalbibliografie; detailed bibliographic data are available on the Internet at https://dnb.dnb.de.

De Gruyter and Walter de Gruyter GmbH are part of De Gruyter Brill.
www.degruyterbrill.com

Questions about General Product Safety Regulation:
productsafety@degruyterbrill.com

Acknowledgements

This volume grew out of a workshop, hosted and funded by the Einstein Center Chronoi Berlin in 2024. The idea behind it was born earlier, during a meeting with Stefanie Rabe overlooking Jerusalem, as we talked about our times. Stefanie Rabe, then Research Associate at the Einstein Center Chronoi, brought our initial idea to institutional life, helping to organize and facilitate the workshop. I am deeply grateful to her, and to the Board of the Einstein Center Chronoi — Eva Cancik-Kirschbaum, Christoph Markschies, and Hermann Parzinger — who, as editors of this series, welcomed the volume with generosity and confidence, and whose support made the whole project possible from the outset. My thanks go equally to Franziska Küster, Research Associate at the Einstein Center Chronoi, whose careful editorial work, attending to language, consistency, and coherence across all contributions, has been essential to bringing this volume to completion.

My deepest gratitude goes to all the contributors to this volume. I am especially grateful to my colleagues of the VISIONIS project, who, when first approached, were perhaps more enthused by the prospect of a trip to Berlin, but who, once gathered, found themselves caught by the question of how vision relates to time. Special thanks are due to Filiz Tütüncü Çağlar and Jack Shardlow for their contributions and for their willingness to think across disciplinary boundaries and bring new perspectives to the conversation. I am also grateful to Sarah Zweig, who, during the opaque time of the Corona pandemic, invited me to join a small reading group on time perception in Late Antiquity — and who, without knowing it, set this entire project in motion.

I am grateful to the editorial team at De Gruyter, and especially to Jessica Bartz and Kalpana Sagayanathan, for their care and professionalism in seeing this book through to publication.

This volume was produced within the framework of the research project VISIONIS (*Vision and Visuality in the Qur'an and Early Islam*), funded by the European Research Council (ERC) under the European Union's Horizon Europe research and innovation programme, Grant Agreement No. 948051.

This book was written and edited in a time of wars, when questions of time, memory, and the observation of erasure of pasts and futures have acquired an urgency far beyond the academy's own horizons of perception. For every human being in Israel, Palestine, Lebanon, Sudan, Iran, Ukraine, and beyond, who could not see their time fulfilled, while we continued to see, to think, and to write.

Jerusalem, April 2026

Content

Part IV: **Philosophical and Comparative Perspectives**

Hannelies Koloska

Introduction: Time and Vision in Islamic Traditions

We speak of time as if it were visible. We say it passes, flows, stands still, or casts shadows. Such metaphors suggest that time is experienced through vision, or at least through modes of perception that react as if we were seeing. Yet, time remains invisible; what we see are its traces: shifting of shadows, fading of colours, or movements of bodies. Our languages and hence our thoughts are filled with this paradox: time is not an object of sight, but through vision we make time sensible.

This volume takes this paradox as its starting point and asks: How is time made visible in Islamic thought and practice? What role does seeing – sensory, intellectual, or spiritual – play in creating, measuring, or transcending time? How do different authors – jurists, poets, exegetes, philosophers, architects, and museologists – translate this relation into authority, form, and experience? It brings together scholars of Islamic thought, art, literature, and contemporary Western philosophy to explore these questions, offering a cross-disciplinary inquiry.

Over the past two decades or so, the study of vision, perception, and the senses in Islamic intellectual and artistic traditions has gained attention. Scholars such as Samir Akkach, Christian Lange, Berenike Metzler, Jamal Elias, or Wendy Shaw have, each in their own way, moved the discussion beyond the realm of art-historical form, iconographic meaning, or ethnological observation, toward the experiential, epistemological, and theological dimensions of seeing.[1] Drawing on sources from theology, philosophy, mysticism, literature, or art, they studied how vision or sensual perception in general mediates different modes of knowing. Vision and perception are not primarily understood as mechanical or biological abilities but as intellectual, cultural, and societal practices.

Parallel to these developments in visual and sensory studies, time and temporality have reemerged as categories in the study of Islam. The fullest accounts written on the relation between time and Islam have been published by Barbara

1 Akkach, Samer, ed. (2021). *Naẓar: Vision, Belief, and Perception in Islamic Cultures.* Leiden: Brill; Lange, Christian (2022), "Introduction: The sensory history of the Islamic world." *The Senses and Society*, 17.1, 1–7; Metzler, Berenike (2024), *Kulturen des Sehens. Begriffsgeschichtliche Untersuchungen zur Visualität im Islam.* Berlin/Boston: De Gruyter; Elias, Jamal J. (2012), *Aisha's Cushion. Religious Art, Perception, and Practice in Islam.* Cambridge, MA: Harvard University Press; Shaw, Wendy M. K. (2019), *What is "Islamic" Art? Between Religion and Perception*, Cambridge: Cambridge University Press.

 | https://doi.org/10.1515/9783112240038-001

Freyer Stowasser and Fadwa El Guindi.[2] The main difference between them is that Stowasser analyzes Islamic perceptions of time primarily through textual sources and historical interpretations, while El Guindi explores the experiential and ritual rhythms of time by emphasizing ethnographic and anthropological perspectives. Both their studies present time as a culturally and theologically constructed phenomenon, where theological consideration, human regulation, and scientific observation converge. Both integrate the distinction between different temporal epistemologies that developed across several overlapping strands in religious, philosophical, and anthropological scholarship and were adapted into Islamic sciences: it might be understood as cyclical or cosmological, reflecting natural recurrence, such as day and night, lunar phases, or seasons, where repetition generates meaning and stability. It can be conceived as linear or teleological, unfolding toward an ultimate goal or fulfilment. Time is also eschatological, oriented towards its own end and thus governed by expectation. Alongside these collective or cosmic perspectives stands a momentary or experiential conception of time, in which the instant becomes the locus of subjective awareness and divine presence. All models are not mutually exclusive; instead, they coexist and relate to one another.

Yet, despite this rich body of work, vision and time have been mainly treated as separate problems: one belonging to the study of visuality and sensory perception, the other to cosmology, history, or anthropology. An exception is Shahzad Bashir and his pathbreaking new form of scholarly publication, "Islamic Pasts and Futures."[3] For Bashir, time is not just measured or narrated, it is *seen from a position* – pasts and futures are imaginative constructs generated from a moving horizon of perception. This approach can be experienced through the digital interface that Bashir developed for his publication, which is deliberately non-linear and asynchronous, unfolding like a web of interlinked perspectives rather than a single temporal line.

What remains underexplored is how seeing itself functions as a temporal practice—how observation, witnessing, or remembrance create, measure, and transform time. This does not refer primarily to the self-explanatory act of measuring time through observation—such as through the movement of celestial bodies or the observation of lunar phases, to which Stowasser has given considerable attention—but rather to the deeper question of how vision itself structures temporal experience. How do acts of seeing or being seen, of bearing witness or recalling what was once seen, generate the right moment of action, temporal relations between past

---

2 Stowasser, Barbara Freyer (2014), *The Day Begins at Sunset. Perceptions of Time in the Islamic World*. London/New York: I.B. Tauris; El Guindi, Fadwa (2008), *By Noon Prayer. The Rhythm of Islam*. Oxford/New York: Berg.

3 Bashir, Shahzad (2022), *A New Vision for Islamic Pasts and Futures*. Cambridge, MA and London: The MIT Press. https://islamic-pasts-futures.org (last accessed on October 30, 2025).

and present, the transient and the eternal, or the visible and the unseen? These questions extend beyond textual or intellectual traditions into the realms of built space and material display. Architecture, for instance, can organize temporal experience through the movement of light, directing the gaze in ways that materialize theological rhythms. Likewise, a museum or an exhibition space stages time for its visitors, framing what is past as visible, ordering sequences, and mediating between historical distance and immediacy. How, then, do architectural and museological practices in Islamic contexts make time perceptible, or even participatory?

This volume brings both subjects into direct conversation and addresses these questions. Unlike previous studies that treated vision and time as distinct domains, this volume argues that, in Islamic thought and material culture, both are inextricably linked. Although the essays assembled here range from pre-Islamic poetry to Ottoman museology and contemporary philosophical reflection, they converge around the shared objective of inquiring into *how seeing and time generate one another*. Perception gives rise to temporality in multiple registers: whether in the sighting of the crescent moon in Mālik's Muwaṭṭaʾ, the witnessing of prophetic dreams, the shimmer of light in the mosque of Damascus, or the gaze of the museum visitor, vision does not merely record time—it constitutes it. Equally central is *the epistemic status of seeing*. From Ibn Qutayba's discussion about *naẓar* to modern Western philosophical debates on perception, sight oscillates between certainty and delusion. Visual immediacy serves both as a guarantor of truth and as a site where truth cannot be obtained without transmission and remembrance. The essays explore this tension, demonstrating how perception serves both as a source of knowledge and a site of doubt. A further thread concerns *the regulation of vision*. Jurists, exegetes, or architects discipline the gaze through the legal timing of prayer, the interpretation of dreams, or the architectural choreography of light. Vision, in these contexts, is never purely individual; it is guided, communal, and framed. To see is to see within a structure of authority. The *temporalities of remembrance* form another connective axis. The Qurʾānic emphasis on *dhikr* and the aesthetics of repetition in architecture and poetry render remembering an act of temporal re-creation: time not as linear succession but as a looping return through perception.

This volume is organized into four sections that examine the relationship between vision and time across different genres and periods of Islamic thought and practice and beyond: the juridical and theological regulation of vision and time, the poetic and scriptural creation of time, the architectural and institutional mediation of time perception, and the philosophical reflection on temporal experience. As you read, you are invited to follow the four sections as perspectives of seeing; from regulated seeing in law and theology (part I), to imaginative seeing in poetry and scripture (part II), embodied seeing in architecture and material culture (part III), and reflective seeing in philosophy (part IV), to explore how time becomes visible and is perceived, experienced, remembered, and understood.

Part I – Vision, Law, and Temporal Order

The opening section examines how early Islamic law and theology established seeing as a regulated act—an operation that grounds communal temporality in visual experience. **Yunus Hentschel**'s essay opens the volume with a study of Mālik's *Muwaṭṭaʾ*, showing how the text trains believers to find the right moment—to grasp *al-sāʿa* not merely as "hour" but as the kairotic instant when an act becomes a divine-human moment of immediate presence. He tracks how observing the sun, or the moon, transforms perception into legal timing, and how juristic procedures convert sight into communal synchrony. The central claim is that the Muwaṭṭaʾ makes vision a technique for producing the timely moment. Hentschel's analysis demonstrates how legal considerations operationalize the concept of seeing, such that actions like prayer or fasting occur when necessary, neither too early nor too late. In his reading, seeing does not just measure duration; it creates obligation by authorizing the moment. **Or Amir**'s essay turns inward, exploring how dream-visions (*ruʾyā*) make chronological time collapse. Working across ḥadīth and juristic materials, he shows that the dream is not a passive imagery but an event in which the temporal distance between the Prophet's age and the dreamer's present collapses into an immediate vision. The key finding is that seeing in dreams reopens the time of revelation—rendering the prophetic past directly accessible—and therefore unsettles the institutional mediation of tradition on which religious authority depends. Amir asks how jurists responded to this danger of immediacy, tracing their efforts to contain the validity of the dreams as such, but refraining from any legal or revelatory meaning of dream-vision: dreams may unveil truth, but only insofar as they confirm what is already revealed. A similar tension between religious authority built on temporal distance and direct interpretation of religious issues is studied by **Yehonatan Yahav.** He examines the polemic of Ibn Qutayba, inquiring how Ibn Qutayba objects to the claim of direct accessibility of knowledge and truth through sight and insight (*naẓar*). His study demonstrates that Ibn Qutayba decisively sides with the traditionists: for him, true knowledge cannot arise from unmediated reasoning or perception (*naẓar*), but only through the accumulated knowledge of the community over time (*tawāṭuʾ*). *Naẓar*, in his view, must be disciplined—helpful in recognizing the signs of God but never autonomous from the transmitted knowledge. Yahav's central insight is that in Ibn Qutayba's writings, time itself becomes the guarantor of truth: the repeated seeing and believing of generations confers certainty that no individual gaze can claim. In this way, Yahav's Ibn Qutayba emphasizes mediation just as Amir's jurists do: visual experiences gain authority only when they are subordinated to the long continuity of tradition.

Part II – Poetic and Qurʾānic Temporalities

The second part turns to the creation of time through words and imagery. **Ula Aweida**'s study of Ṭarafa ibn al-ʿAbd's Muʿallaqa brings the discussion to the pre-Islamic Arabic horizon of vision and time. Her essay is especially noteworthy for grounding itself in both primary and secondary Arabic sources—a body of scholarship that is often neglected. She examines how pre-Islamic poetic vision already formulates many of the questions that later theological and philosophical texts will formalize: how does one see and understand time, and how does the gaze transform transience into meaning? Aweida shows that Ṭarafa's descriptions perform time; the ruins (*aṭlāl*) make the past visible, the caravan embodies movement through the present, and the she-camel carries the poet toward the future; together they form a visual language and imagery of time. She explores how perception becomes an ethical and existential response to the erosion of life under *al-dahr* (fate, active time force). Ṭarafa's seeing is immediate and individual, yet it already anticipates the later tension between fleeting perception and enduring remembrance. Aweida's study thus demonstrates that the Arabic poetic tradition reminds us that Islamic debates on vision, law, and revelation are deeply rooted in a visual poetics of finitude and renewal. Continuing from Aweida's exploration of poetic vision, **Hannelies Koloska**'s study turns to the Qurʾān and its visualization of time. Her essay, based on both textual analysis and visual afterlives in miniature painting, examines how memory (*dhikr*), vision, and visualization operate together to create time as a textually anchored experience. Her central argument is that the Qurʾānic texts produce a simultaneous temporality of past, present, and future through narration techniques that include acts of seeing and recalling. The story of the Companions of the Cave (Q 18:9–26) serves as her key object, where sleep, awakening, and divine concealment turn perception into a measure of time. Her essay links literary and visual cultures, demonstrating how a later Falnāmah miniature continues Qurʾānic simultaneity by translating layered temporalities into spatial form.

Part III – Material Cultures and Time Perception

The third part inquires about spatial and institutional forms of visualized, embodied, or exhibited time. **Inbal Kol** examines how early mosque architecture conveyed theological and cosmological concepts of time through the medium of light, creating a sensory experience. Building on Wendy Shaw's concept of "seeing with the heart" and Henry Corbin's notion of the visible as a gateway to the invisible, Kol shows that early Islamic architects used natural and artificial light to synchronize human temporality with divine order. Her close reading of sites such as the Great Mosque of Damascus and Córdoba demonstrates how the modulation of light and shadow materialized the theology of time as both cyclical and ever-renewed. Kol's essay provides a crucial bridge to the textual analyses of earlier chapters: like Hentschel's juristic observation of time in Mālik's *Muwaṭṭaʾ* or Koloska's Qurʾānic visualization of simultaneity, Kol shows how theological temporality is translated into lived perception. Her contribution shows that mosque architecture not only shelters worship but performs theology. **Filiz Tütüncü Çağlar**'s essay turns to the establishment and creation of the Ottoman Imperial Museum (*Müze-i Hümâyûn*) as the modern arena in which time itself is curated and displayed. Her study examines how, during the late Ottoman period, practices of ordering time and establishing chronologies are translated into architectural and archaeological forms of perception, as well as into a historical logic of the museum. Her essay shows how the guided gaze becomes a tool of historical consciousness and political authority. Drawing on Ottoman archival records, catalogues, and contemporary commentaries in Arabic, Ottoman Turkish, and French, Tütüncü Çağlar demonstrates that the museum did not simply collect antiquities: it produced a specific outlook on time and history. Through acts of classification, labeling, and display, the museum arranged objects to visualize the empire's past as a continuous narrative of civilization. In Tütüncü Çağlar's reading, the museum in its own way extends the Qurʾānic and architectural logic of seeing as remembrance, set out by Koloska and Kol into the institutional age: what once appeared as divine pedagogy or luminous presence now emerges as curatorial vision. The gaze is here reconfigured as state vision, a bureaucratic seeing that organizes collective memory. Her essay thus closes the historical arc of the volume: from the poet's personal eye and the jurist's regulated sight to the curator's administrative gaze, where the act of seeing itself is absorbed into the apparatus of displaying history.

Part IV – Philosophical and Comparative Perspectives

Concluding the volume, **Jack Shardlow**'s essay steps back to reflect on the entire constellation of studies, asking what happens when Islamic and Western philosophies of time and perception are brought into conversation. His paper serves as a philosophical mirror, examining how the various forms of seeing explored in this volume—poetic, juridical, visionary, architectural, and institutional—illuminate fundamental questions about how humans experience and think about time. Shardlow's guiding question is how seeing time differs from thinking time, and how Islamic concepts relate to contemporary debates about the "now," the flow of time, and the nature of temporal consciousness. Drawing on the analytic and phenomenological traditions of Western philosophy, Shardlow traces how Islamic reflections on vision and temporality resonate with—and challenge—modern notions of the *nunc fluens* (the flowing now) and the *nunc differens* (the extended now). Time, he argues, is never simply "seen" from outside but always *inhabited* through embodied acts of seeing, remembering, and witnessing. In his reading, each essay contributes a distinct model of perceiving time: Hentschel's disciplined seeing of the right moment; Amir's dream-vision collapsing mediation; Yahav's transmission-bound gaze; Aweida's poetic eye; Koloska's revelatory remembrance; Kol's luminous architecture of the moment; and Çağlar's curatorial ordering of history. Shardlow reinterprets these as variations on the problem of the "flowing present", where perception both creates and confines temporal experience. His reflection transforms the volume's case studies into a philosophical argument: that to see in Islamic thought is never a neutral perception, but always an act of temporal participation.

Part I: **Vision, Law, and Temporal Order**

Yunus V. Hentschel

Observing the Moment

Time and Seeing in the *Muwaṭṭa'* of Mālik b. Anas (d. 179/795)

> According to Mālik, [. . .] the Messenger of God (pbuh) would supplicate saying, 'God, Cleaver of dawn from darkness, who makes the night a time of repose and who made the sun and the moon the means to reckon the passage of time (*wa-sh-shamsi wa-l-qamari ḥusbānan*)! Discharge my debts, free me from need, and enable me to use my sight (*baṣarī*), hearing, and strength in Your cause!'[1]

Muslim worship is fundamentally based on awareness of time. By harmonizing body and mind with cosmological movement, the believer enters the right moment for prayer. Islamic time is not organized by an arithmetical construction of equal-length time units. Rather, it continuously re-emerges through the ever-changing position of the believer in relation to the celestial bodies. The criteria for detecting the timely instant for prayer rest on sight-based perception. This includes observing the position of the sun and the stage of the moon phase, which also marks the start and end points of consecrated timeframes. The moments of time for Muslim prayer and ritual are therefore never fixed but continually shift in relation to celestial movement. This contrasts sharply with contemporary standardized clock time and a globalized calendar. Yet Islam's dynamic time is not obstructed by this standardization; it operates on its own level as a lived practice rather than an abstract system. This practice is rooted in Islam's foundational sources and has been performed by Muslims since then.

Among these foundational sources stands the *Muwaṭṭa'* of Mālik b. Anas (d. 179/795). The *Muwaṭṭa'* is the earliest surviving Islamic legal treatise, which became formative for Muslim jurisprudence and ritual regulation.[2] This collection contains reports about the Prophet Muḥammad, his companions, the following generations, as well as legal and exegetical interpretations by Mālik. Mālik declared the practice of the people of Medina (*'amal ahl al-madīna*)—safeguarded by the local scholars—as the guarantee for the authenticity of the Prophet's tradition. He, thereby, expands the sayings and deeds of the Prophet (*ḥadīth*, pl. *aḥādīth*) with those of esteemed early Muslims, who were active in Medina until Mālik's time. Mālik's presentation and interpretation of the Prophetic and Medinese traditions aim to

1 Mālik, *al-Muwaṭṭa'*, 203 [142]. The first page number refers here and in the following to the 2019 edition and English translation by Fadel and Monette. The page number in the square brackets refers to the Arabic edition of 2013, when I cite the transliterated Arabic terms.

2 Cf. El Shamsy 2013, 17–22; Melchert 2001; Schacht 2012; Tottoli 2014; Wymann-Landgraf 2013.

serve as a blueprint for Muslim ritualistic, juridical, and societal conduct, and—as I explore here—time reckoning.

In the course of my analysis of the *Muwaṭṭa*ʾ's temporal consciousness, I demonstrate that its time observance is realized through the believer's awareness of the right moment for worship and socioreligious behavior. Visual perception is key to detecting these moments: the positions of the sun and moon, light-quality, color, and the casting of shadows all serve as temporal markers. These junctures open timeframes in which one of the five prayers and other ritual practices should be performed. Recognizing the temporal-observational markers allows the believer to enter and leave sacred time-spaces, which are actualized through obligatory prayers, vigils, the fasting period of Ramaḍān, and the Pilgrimage (*ḥajj*). To conceptualize these time-spaces, I begin my analysis by presenting the categories of time in the *Muwaṭṭa*ʾ and how they are utilized there. These categories give structure to ritual, while also facilitating societal and financial communal interests. Next, I inquire into the connection between time reckoning and visuality. Subsequently, I explore the tension between the immediacy of the prescribed time and the fluidity of time phases, in which a prayer is valid. Based on this, I reflect on the term *sāʿa* as a special moment and sacred time-space, which correlates semantically with the unforeseeable, but perpetually possible coming of the Last Hour.

While scholars have noted the importance of time in Islamic practice,[3] no detailed analysis has examined how the *Muwaṭṭa*ʾ specifically constructs temporal consciousness through visual observation.[4] This study fills that gap by demonstrating that Mālik's time reckoning model operates through a sophisticated system of sight-based markers that enable believers to navigate between ordinary and sacred time.

1 Time Structure in the *Muwaṭṭa*ʾ

How did early Muslims structure time? To answer this question requires first acknowledging the dominance—and particularity—of contemporary temporal frameworks. In the modern globalized understanding, time is organized by abstracted, standardized units of 24 hours, 60 minutes, and 60 seconds, which are

3 Cf. the scholars cited in this article, particularly El Guindi 2008. Additionally, cf. Bashir 2014 on the multi-strand historiographies in post-classical Islam; and Bauer 2003 on the explorative, semantic-temporal play in Ottoman chronogram-composing.

4 Claire Gallien briefly addresses the visuality of the *Muwaṭṭa*ʾ's time reckoning in her forthcoming article on Sacred Time in Islam in the St Andrews Encyclopaedia of Theology.

uncoupled from the celestial bodies' asymmetrical and therefore changing intervals. Moreover, the prevailing Gregorian Calendar and Christian historiography are disguised as being universal in calling it the Common Era. Although overshadowed by the current hegemony of Western time standardization, human beings have developed a multitude of systems of time reckoning and "different cultural conceptualizations of time".[5] Muslims have managed their time throughout 1400 years, often negotiating with multiple other time models. The Islamic time model and calendar reform were already a crucial marker in the emergence of Islam.[6] Although different from the Western model, Islamic time is structured and standardized but in different ways. According to Eviatar Zerubavel, "if time is to be shared as an intersubjective social reality, it ought to be *standardized*"[7] and translated into a "*standard time language*".[8] Early Muslims, represented here through Mālik's interpretation of the Medinese tradition, accordingly, structured their temporal experience by applying specific categories and nomenclature.

In the *Muwaṭṭa'*, the day (*yawm*) is the primary unit for time management. The day (*yawm*) stands either for the full night-daylight cycle (*al-laylu wa-n-nahār*)[9] or—like the term *nahār*—expresses the daylight part of the day (*fī l-yawmi wa-l-laylati*).[10] There are relational subdivisions of this daylight-night unit, like the early parts of the day (*awwal nahārihi*)[11] or divisions of the nighttime in thirds, halves, or "the end of the night (*ākhir al-layl*)".[12] Some of these sub-daylight/night divisions can contain a special status for spiritual elevation:

> When only one-third of the night remains (*ḥatta yabqā thulthu l-layli l-ākhiru*), our Lord, Blessed and Sublime is He, descends to the lowest heaven of this world and says, 'Who is supplicating Me, so that I may fulfill his request? [. . .] Who is seeking My forgiveness, so that I might forgive him?'[13]

The night has a special quality for voluntary prayers as reflected in the *Muwaṭṭa'*'s separate chapter on vigils (*kitāb ṣalāti l-layl*).[14] Additionally, the night (*layl*) can—like *yawm*—also serve as a counting marker for a whole day. This is particularly the case when the number of nights someone stays in a place determines their status as

5 El Guindi 2008, 31; cf. El Guindi 2008, 81–89, and *passim*; Stowasser 2014, 4–13.
6 Böwering 1997, 63–65; El Guindi 2008, 102–109, 124–126.
7 Zerubavel 1982a, 2; italics in the original.
8 Zerubavel 1982a, 3; italics in the original.
9 Mālik, *al-Muwaṭṭa'*, 142 [80], also 172 [115].
10 Mālik, *al-Muwaṭṭa'*, 174 [118].
11 Mālik, *al-Muwaṭṭa'*, 132 [70].
12 Mālik, *al-Muwaṭṭa'*, 142 [80].
13 Mālik, *al-Muwaṭṭa'*, 203 [143].
14 Mālik, *al-Muwaṭṭa'*, 141–147 [79–86].

resident or traveler, and consequently, whether prayer can be shortened: "Whoever decides to stay in a place for at least four nights (*iqāmata arbaʿa layālin*) when travelling should perform the prayer in full."[15] The night can also define other time periods like being in the consecrated state of a pilgrim. ʿĀʾisha (d. 58/678), one of the Prophet's wives and a prime Hadith-transmitter, said: "The restrictions of the consecrated state last only ten days [in Arabic: nights] (*ʿashru layālin*)".[16] Usually, however, *yawm* is the category for counting (*ʿaddad*) the days to indicate the right point in time for entering and leaving a ritualistic time-phase, like the consecrated state of the Pilgrimage.[17] The counting of days is crucial for assessing the starting and ending of the fasting month Ramaḍān.

During Ramaḍān, the daylight time serves as the main regulatory unit, constituting the period of fasting. From the breaking of dawn until sunset, Muslims refrain from eating, drinking, smoking, and having sexual intercourse. If a believer breaks the abstention during daylight hours, the fast of the whole day is broken and should be compensated for.[18] Accordingly, a full day is the unit to be counted when a believer is not able to fast and has to make up this day later instead (*yawman makānahu*):[19] "Whoever does not observe the Ramaḍān fast because of an illness or travel should make up the days he missed by fasting them consecutively, as though they were in the month of Ramaḍān."[20] If the person is incapable of fasting, he or she must give charity for every day missed.[21] A believer should also fast a fixed number of days, which means the daylight time of these days, when he or she does not fulfill the correct sacrifice during the Pilgrimage: "He must fast three days during the Pilgrimage (*thalāta ayyāmi fī l-ḥajji*) and seven days when he returns home (*wa-sabʿatin idhā rajaʿa*)."[22] These regulations depend on accurately determining when days begin and end.

In Islam, the start and end of a day and a month are counted by sunset.[23] Mālik nuances this understanding by elaborating on the case when the crescent moon is seen already during daylight on the last fasting day of Ramaḍān. Seeing the new moon signals the beginning of the new month, in this case of Shawwāl, and, therefore, the end of the fasting period. Mālik clarifies, however, that one has to fast until

15 Mālik, *al-Muwaṭṭaʾ*, 160 [101]; next to other reports with different numbers of nights and estimations when the prayer-shortening is applicable due to travelling.
16 Mālik, *al-Muwaṭṭaʾ*, 304 [241].
17 Mālik, *al-Muwaṭṭaʾ*, 311 [247].
18 Mālik, *al-Muwaṭṭaʾ*, 260, and *passim*.
19 Mālik, *al-Muwaṭṭaʾ*, 264 [205].
20 Mālik, *al-Muwaṭṭaʾ*, 264 [205].
21 Mālik, *al-Muwaṭṭaʾ*, 267, 306.
22 Mālik, *al-Muwaṭṭaʾ*, 297 [234].
23 Stowasser 2014, 21, and *passim*.

sunset. Although the moon has been sighted, the new month is counted from the following sunset. Mālik rules that despite the visibility of the moon during daylight, "the crescent moon belongs to the coming night (*fa-innamā huwa hilālu l-laylata llatī ta'atī*)".[24] To further define how the days are counted as wholes, Mālik discusses the case of a man who converts to Islam on the last day of Ramaḍān. Mālik says: "He is under no obligation to make up any prior fasting days. Rather, he begins fasting from that day onward. I prefer that he make up the fasting day on which he embraced Islam insofar as he was a Muslim for part of that day (*an yaqḍiya l-yawma lladhī aslama fīhi*)."[25]

In a narration, *yawman* can mean someday, an unspecified day at a particular time,[26] or the present day, the contemporary.[27] *Yawm* can also serve as a carrier of a historiographic specification (see below). The Arabic names of ordinary weekdays, though, express the simple counting from the first to the seventh day, except for the sixth, the day of the Islamic Friday-prayer-congregation (*yawm al-jum'a*). This day is distinctly "marked,"[28] the significance of which I discuss in the next section. In the *Muwaṭṭa'*, only Monday, the second day of the week (*yawm al-ithnayn*), and Tuesday, the third day (*yawm al-thulāthā'*), are named. This means that the naming of the days and the concept of the seven-day week were in existence and used during the time of Mālik. In the example given, however, spelling out the weekdays does not reveal a specific inherent meaning of these days but that something substantial happened on two subsequent days and not later: "According to Mālik, it reached him that the Messenger of God (pbuh) died on a Monday and was buried on a Tuesday (*tuwuffī fī yawma l-ithnayni wa-dufina yawma th-thulāthā'ī*)."[29] While this example illustrates the functional use of weekday names, certain days in the *Muwaṭṭa'* transcend mere chronological marking to embody hallowed significance.

2 Days with Special Status

In contrast to the unmarked weekdays, the *Muwaṭṭa'* singles out days attributed with special sacred status, which require distinct ritual behavior. Most importantly, Friday—the Day of Congregation (*yawm al-jum'a*) —is not only the pulse-giv-

24 Mālik, *al-Muwaṭṭa'*, 254 [194].
25 Mālik, *al-Muwaṭṭa'*, 266 [206].
26 Mālik, *al-Muwaṭṭa'*, 74, 371 [9, 305].
27 Mālik, *al-Muwaṭṭa'*, 177 [119].
28 Zerubavel 1987, 349.
29 Mālik, *al-Muwaṭṭa'*, 214 [154].

ing "peak day"[30] of the Islamic week but also possesses a supra-temporal quality. According to one prophetic discourse in the *Muwaṭṭa'*, Friday is the day on which Adam was created and when the Last Day will occur. Friday, thereby, marks both the beginning and end of worldly time. In between, Fridays are a cyclic condensation of the human struggle of closeness and distance from God represented by Adam.

> The most auspicious day upon which the sun rises is Friday (*khayru yawmin ṭalaʿat ʿalayhi sh-shamsu yawmu l-jumuʿati*). Adam was created on that day, and on it he fell from the Garden to the Earth; repentance was granted to him on that day, and on that day he died. The Hour of Divine Judgement is on that day (*fīhā taqūmu s-sāʿatu*). Every moving creature is attentive on Friday, from morning to sunset (*min ḥīni tuṣbiḥu ḥattā taṭluʿa sh-shamsu*), in fear of the Hour, except for jinn and humans (*shafaqan min as-sāʿati illā l-jinna wa-l-insa*).[31]

This Hadith continues to discuss the *sāʿa* as both the eschatological Hour and a particular, recurring moment in time, which I will examine later. For now, I highlight the special status Friday has in Muslim creed and practice through the congregational prayer, established in the *Muwaṭṭa'*, which contains two separate chapters for the rules governing *yawm al-jumʿa*.[32]

Beyond Friday's weekly recurrence, the *Muwaṭṭa'* designates certain days as possessing heightened spiritual significance. Notably, the ten-day period of the Pilgrimage in the month Dhū l-Ḥijja contains a condensation of days with special status. During this time, the pilgrim enters a consecrated state, subject to special rules regarding purity, clothes, and behavior.[33] The peak of the Pilgrimage is the ninth day, the Day of ʿArafa (*yawm ʿarafa*), which is seen as the "best day for supplications."[34] The exit point of the consecrated state happens on *yawm al-naḥr* when the sacrifice animal is slaughtered. Mālik specifies that the slaughter concludes the consecrated state but must not happen "before dawn breaks (*qabla fajri yawma n-naḥri*)" and that "everything should take place on that day—slaughter, donning clothes, grooming the body, and shaving—and none of it should occur before that day".[35]

Following the Pilgrimage and the fasting month of Ramaḍān, there are two sets of festive days: the Feast of Sacrifice (*ʿīd al-aḍḥā*) and the Feast of Breaking the Fast (*ʿīd al-fiṭr*). "Festivals often function as the main temporal reference point around which calendars revolve."[36] As the Islamic calendar strictly follows the lunar month,

30 Zerubavel 1987, 349.

31 Mālik, *al-Muwaṭṭa'*, 136 [74].

32 Mālik, *al-Muwaṭṭa'*, Book 5, 131–138 [69–76]; Book 8, 149–156 [87–96].

33 Mālik, *al-Muwaṭṭa'*, 281–356.

34 Mālik, *al-Muwaṭṭa'*, 204 [144]; on the special status of the Day of ʿArafa, cf. also 353.

35 Mālik, *al-Muwaṭṭa'*, 335 [270].

36 Durkheim acc. Zerubavel 1982b, 284–285.

its festive days are not related to seasons, equinoxes, etc., but are "movable".[37] Subsequently, there is no debate about coincidences with festivals of other religious traditions to establish a collective identity through differing dating, as it occurred in Christianity regarding Easter and Jewish Passover.[38] Still, the festive days seem to be crucial for Mālik, who puts a lot of effort into noting their special status.

Whereas Mālik names reports featuring different opinions on whether one should fast on *yawm ʿarafa*,[39] Mālik argues with several Hadiths that it is forbidden to fast on the first of the festival days (*ayyām at-tashrīq*),[40] and that "these are days for eating and drinking and for the remembrance of God."[41] Mālik supports the special ranking of the festive days with an exegetical alignment with the Qur'ān: "Magnifying God during the three Festival Days is obligatory for both men and women, whether in a group or individually, and whether they are present at Mīna or far away in distant lands. [. . .] The 'numbered days' (*al-ayyām al-maʿdūdāt*) [mentioned in Q 2:203] are the three Festival Days."[42] Mālik perceives only a limited number of days as religiously elevated, like *yawm al-jumʿa*, *yawm an-naḥr*, *yawm ʿarafa*, and the festive days (*ayyām at-tashrīq*). Additionally, Mālik cites reports that encourage the voluntary fasting on the Day of ʿĀshūra' (*yawm ʿāshūra'*).[43] He is, however, critical about common practices to attribute other days with specific practices, like the Six Days (*sittatu ayyām*) of Shawwāl on which people tend to fast. Mālik disapproves of this practice and declares it to be an "unauthorized innovation (*bidʿa*)".[44]

Having established the sacred significance of certain days, I now turn to the larger temporal units of months and years, which provide the cyclical framework for Islamic ritual life.

3 Month and Year

Just as certain days possess sacred status, so too do a number of months in the *Muwaṭṭa'* of which the month of Ramaḍān is the most distinct. The following two reports on the length of Ramaḍān not only contain the number of required fasting days but also define the length of a lunar, synodic month (*shahr*) as twenty-nine and

37 Stowasser 2014, 115.
38 Zerubavel 1982b; Zerubavel 1987, 350.
39 Mālik, *al-Muwaṭṭa'*, 320–321.
40 Mālik, *al-Muwaṭṭa'*, 320–321 [257].
41 Mālik, *al-Muwaṭṭa'*, 321.
42 Mālik, *al-Muwaṭṭa'*, 340–341 [276].
43 Mālik, *al-Muwaṭṭa'*, 260–261 [202].
44 Mālik, *al-Muwaṭṭa'*, 269–270 [210].

a half days. As days are counted as full units, the month in Muslim reckoning has either twenty-nine or thirty days. The start and end of the month are marked by the (theoretical) visibility of the crescent moon.[45]

> The month has twenty-nine days (*ash-shahru tisʿun wa-ʿishrūna*) so don't fast until you see the crescent moon of Ramadan (*fa-lā taṣūmū ḥattā taraw l-hilāla*), and don't celebrate the Feast of Breaking the Ramadan Fast (*ʿīd al-fiṭr*) until you see the crescent moon of Shawwāl. If the sky above you is cloudy, estimate when the moon should appear (*fa-in ghumma ʿalaykum fa-qdurū la-hu*) [...and according to the following report:] If the sky above you is cloudy, then fast a complete month of thirty days (*fa-in ghumma ʿalaykum fa-akmilū l-ʿadada/l-ʿiddata thalāthīna*).[46]

In addition, Mālik enlists the months for the "pilgrimage season" (*fī ashhuri l-ḥajj*), which lead from Ramaḍān to the time for the Pilgrimage (*ḥajj*), as having a special status: *Shawwāl, Dhū l-Qaʿda, Dhū l-Ḥijja.*[47] The Pilgrimage can only be performed in the first ten days of *Dhū l-Ḥijja.* By contrast, the *Muwaṭṭaʾ* contains differing estimations regarding the optimal time for the small pilgrimage or Visitation (*ʿumra*). If somebody performs the Visitation within the "pilgrimage season" and stays in Mecca until performing the Pilgrimage in the same year, this practice is called *tamattuʿ*, which requires distinct rulings.[48] The reports indicate that the Visitation can be performed at any time.[49] Mālik asserts, however, that the Visitation should not be performed "more than once a year."[50] Besides the months with special status, the 29/30-day period from a new moon to the next (*shahr*) can also serve as a measurement equivalent to the day regarding compensation, for instance, that one has to fast for two consecutive months (*shahrayn*).[51]

Twelve lunar months constitute one year (*ʿām* or *sana*). From a ritualistic standpoint, the Islamic year is a cyclical timeframe for locating the reoccurrence of Ramaḍān and the pilgrimage season, and the respective festive days. If compensation is due for missed fasting it must happen before the start of Ramaḍān in the coming year.[52] If one insufficiently performs the Pilgrimage, the Pilgrimage should be repeated in the following year (*ḥajj qābil/ʿāman qābilan*) to complete the current,

---

45 El Guindi 2008, 111–112; Stowasser 2014, 21–22.

46 Mālik, *al-Muwaṭṭaʾ*, 253 [193].

47 Mālik, *al-Muwaṭṭaʾ*, 297 [234]. Mālik's reports do not name Rajab as a month with a special status, which it had in pre-Islamic time, and was contested in early Islamic practice, cf. Talmon-Heller 2020, 134–147.

48 Mālik, *al-Muwaṭṭaʾ*, 297–298 [233–235], 356.

49 Mālik, *al-Muwaṭṭaʾ*, 297–299.

50 Mālik, *al-Muwaṭṭaʾ*, 299.

51 Mālik, *al-Muwaṭṭaʾ*, 259 [200].

52 Mālik, *al-Muwaṭṭaʾ*, 268.

failed Pilgrimage.[53] Further, the number of years can determine the status of being a resident. This is also relevant for the Pilgrimage, because there are variations in regulations of entering the consecrated state for residents of Mecca. In this context, Mālik gives the example of ʿAbd Allāh b. al-Zubayr, who "lived in Mecca for nine years (*aqāma bi-makkata tisʿa sinīn*)."[54]

The year is the standard unit of financial interest. The course of a year is the prime unit for executing the alms-tax (*zakāt*) and charity alms (*sadaqa*), as well as the corresponding assessment of property. The starting date of this course of the year (*yaḥūla ʿalayhi l-ḥawlu*) is the exact day (*min yawmihi dhālika*)[55] on which something is gained through buying, selling, or when something is coming out of the ground, like metal or grain in the harvest.[56] Payment is due on the very day the course of the year ends, or also during the month of the last day of the year's course.[57] The additional alms in connection with the Feast of Breaking the Fast should be paid from three days before the feast or, at the latest, before or immediately after the morning prayer of the Feast.[58] The tax of non-Muslims (*jizya*) is likewise collected annually.[59] Moreover, Mālik assesses that "alms-tax is due on gold ore and on any gold or silver jewelry that is not worn [and is above a certain amount, and that it] must be weighedt annually (*fī kulli ʿāmin*)."[60] Property and debt can be accumulated, and money borrowed over years (*sinīna* or *aʿwāman*).[61] If alms are paid with animals, their age matters and have a specific name: a yearling lamb (*shāt*), a she-camel in the second year (*maḥāḍ*), a camel in third year (*labūn*), etc.[62]

These temporal categories—days, months, years—not only structure ritual and taxation but also provide the framework for historical consciousness.

---

53 Mālik, *al-Muwaṭṭaʾ*, 310–312 [247], 324 [261].

54 Mālik, *al-Muwaṭṭaʾ*, 293 [230]. It is not to be assumed that nine years are the decisive criterion for becoming a resident of Mecca. Rather, it stresses that al-Zubayr lived there for a long time, in his case nine years, and enters the consecrated state as a Meccan would do.

55 Mālik, *al-Muwaṭṭaʾ*, 225 [166].

56 Mālik, *al-Muwaṭṭaʾ*, 222–246.

57 Mālik, *al-Muwaṭṭaʾ*, 227, 230.

58 Mālik, *al-Muwaṭṭaʾ*, 251.

59 Mālik, *al-Muwaṭṭaʾ*, 246–248 [187].

60 Mālik, *al-Muwaṭṭaʾ*, 226 [167].

61 Mālik, *al-Muwaṭṭaʾ*, 228 [169–170].

62 Mālik, *al-Muwaṭṭaʾ*, 231 [172].

4 Historiographic and Calendar Awareness

The *Muwaṭṭaʾ* is not a historiographic treatise but does reflect historical awareness. This awareness is, however, concerned with a relatively limited time period: the roughly 150 years from the time of the Prophet until Mālik, expressed as "from the time of the Messenger of God (pbuh) down to this day (*mundhu zamāni rasūli llāhi ṣws ilā l-yawmi*)".[63] When reports in *Muwaṭṭaʾ* address the time before Islam, they typically refer to it as *al-jāhilīya*, the "Days of Ignorance".[64] This terminology does not result from historical disinterest. Rather, it serves as a contrasting tool to define Muslim socioreligious identity.[65] It highlights the differences in legal and ritualistic conduct between the time prior to and during the coming of Islam. When Mālik refers to the time of the Prophet, he either stresses the continuity of a practice, like in the quote above, or changes between "the early days of Islam (*fī z-zamāni l-awwali/fī awwal al-Islām*) or the "time of the Prophet" (*fī zamāni rasūli llāhi*) and his time.[66] More generally, the term *zamān* means a period of time like a life-time or the term of caliphs, for example "during the term of ʿUmar b. al-Khaṭṭāb (*fī zamāni ʿUmara*)".[67]

Although it has been argued that the Ḥijra calendar—starting with the migration of the Prophet from Mecca to Medina, in 622 CE—was already introduced by the second caliph ʿUmar b. al-Khaṭṭāb (d. 23/644),[68] Mālik does not apply this form of dating in the *Muwaṭṭaʾ*, so that he would have said that an event happened in the year so-and-so of the Ḥijra. Rather, numerous particular events are historical markers to date something. In the following example, the Prophet's establishment in Medina is such a marker without referring to it as the Ḥijra though: "The Messenger of God (pbuh) prayed toward Jerusalem for sixteen months after his arrival in Medina (*in qadima l-madīnata sittata ʿashara shahran*). Then the prayer direction was changed two months before the Battle of Badr (*qabla badrin bi-shahrayni*)."[69] In the *Muwaṭṭaʾ*'s general historiographical records, a day (*yawm*) or a year (*ʿām*) are attributed with a sociopolitical event, which was common in pre-Islamic and early Islamic historiography.[70] Often, these events are battles such as the Day of the Battle of Badr (*yawma badrin*)[71] or the Day of the Battle of Uḥud (*yawm uḥud*),[72] the

---

63 Mālik, *al-Muwaṭṭaʾ*, 177 [119].
64 Mālik, *al-Muwaṭṭaʾ*, 226 [167], 248, 261.
65 On Qurʾānic historiography, cf. Stewart 2024.
66 Mālik, *al-Muwaṭṭaʾ*, 111 [50], 343, 383 [322], and 378 [320].
67 Mālik, *al-Muwaṭṭaʾ*, 132 [70], 248, cf. also 229.
68 El Guindi 2008, 113; Stowasser 2014, 15–16; Gallien (forthcoming).
69 Mālik, *al-Muwaṭṭaʾ*, 192 [132].
70 El Guindi 2008, 96.
71 Mālik, *al-Muwaṭṭaʾ*, 353 [288].
72 Mālik, *al-Muwaṭṭaʾ*, 372 [306], 374.

Year or also the Day of the Battle of Ḥunayn (*ʿāma/yawma ḥunaynin*).[73] The markers can be other sociopolitical events like treaties as in the Year of the Conquest of Mecca (*ʿām al-fatḥ*),[74] the Year of the Treaty of Ḥudaybiya (*ʿāma ḥudaybiyati*),[75] or they are of socioreligious relevance, like the Year of the Farewell Pilgrimage (*ʿāma ḥajjati l-wadāʿi*),[76] the last pilgrimage of the Prophet before he died. Dating, in the *Muwaṭṭa'*, can also be executed through referring to other biographical data and in relation to time periods of special status. For example, Mālik dates the day and the year when the first Umayyad caliph Muʿāwiya b. Abī Sufyān (d. 60/680) communicated a specific ruling as "on the day of ʿAshūrā' in the year in which he [Muʿāwiya] performed the Pilgrimage".[77]

The *Muwaṭṭa'* does contain historiographic elements; its calendrical quality is, however, primarily of a religious and ritualistic nature, and in this regard, it is cyclic. Simultaneously, the *Muwaṭṭa'* has a strong teleological aspect in stressing the coming of the Last Hour (*sāʿa*) (see below). At times, it delivers other visions of the future, probably reflecting Mālik's and his immediate predecessors' estimations of their contemporaries' starting decline in practice:

> You are living in a time (*innaka fī zamānin*) when those who understand the Quran are many, but those who recite it are few; [. . .] when prayers are long, but sermons are short (*yuṭīlūna fīhi ṣ-ṣalāta wa-yuqṣirūna l-khuṭbata*); and when good deeds are preferred over desires. There will come a time (*wa-saya'atī ʿalā n-nāsi zamānun*), however, when those who understand the Quran will be few, but those who recite it many; [. . .] when the sermons are long, but the prayers short (*yuṭīlūna fīhi l-khuṭbata wa-yaqṣurūna ṣ-ṣalāta*); and when desires are preferred over good deeds.[78]

This report juxtaposes present and future time-periods (*zamān*), determining the quality of religious observance through temporal duration. This intrinsic relationship of time and religious observance leads directly to the central concern of my analysis: the visual perception of temporal changes. The *Muwaṭṭa'*'s system of days, months, and years, and its designation of sacred times, all depend fundamentally on the believer's capacity to see and interpret the changing positions of sun and moon.

---

73 Mālik, *al-Muwaṭṭa'*, 364, 366–368 [299–300].

74 Mālik, *al-Muwaṭṭa'*, 162 [103], 258, 353.

75 Mālik, *al-Muwaṭṭa'*, 296 [232], 309, 379.

76 Mālik, *al-Muwaṭṭa'*, 344 [280].

77 Mālik, *al-Muwaṭṭa'*, 261, also 297.

78 Mālik, *al-Muwaṭṭa'*, 173 [116]; cf. also Mālik, *al-Muwaṭṭa'*, 117, 147, 183, 196, where time-duration is measured against reciting the Qur'ān in different tempos.

5 Seeing the Moment—The Visuality of Prayer Times

Observing the right time and worship are closely interconnected in Islam. As Otfried Weintritt has formulated it, Islamic "time is a means of carrying out divine law",[79] achieved by aligning ritual with divinely ordered cosmological movement. Gerhard Böwering addresses the importance of what he calls "the intricate timing of ritual prayer in Islam" but refrains from exploring it.[80] In what follows, I argue that the time of prayer (*waqt al-ṣalāt*)[81] serves as the essential timekeeper structuring the daily life of observant Muslims in the *Muwaṭṭaʾ*. The five obligatory prayers are all semantically folded with stages of the day in relationship to the sun and the darkness of the night: Morning/Dawn Prayer (*ṣalāt-aṣ-ṣubḥ/ṣalāt al-fajr*), Noon Prayer (*ṣalāt aẓ-ẓuhr*), Afternoon Prayer (*ṣalāt al-ʿaṣr*), Sunset Prayer (*ṣalāt al-maghrib*), Evening Prayer (*ṣalāt al-ʿishāʾ*). An additional division is applied for Night and Daylight (voluntary) Prayers: *ṣalātu l-layli wa-n-nahāri.*[82]

To detect the times of the obligatory prayers, sight is crucial. The visual perception of sunlight, the darkness of night, sunrise, and sunset marks the starting points of the timeframes in which the prayers can be performed. This perceptual mode of religious time reckoning is rooted in the Qur'ān (Q. 6:96, 31:29, 55:5, et al.), where it is enunciated that the celestial bodies move on divine order and serve humanity as temporal indicators. As I will demonstrate, the *Muwaṭṭaʾ* contains multiple reports delivering guidelines on how observing celestial movements can be translated into assessing the points of juncture for prayer. These optical indicators also mark the beginning and end of months, especially those with sacred status.

Before I delve into these reports, it is worth noting that the *Muwaṭṭaʾ* is not concerned with sophisticated mathematical procedures or astronomical devices for calculating time. The ecliptic course of the earth and the consequent change of seasons and lengths of day and nighttime, latitudes and the differences of shadows, longitudes and the differences in starting and ending points of months relative to the possible visibility of the moon, etc., do not seem to bother Mālik. Later Muslim scholars, championed by Abū Rayḥān al-Bīrūnī (d. 440/1048), put great effort into accounting for these challenges in time reckoning.[83] Rather, by presenting visual reports, the *Muwaṭṭaʾ* deploys a manageable approach through practical examples,

79 Weintritt 2008, 87.
80 Böwering 1997, 66.
81 Mālik, *al-Muwaṭṭaʾ*, 74–76 [10–11].
82 Mālik, *al-Muwaṭṭaʾ*, 142 [80].
83 Stowasser 2014, 143, 149–156; Wishnitzer 2021.

enabling every believer to orient themselves regarding prayer timeframes. Yet, the awareness of time and the prioritizing of performing the prayer within the accurate timeframes are indispensable for the early Muslim authorities, according to Mālik. The measurements for the instants of altering timeframes are defined by seeing how the sunlight falls, which color it has, and which length shadows have in relation to one's own body and architectural environment.

> ʿUmar b. al-Khaṭṭāb wrote to his governors, 'In my estimation, your most important duty is the obligatory prayer. Whoever guards it and performs it diligently guards his religion; whoever neglects his prayer is likely to be even more heedless of his other duties.' He then added, 'Perform the Noon Prayer [. . .] beginning when a person's shadow is one arm's length until his shadow is equal to his own height (*idhā kāna l-fayʾu dhirāʿan ilā yakūna ẓillu ahadikum mithlahu*); the Afternoon Prayer when the sun is high in the sky, white and clear (*murtafiʿatun bayḍāʾu naqayyatun*), and when there is still enough time for a rider to travel six to ten kilometers before the sun sets; the Sunset Prayer [. . .] when the sun sets; and the Evening Prayer between the time that twilight disappears and the end of the first third of the night (*idhā ghāba sh-shafaqu ilā thulthi l-layli*). Whoever goes to bed without performing the Evening Prayer—may his night be restless [in Arabic lit.: who sleeps, his eye won't sleep] (*fa-man nāma fa-lā nāmat ʿaynuhu*)! [. . .] Perform the morning prayer when the stars are clear and fill the sky.[84]

Mālik adds another epistle by ʿUmar b. al-Khaṭṭāb to further clarify: "Perform the Noon Prayer when the sun begins its descent from its zenith; the Afternoon Prayer when the sun is white and clear, before it comes yellowish-orange (*ṣufratun*)."[85] In a report leading back to ʿĀʾisha, it is narrated that the Prophet "would perform the Afternoon Prayer [. . .] while the sun was still shining in her chamber, before it faded there (*wa-sh-shamsu fī ḥujratihā qabla an taẓhara*)."[86] In another report, on the authority of Abū Hurayra (d. ca. 59/679), it is stated:

> Perform the Noon Prayer when your shadow equals your height (*idhā kāna ẓilluka mithlaka*); the Afternoon Prayer when your shadow is double your height (*idhā kāna ẓilluka mithlayka*); the Sunset Prayer when the sun sets; the Evening Prayer in the first third of the night; and the Morning prayer when it is still dark (*bi-ghabashin*), meaning when dawn is just breaking (*al-ghalasa*).[87]

All these reports contain highly visual elements; with the following reports from the *Muwaṭṭaʾ*, I argue that this visuality is not arbitrary, but that early Muslims per-

84 Mālik, *al-Muwaṭṭaʾ*, 75–76 [11]. Measuring time by travel distance was a common form of premodern time reckoning, cf. El Guindi 2008, 96.

85 Mālik, *al-Muwaṭṭaʾ*, 76 [11].

86 Mālik, *al-Muwaṭṭaʾ*, 74 [10].

87 Mālik, *al-Muwaṭṭaʾ*, 76–77 [12].

ceived the act of sight-based observation and gazing as crucial. Mālik's grandfather reported:

> I used to notice [in the Arabic lit.: see] (*kuntu arā*) that on Fridays, a cushion belonging to ʿAqīl b. Abī Ṭālib would be placed along the western wall of the Prophet's Mosque. Only when the shadow of the wall (*ẓillu l-jidāri*) had completely covered (*ghashī*) the cushion would ʿUmar b. al-Khaṭṭāb enter the mosque for the Friday Congregational Prayer.[88]

Another report on the practice of ʿUmar b. al-Khaṭṭāb highlights his observational inspection (*naẓara*), which leads to seeing (*raʾā*) the decisive criterion for his further decision-making when to perform a prayer:

> When ʿUmar finished his circumambulation [of the Kabah in the morning], he looked up and saw that the sun had not yet risen (*naẓara fa-lam yara sh-shamsa ṭalaʿat*), so he mounted his camel and rode until he reached Dhū Ṭuwā, where he dismounted and performed two cycles (*rakʿa*) of prayer.[89]

The centrality of seeing to indicate the right moment for prayer due to the position of the sun and the course of day and night becomes even clearer when the question of blindness is addressed. In this report, a blind person has to rely on others to determine the time, even if he is in charge of calling for the prayer: "Ibn Umm Maktūm was blind (*rajulan aʿmā*), and he would make the call to prayer only after someone told him, 'It is morning, it is morning'",[90] meaning that they saw that the dawn is going to break and informed him about that.

As demonstrated in the preceding sections, the *Muwaṭṭaʾ* applies defined categories of time and provides visual markers indicating the frameworks in which prayer should be performed. These examples sometimes refer to concrete places—such as ʿĀʾisha's chamber—to which most readers of the *Muwaṭṭaʾ* would not have had access. Nevertheless, these reports provide suitable guidelines enabling believers to deduce their own assessment of the correct moment for prayer. Considerations regarding prescribed times are consequently at the center of many narrations in the *Muwaṭṭaʾ*.

---

88 Mālik, *al-Muwaṭṭaʾ*, 77 [12].
89 Mālik, *al-Muwaṭṭaʾ*, 315 [251].
90 Mālik, *al-Muwaṭṭaʾ*, 113 [52].

6 The Prescribed Time—*waqt*

The opening section of the *Muwaṭṭa'*—the book of prayer times (*kitāb wuqūt aṣ-ṣalāt*)[91]—begins with a debate on whether prayer must be performed at the exact time or can be delayed or deferred. Reflecting Mālik's particular approach of perceiving the practice of the people of Medina as normative (in addition to prophetic conduct), the *Muwaṭṭa'* does not begin with a direct report of the Prophet Muḥammad. Rather, it refers to the later Umayyad caliph ʿUmar b. ʿAbd al-ʿAzīz (r. 99–101/717–720), who "one day [. . .] deferred the performance of an obligatory prayer (*akhkhara ṣalāta yawman*)" and was then confronted by ʿUrwa b. al-Zubayr (d. 94/713), one of the "seven jurists of Medina"[92] and a prime source for Mālik. This report contains a dispute between ʿUmar b. ʿAbd al-ʿAzīz and the jurist if the angel Gabriel taught the Prophet the five prayer-times (*a-wa inna Jibrīla huwa lladhī aqāma li-rasūli llāhi (ṣws) waqta ṣalāti*).[93] Without explicitly stating it, the composition of the report suggests that the prayers should be performed promptly and not deferred. Subsequently, Mālik's compilation of reports lists decisive markers for the starting points of the prayer times and the corresponding timeframes in which the obligatory prayers are permissible. Flexibility to pray and to prepare for ritual at any point within these timeframes—"early or late (*mu'ajjilan aw mu'akhkhiran*)"[94] —is granted. While deferring prayer is justified (and even obligated) to avoid, for example extreme conditions such as midday heat,[95] the reports nevertheless support a clear preference for immediate performance over the deferral:

> Many a worshipper will perform an obligatory prayer toward the end of its prescribed time (*wa-mā fātahu waqtuha*), yet had he prayed it earlier, his reward for doing so would have been superior to, and greater than, his family and his wealth.[96]

Utilizing the same criteria of valorization, the intentional omission of a prayer in its timeframe is considered "equivalent to losing his family and all his wealth."[97] Simultaneously, the reports in the *Muwaṭṭa'* acknowledge human fallibility and allow for some vagueness, for example, when, as shown before, the sight of the moon is obstructed through clouds, and one must estimate the time. The prophetic tradition also justifies several reasons for when a prayer is missed. This is primarily the case

91 Mālik, *al-Muwaṭṭa'*, 73–82 [9–17].
92 Mālik, *al-Muwaṭṭa'*, 74, fn. 5.
93 Mālik, *al-Muwaṭṭa'*, 74 [9].
94 Mālik, *al-Muwaṭṭa'*, 132 [70].
95 Mālik, *al-Muwaṭṭa'*, 82.
96 Mālik, *al-Muwaṭṭa'*, 79 [14].
97 Mālik, *al-Muwaṭṭa'*, 79.

when it is beyond the believer's control. If somebody is unconscious, forgets, or oversleeps "he should perform the prayer as he would normally have performed it during its prescribed times (*fī waqtihā*)."[98] Islamic guidelines for correct ritual conduct—in this case, regarding time reckoning—contain flexibility if the believer's best effort and intention are given. This somewhat lenient legal approach is supported by Mālik by giving the following report, which is not about time but the direction of prayer: "According to Mālik, [. . .] ʿUmar b. al-Khaṭṭāb said [in Medina], 'Anywhere between the east and the west is an appropriate direction of prayer, as long as the worshipper is facing south toward God's House (the Kabah).'"[99] However, when this flexibility is exploited—when wrong intentions take precedence over the promptness of prayer without justified reason—the prophetic tradition is highly critical. The association of improper prayer timing with satanic pitfalls underscores the spiritual stakes of temporal awareness:

> That is the prayer of the hypocrites! They sit indifferently until the sun becomes yellow and is between the Devil's horns (or 'on the Devil's horn') (*ḥattā idhā ṣfarrati sh-shams wa-kānat bayna qarnay sh-shayṭāni, aw ʿalā qarni sh-shayṭāni*). Then the hypocrite finally gets up and knocks out four cycles of prayer, pecking up and down like a bird (*qāma fanaqara arbaʿa*), hardly remembering God at all (*wa-lā yadhkuru llāha fīhā illā qalīlan*).[100]

The reference to the sun between the devil's horns resonates with two other reports. There, the Prophet forbids the performance of additional prayers in two periods of time (*sāʿatayn*).[101] These two periods are after the Morning Prayer until the sun reaches its zenith and after the Afternoon prayer until the sun has set:

> 'The sun rises, and with it the Devil's horns (*inna sh-shamsa taṭluʿu wa-maʿahā qarnu sh-shayṭāni*), but when it rises high, the horns leave it (*fa-idhā rtafaʿat fāraqahā*). When the sun reaches its zenith, the horns rejoice it (*qāranahā*). When the sun begins to decline, however, the horns again leave it. When the sun draws near the western horizon, the horns return, but when the sun disappears below the western horizon, the horns leave it again.' The Messenger of God (pbuh) prohibited the performance of prayer at these times (*wa-nahā rasūlu llāhi ṣws ʿani ṣ-ṣalāti fī tilka s-sāʿāti*).[102]

According to the later pioneering Muslim scholar of calendars as culturally specific "mental constructs"[103] and as objects of "ethnological cross-cultural compari-

98 Mālik, *al-Muwaṭṭa'*, 81 [16], cf. also 80, 344.
99 Mālik, *al-Muwaṭṭa'*, 192.
100 Mālik, *al-Muwaṭṭa'*, 206–207 [147].
101 Mālik, *al-Muwaṭṭa'*, 200 [139].
102 Mālik, *al-Muwaṭṭa'*, 206 [146].
103 Stowasser 2014, 105.

son",[104] al-Bīrūnī, this prohibition on conducting prayer when the sun rises, when it is exactly at its zenith, and before it sets serves as a demarcation from non-Muslim forms of sun worship.[105] Besides this socioreligious identity demarcation, this regulation adds a further restriction on the prescribed daylight prayer times: "No one should plan to pray when the sun is rising or when it is setting."[106] Through a restriction, the Prophet's suggested time reckoning encourages cultivating the awareness of the right time. Thus, Mālik repeatedly calls for attentiveness to the prayer times and their boundaries, which should be prioritized over all other considerations.

> No one should pass through Muʿarras on his way back to Mecca from Minā without praying there. If he passes through it outside the scheduled prayer times (*wa-in marra bi-hi fī ghayri waqti ṣalāti*), he should stay there until it is time for the performance of a prayer (*fa-l-yuqim ḥattā taḥilla ṣ-ṣalātu*) and then pray there in a manner that seems appropriate to him.[107]

For Mālik, the prescribed time—particularly for the Feast Prayers—is sacrosanct. Therefore, even the "ruler" must prioritize them and "sets out from his home to the place where the Feast Prayer is to be performed at a time that allows him to arrive there shortly after the sun rises, when it has become permissible to perform the Feast Prayer (*fī waqti l-fiṭri wa-l-aḍḥā*)".[108] Likewise, during the pilgrimage, it is crucial to be on time to fulfill its obligations:

> Whoever fails to reach ʿArafāt prior to the breaking of dawn on the night of Muzdalifa (*min laylati l-muzdalifati qabla an yaṭluʿa l-fajru*) has missed the Pilgrimage, and whoever manages to reach it before the breaking of dawn (*min qabli an yaṭluʿa l-fajru*) on the night of Muzdalifa has fulfilled the pilgrimage (*fa-qad adraka l-ḥajja*).[109]

Similarly, Mālik emphasizes punctuality to properly carry out the practice of pious seclusion in the last ten nights of Ramaḍān:

> The person desiring to engage in pious seclusion should enter his desired place of seclusion before the sun sets on the night in which he wishes to begin his seclusion (*qabla ghurūbi sh-shamsi mina l-laylati llatī yurīdu an yaʿtakifa fīhā*), so that he is ready to begin it at the beginning of the night (*awwala l-laylati*).[110]

---

104 El Guindi 2008, 170.
105 Stowasser 2014, 148.
106 Mālik, *al-Muwaṭṭaʾ*, 207.
107 Mālik, *al-Muwaṭṭaʾ*, 341 [277].
108 Mālik, *al-Muwaṭṭaʾ*, 180 [122]. The morning feast prayer is a striking exception to the rule that one should not pray when the sun rises, like in the reports presented above. This further emphasizes the special status of the festival days.
109 Mālik, *al-Muwaṭṭaʾ*, 332 [267].
110 Mālik, *al-Muwaṭṭaʾ*, 276 [212].

The believer must not be late, but also must not be too early, before the due time, like in this case of someone who hastens over the imam, who gives the time-beat of the prayer: "As for the one who changes positions in prayer prior to the imam, a demon has grabbed him by the forelock."[111] The observant Muslim should be punctual, maintaining constant awareness that worship is actualized through bodily alignment with celestial movements, fellow believers in communal prayer, and the prescribed moments of time. Confronting a person who came late for the sermon (*khutba*) of the Friday congregational prayer, ʿUmar b. al-Khaṭṭāb calls him out: "What time do you think it is? (*ayyatu sāʿatin hādhihi*)?"[112] The caliph, of course, was not asking about clock time. He also was not only asking why the man was late and if he was unaware that it is late. The reference to the term *sāʿa*, the extraordinary moment in time, goes deeper. This moment—*as-sāʿa*—represents the conceptual culmination of the *Muwaṭṭa*'s time understanding, embodying both the fleeting instant of immediate divine encounter and the eschatological Hour toward which all time moves.

7 The Ultimate, Sacred Moment—*sāʿa*

Although the term *sāʿa* in the *Muwaṭṭa'* does not correspond to one of the 24 hours as it does in contemporary Arabic, it can still indicate a division of time. Regarding the merits of setting out to join the Friday congregational prayer, the Prophet names five subdivisions of the morning before the prayer (*fī sāʿati l-ūlā*; *ath-thāniya*; *ath-thālitha*; *ar-rābiʿa*; *al-khāmisa*). The Prophet declares that leaving in the first *sāʿa* is equivalent to offering "a camel as charitable sacrifice." Leaving in a later *sāʿa* is equivalent to a gradually smaller sacrifice.[113] Whereas *sāʿa* here serves as a divider of a certain timeframe, it can also mean a brief period of time (*sāʿatan*),[114] and, in this function, contrasts a long period of time (*zamānan*).[115] In other contexts, *sāʿa* means the concrete moment of time in which something occurs or should occur, as in the question: "right now (*a hādihi s-sāʿata*)?"[116] In the following ruling by Mālik, the term *sāʿa* refers to the instants when a woman, whose menstruation starts and ends, leaves and re-enters the consecrated state of seclusion.

111 Mālik, *al-Muwaṭṭa'*, 122.
112 Mālik, *al-Muwaṭṭa'*, 131 [69].
113 Mālik, *al-Muwaṭṭa'*, 131 [69].
114 Mālik, *al-Muwaṭṭa'*, 256 [196].
115 Mālik, *al-Muwaṭṭa'*, 217 [159].
116 Mālik, *al-Muwaṭṭa'*, 337 [273].

> A woman who goes into pious seclusion and then menstruates during the time of seclusion should return to her house. When her period finishes, she should immediately return to the mosque. She should not delay, and she should resume her seclusion from where she previously left off (*ayyata sāʿatin ṭahurat wa-lā tuʾakhkhiru dhālika thumma tabnī ʿalā mā maḍā min ʾitikāfihā*).[117]

According to this legal ruling of Mālik, menstruation is a valid reason to leave the consecrated state of seclusion. However, the consecrated state must be resumed in the very instant (*sāʿa*): it ends and ritual purity is re-established, without unjustified delay. Minute time awareness stands at the center of this assessment, as it does in reports concerning the detection of starting and ending points of prayer and ritual timeframes. The reports of the *Muwaṭṭaʾ* repeatedly emphasize that attentiveness to the moment is crucial for fulfilling Muslim ritual conduct, especially prayer.

After the Qur'ān, the *Muwaṭṭaʾ* is probably the earliest Islamic textual source that lays the foundation of what Fadwa El Guindi has called the rhythm of Islam. She argues that "Muslims weave in and out, from ordinary space and time to sacred space and time, throughout the day, every month, throughout the year for a lifetime."[118] This "fluid, interwoven temporality"[119] between the movement of the celestial bodies and the believer's life-structure through observing prayer in relation to the "fundamental" or "perfect instant"[120] creates a "moment-by-moment awareness."[121] The centrality of this moment, and the difficulty to grasp it, is captivatingly communicated within the discourse of the *Muwaṭṭaʾ* also through the following saying of the Prophet:

> 'There is a moment (*fīhi sāʿatun*) on Friday when God grants to any Muslim who is standing in prayer, beseeching Him for something at that very moment, whatever he asks.' The Messenger of God (pbuh) used his hand to indicate how fleeting that moment is (*wa-ashāra rasūlu llāhi ṣws bi-yadihi yuqalliluhā*).[122]

This qualification of the moment—*sāʿa*—in which God answers the supplication of the praying believer occurs also in the Hadith, which I have already presented in connection with the special status of Friday. There, it follows, that companions discuss at which part of Friday this special moment occurs. One of them argues that it is in "the last moments of Friday (*ākhiru sāʿatin fī yawmi l-jumuʿati*)." However, at the end of the report, it is hinted at that it could be at any moment and one should

---

117 Mālik, *al-Muwaṭṭaʾ*, 279 [214].
118 El Guindi 2008, 20, cf. also El Guindi 2008, 134–137.
119 El Guindi 2008, 137.
120 El Guindi 2008, 126.
121 El Guindi 2008, 138.
122 Mālik, *al-Muwaṭṭaʾ*, 135 [73].

be in attentive readiness for the coming of this moment. This conclusion circles back to the beginning of the Hadith where it is stated that "every moving creature is attentive (*muṣīkhatun*) [. . .] in fear of the Hour (*as-sāʿa*) [. . .] except for jinn and humans".[123]

The Hadith singles out jinn and humans because they have free will and are, therefore, enabled to alienate themselves from an intrinsic God-consciousness that other creatures live by. According to the Qur'ān 17:11, human beings are hasty (*ʿajūlan*). In the following verse, 17:12, it is proclaimed that God created day and night and the measurements of time reckoning (*ʿadada s-sinīna wa-l-ḥisāba*) to seek for God's bounty. To adjust one's life to the created cosmological rhythm allows one to overcome the disposition of haste. Entering the sacred moment of prayer[124] enables the believer to defy the transitoriness of their own timespan. According to the prophetic tradition featured in the *Muwaṭṭaʾ*, time folds through sincere prayer: the very moment (*sāʿa*) the believer is standing in full God consciousness, asking for His mercy, he anticipates the coming of the Hour (*sāʿa*) of the Last Day as an absolute truth against which all worldly considerations fade.[125] This is exemplified by the Prophet, who prayed during his vigils:

> God! All praise belongs to You. [. . .] You are the Maintainer of the heavens and the earth, [. . .] You are the Truth; [. . .] the Hour of Judgement is real (*as-sāʿatu ḥaqqun*). God! To You I have given myself up [. . .]. To You I have returned.[126]

The recurring and underlying principle within multiple reports of the *Muwaṭṭaʾ* is the intention to find the right moment for spiritual closeness to God. Yet, this very moment (*sāʿa*)—equivocal with the Last Hour (*as-sāʿa*), which coming only God knows[127]—is beyond human control. The believer can only put effort into approaching this moment of complete spiritual sincerity and transparency. In response, the *Muwaṭṭaʾ* provides categories of time and visual criteria to assess the correct period of time for performing prayers and consecrated states to come as close as possible to this instant. It outlines an accessible and all-present time-space structure, in which worship can be constantly performed and experienced.

---

123 Mālik, *al-Muwaṭṭaʾ*, 136 [74].

124 On entering and exiting a spiritually elevated space through prayer, cf. Neuwirth and Hartwig 2021, 132–133. I thank Hannelies Koloska for putting my attention to this interpretation of the verses 17:78–81 of the same Sūra 17 of the Qur'ān, I refer to in the main text. Q 17:78–81 address the interwovenness of devotion, prayer, daylight- and nighttime.

125 Cf. also Q 31:33–34.

126 Mālik, *al-Muwaṭṭaʾ*, 204 [144]. This Hadith can be seen as an embodied realization of the verses Q 17:78–81, performed by the Prophet.

127 Q 31:34 et al.; cf. also Stewart 2024, 55; Stowasser 2014, 26, 38.

Mālik's *Muwaṭṭa'* is not a philosophical or theological reflection on time,[128] and it does not hold a tendency to intellectually transcend time like in Ancient Greek thought.[129] Rather, time reckoning as proposed in the *Muwaṭṭa'* builds on the everyday human experience through the senses, the body, and space.[130] In this regard, it does align with certain Byzantine Christian thinkers, with the essential difference that Muslims do not perceive Jesus Christ and the Church as the access points[131] to sacred time as an "endless and unbroken temporal extension".[132] In the *Muwaṭṭa'*, the individual believer has the possibility to integrate him- or herself directly into such temporal extension through the daily prayers, when he or she applies the visual markers to detect the right moment to enter sacred time-space. Time in the *Muwaṭṭa'* does also not aim to optimize human productivity, as contemporary capitalistic time regimes do.[133] Rather, the *Muwaṭṭa'* equips believers with a framework to optimize their surrender in worship (*taslīm*) through harmonizing themselves with Islam's sacred temporal structure. This distinction illuminates the fundamental character of *Muwaṭṭa'*'s time reckoning system: it is neither abstract calculation nor arbitrary convention, but an embodied, visually mediated practice that positions the believer within the rhythm of divine cosmological order. Having traced how this system operates through its categories, visual markers, prescribed times, and sacred moments, I now synthesize these findings to assess the *Muwaṭṭa'*'s distinctive contribution to Islamic temporal consciousness.

8 Conclusion—Sacred Time-Spaces

Through analyzing time-related reports from the *Muwaṭṭa'*, I have shown the central importance Mālik attributes to temporal observance in Muslim conduct. Islamic time—as presented in the reports compiled in the *Muwaṭṭa'*—seeks to align human consciousness with God-willed cosmological movement through visually discernible phenomena. Optical indicators—the position of the sun, the phase of the moon, the sun's color, and shadow length—open time zones that extend until the next boundary arrives. Muslim time reckoning thus traverses from one temporal zone to another, with certain time stretches possessing special sacred status.

128 On Islamic philosophies and theologies on time, cf. Altaie 2018; Böwering 1997, 57–62; Gallien (forthcoming); Steiris 2018; Stowasser 2014, 41–45; Yousef 2019.

129 Markov 2019, 27.

130 On the connection of space, time, and selfhood, cf. Mensch 2015, 691–692.

131 Markov 2019, 38.

132 Markov 2019, 35.

133 El Guindi 2008, 27, 85; Stowasser 2014, 161–162.

Fridays, in particular, hold the possibility of experiencing the concrete moment of human-divine encounter, ultimately realized in the coming Hour of the Day of Resurrection (*yawm al-qiyāma*).

The *Muwaṭṭa'*'s model for Muslim time-management represents an ongoing effort to capture the exact moment within shifting timeframes. These timeframes materialize as time-spaces primarily structured by the five daily prayers. By providing visual criteria for detecting the starting- and endpoints of consecrated intervals, the *Muwaṭṭa'* enables believers to navigate fluid temporal boundaries that shift with the changing relational positions of earth, sun, moon, visible planets, and the observer. This creates a socioreligious temporal framework encouraging Muslims to enter the reoccurring sacred moment with every prayer and consecrated state.

The prophetic and early Muslim reports compiled in the *Muwaṭṭa'* invite reflection on time as a multilayered structure integrating everyday life, prayer, and consecrated states. The *sāʿa* emerges as the pivotal concept, signifying both the fleeting moment that dissolves ordinary time through the liminal experience of prayer and the ever-present yet elusive coming of the final Hour. Within each time-space lies the possibility of capturing this absolute moment—a possibility forfeited through delay or inattention. In correspondence with the movement of celestial bodies, the Muslim believer transcends subjective time by entering sacred time.

Returning to the Prophet's supplication that opened this study, we now grasp the full significance of requesting God's enablement "to use my sight [...] in Your cause." Within the *Muwaṭṭa'*'s framework, sight functions not merely as a physical faculty but as the primary means through which believers apprehend sacred temporality. Visual observation becomes a crucial practice synchronizing worship with divine creative order, transforming each moment of seeing into an act of devotion and each prayer into a threshold between the transient and the eternal.

Bibliography

Altaie, Mohamed Basil (2018), "Time in Islamic Kalām." In *Christian and Islamic Philosophies of Time*, edited by Sotiris Mitralexis and Marcin Podbielski. Delaware/Malaga: Vernon Press, 119–133.

Bashir, Shahzad (2014), "On Islamic Time: Rethinking Chronology in the Historiography of Muslim Societies." *History and Theory* 53.4, 519–544.

Bauer, Thomas (2003), "Vom Sinn der Zeit aus der Geschichte des arabischen Chronogramms." *Arabica* 50.4, 501–531.

Böwering, Gerhard (1997), "The Concept of Time in Islam." *Proceedings of the American Philosophical Society* 141.1, 55–66.

El Guindi, Fadwa (2008), *By Noon Prayer. The Rhythm of Islam.* Oxford/New York: Berg.

El Shamsy, Ahmad (2013), *The Canonization of Islamic Law. A Social and Intellectual History.* Cambridge: Cambridge University Press.

Gallien, Claire (forthcoming), "Sacred Time." In *St Andrews Encyclopaedia of Theology*.

Mālik b. Anas. *al-Muwaṭṭaʾ*, edited by Ḥāmid Aḥmad al-Ṭāhir. Cairo: Dār al-Fajar li-l-Tirāth, 2013.

Mālik b. Anas. *al-Muwaṭṭaʾ by Mālik b. Anas (d. 179/795). The Recension of Yaḥyā al-Laythī. A translation of the Royal Moroccan Edition*, edited and translated by Mohammed Fadel and Connell Monette. Cambridge: Program in Islamic Law, 2019.

Markov, Smilen (2019), "The Byzantine Concept of Historical Time: Origin and Development." In *Christian and Islamic Philosophies of Time*, edited by Sotiris Mitralexis and Marcin Podbielski. Delaware/Malaga: Vernon Press, 27–46.

Melchert, Christopher (2001), "Traditionist-Jurisprudents and the Framing of Islamic Law." *Islamic Law and Society* 8.3, 383–406.

Mensch, James (2015), "Desire and Selfhood." *The European Legacy* 20.7, 689–698.

Neuwirth, Angelika, and Dirk Hartwig (2021), *Der Koran. Band 2/2. Spätmittelmekkanische Suren. Von Mekka nach Jerusalem: Der spirituelle Weg der Gemeinde heraus aus säkularer Indifferenz und apokalyptischem Pessimismus. Handkommentar mit Übersetzung von Angelika Neuwirth und Dirk Hartwig*. Berlin: Verlag der Weltreligionen.

Schacht, Joseph (2012), "Mālik b. Anas." In *The Encyclopedia of Islam 2 Online*. Accessed 5 November 2025, https://doi.org/10.1163/1573-3912_islam_COM_0649.

Steiris, Georgios (2018), "Al-Fārābi on the Role of Philosophy of History in the History of Civilization." In *Christian and Islamic Philosophies of Time*, edited by Sotiris Mitralexis and Marcin Podbielski. Delaware/Malaga: Vernon Press, 135–144.

Stewart, Devin J. (2024), "'Signs for Those Who Can Decipher Them.' Ancient Ruins in the Qur'ān." In *Behind the Story: Ethical Readings of Qur'ānic Narratives*, edited by Samer Rashwani. Leiden/Boston: Brill, 44–92.

Stowasser, Barbara Freyer (2014), *The Day Begins at Sunset. Perceptions of Time in the Islamic World*. London/New York: I.B. Tauris.

Talmon-Heller, Daniella (2020), *Sacred Place and Sacred Time in the Medieval Islamic Middle East. A Historical Perspective*. Edinburgh: Edinburgh University Press.

Tottoli, Roberto (2014), "Interrelations and Boundaries between Tafsīr and Hadith Literature: The Exegesis of Mālik b. Anas's *Muwaṭṭaʾ* and Classical Qur'anic Commentaries." In *Tafsīr and Islamic Intellectual History: Exploring the Boundaries of a Genre*, edited by Andreas Görke and Johanna Pink. Oxford/New York: Oxford University Press, 147–185.

Weintritt, Otfried (2008), "Interpretations of Time in Islam." In *Time and History: The Variety of Cultures*, edited by Jörn Rüsen. New York/Oxford: Berghahn Books, 85–92.

Wishnitzer, Avner (2021), "Timekeeping: socio-political and cultural aspects." In *Encyclopedia of Islam 3 Online*. Accessed 5 November 2025, https://doi.org/10.1163/1573-3912_ei3_COM_36706.

Wymann-Landgraf, Umar F. Abd-Allah (2013), *Mālik and Medina. Islamic Legal Reasoning in the Formative Period*. Leiden/Boston: Brill.

Yousef, Mohamed Ali (2019), "Zeno's Paradoxes and the Reality of Motion According to Ibn al-Arabi's Single Monad Model of the Cosmos." In *Christian and Islamic Philosophies of Time*, edited by Sotiris Mitralexis and Marcin Podbielski. Delaware/Malaga: Vernon Press, 145–176.

Zerubavel, Eviatar (1982a), "The Standardization of Time: A Sociohistorical Perspective." *American Journal of Sociology* 88.1, 1–23.

Zerubavel, Eviatar (1982b), "Easter and Passover: On Calendars and Group Identity." *American Sociological Review* 47.2, 284–289.

Zerubavel, Eviatar (1987), "The Language of Time: Toward a Semiotics of Temporality." *The Sociological Quarterly* 28.3, 343–356.

Or Amir

Dreams as Collapsing Time and the Question of Tradition

"We have taken off thee thy covering,
and thy sight today is sharp"
(Q 50:22)

1 Introduction

Islamic tradition views visual perception as multilayered, noting that our physical senses can only partially grasp the universe.[1] Not only that, but our visual perception is often regarded as flawed, misleading, and deceptive. It is only through the ongoing transmission of "Tradition," which constructs our relations to the sacred time of revelation, that sensual perception receives certainty.[2] Surely, "Islamic tradition" is a problematic, even redundant term, being such a remarkably diverse mosaic of legal, mystical, philosophical, and other approaches to, and engagements with revelation, some highlighting its exoteric meaning(s) while others focusing on more esoteric interpretations. However, all these hermeneutical currents acknowledge the significant role of the unseen (*al-ghayb*), not just in its transcendent sense, but also in our earthly, tangible world. Thus, when studying Islamic visual culture, it would be misleading not to reserve a central place for the unseen and for the Islamic awareness that our temporal perception of reality is but a link in a chain stretching back to the foundational moment of revelation.

The plurality of Islamic tradition is evident in the variant hermeneutical engagements with the above-cited verse: does it refer to the sense of sight in the hereafter, or to persons of an elevated spiritual rank in this world, for whom God removes the veil, thus opening their sight to the hidden secrets of the universe—past, present, and future? The latter interpretation was naturally appealing to Sufi exegetes.[3] Abū Ḥāmid al-Ghazālī (d. 505/1111), the great synthesizer of Sufi mysticism and Sunni jurisprudence, refers to this verse in one of his discussions on the inferiority of sensual perception compared to the "inner-eye", through which the spiritual elite—namely, the saints or "friends of God" (*awliyāʾ*)—can perceive

1 Ormsby 1984, 58–60.
2 See Yahav's article in this volume.
3 See, e.g., Ibn ʿAjība, *al-Baḥr*, 5:452.

© 2026 the author(s) | https://doi.org/10.1515/9783112240038-003

that which is not seen by the physical organ, the eye.[4] While al-Ghazālī discusses the spiritual cultivation necessary for this "inner-eye" to open through the light of God or the Prophet,[5] he also acknowledges another, more egalitarian, path to achieve such vision that is accessible to all. This is achieved through dreams, when the ordinary senses are asleep, and the soul is free from their restraints. It is then that ordinary men could see into the un-seen.[6] To see, indeed, as the Arabic term for dream-vision, *ru'ya*, clearly suggests.[7]

Dreaming is a universal phenomenon which, paradoxically, provides the dreamer a unique visual experience while his or her eyes are shut. But, as dreams are "seen", they were consistently assigned by pre-modern societies a high epistemic value, often deemed more trustworthy than the vision in a state of wakefulness.[8] That the visual aspect of the dream is key to the trust assigned to it is evident in the Arabic-Islamic terminology for different types of dreams. As Nadia al-Bagdadi pointed out, "a good dream is seen, a bad one – heard, as in the whispering of Satan."[9] This is evident not only in Islamic societies. As Roger Caillois, who approaches the phenomenon of dreaming from a universal perspective, writes:

> the so-called primitive peoples [. . .] attribute no lesser degree of reality to the dream than to the waking experience. Sometimes, rather more impressed by dreams, they accord them greater weight than they do a simple, banal perception, and they are convinced that the dreams bear witness to a superior reality [. . .] From this authority several consequences derive, the first of which is that the events in a dream do not seem less true than those of the waking state. Everything seen in a dream is held believable. . . What evidence can you present against what has been seen?[10]

In what follows, I will focus on the epistemic and temporal value ascribed to dream-visions in the Islamic tradition, in its narrower sense, that is, the traditional views of the Sunni jurisconsults (*fuqahā'*), while not losing sight of the universal aspect of dreams and their value in other traditions, namely the two other monotheistic ones – Judaism and Christianity. I argue that, since dreams function as a bridge between the human limited temporality (*waqt*) and the eternal time of God (*dahr*),[11] they are not only an epistemic phenomenon but moments of collaps-

---

4 Al-Ghazālī, *Iḥyā' 'ulūm al-dīn*, 4:504–506.
5 Lazarus-Yafeh 1975, 295–297.
6 Al-Ghazālī, *Iḥyā' 'ulūm al-dīn*, 4:504–511; al-Bagdadi 2006, 135–136; Montgomery Watt 1953, 22–25.
7 Al-Bagdadi 2006, 131–132.
8 Caillois 1966, 29.
9 Al-Bagdadi 2006, 122–123.
10 Caillois 1966, 28–29.
11 Böwering 1997, 58, 61.

ing time, challenging linear conceptions of history and the authority derived from them. Then, building on Hannah Arendt's thesis, that authority was historically understood as inherently temporal, shaped by the dynamics of simultaneous distance and proximity to a founding event, I argue that the *fuqahāʾ*, who considered themselves as guardians of tradition, derived their authority from a maintained temporal string stretching from the moment of revelation to their temporal present, as the ones authorized to bridge this historical distance through the transmission of tradition. Dreams, by contrast, could offer immediate access to the moment of sacred origin, collapsing that distance instantly, and thereby posing a fundamental challenge to the *fuqahāʾ*'s institutional authority. First, I will briefly outline the attitude to dreams within the Islamic tradition, focusing on the Qurʾān and, especially, the hadith. As will be discussed below, a special place is reserved in this tradition for dreams in which the Prophet Muhammad is seen. Then, I will consider the temporal dimension of dreams as a possible bridge between present, past, and future. Finally, I will consider the challenges dreams could have posed to "tradition," and especially to the authority of religious scholars, as guardians of tradition, both in Islam and other religions.

2 Dreams and Islamic Tradition

Dreams appear in the Qurʾān on several occasions, notably in relation to the Prophet Joseph (Yūsuf). Nonetheless, the authority ascribed to dreams is mainly anchored in the hadith literature. While most canonical collections of hadith feature a chapter dedicated to dreams, in which dozens of traditions are narrated, two traditions stand out prominently throughout the hadith literature, and in them the high epistemic value Islamic tradition ascribes to dreaming is most prominently established. The first hadith has the Prophet saying: "The dream of the believer is 1/46 of prophecy," thus establishing a connection between dreams and revelation.[12] With the Sunni dogma that the Prophet Muhammad was the seal of prophethood, and the consequent spiritual void left after the completion of his mission, this hadith made dreams an especially cherished channel for the continuance of revelation in the post-prophetic age.[13] The second hadith, which plays a key part in every discussion of dreams, relates specifically to dreams featuring the Prophet. In it, the Prophet

12 Ibn Ḥajar al-ʿAsqalānī, *Fatḥ al-bārī*, 16:312–315. There are several variants of this hadith, but the essence remains.

13 Another favorite hadith is: "Nothing of prophethood will remain after me except righteous nightly dreams." See: Brown 2009, 110; Friedmann 1989, 83–93.

states: "Whoever has seen me [in a dream] has seen me truly, as Satan cannot take my form."[14] The implication of this hadith is that any dream in which the Prophet is seen is, *a priori*, a true dream, a direct message from the *Abode of Truth*, and a glance into the realm of the unseen.[15] In temporal terms, it means re-connecting to the prophetic golden age, or moment of revelation.

While these two hadiths form the core of Islamic tradition's attitude to dreams, there are many other hadiths which relate to the veracity of dreams, their source (whether divine or mundane), their role in the revelation of the Qur'ān, the role of the Prophet as dream interpreter for his companions, and much more.[16] Thus, from the earliest stages of its development, Islamic tradition assigned a high value, and a key role, to dreams. Among the consequences of this, we may mention the prosperous science of dream interpretation, which developed in Islamic societies,[17] and the repeated use of dreams as a legitimizing device in various genres of literature and in every conceivable aspect of life: from legitimizing rulers, their ascension to the throne, and their actions, to assessing the authenticity of hadiths, legitimizing the various schools of law (*madhāhib*), and so on.[18] In this regard, dreams filled a legitimizing role similar to that of hadith in Islamic tradition.[19]

Islamic discourse on dreams did not develop in a vacuum and was part of the oneiric landscape of Late Antiquity, especially that of the Hellenic and monotheistic traditions. One example is that classic Islamic typology of dreams is clearly compatible with the Antique Greek and the Late Antique Christian typology. According to this classification, dreams are of three types: (1) dreams that are communications from God, which are truthful; (2) dreams which are the fruit of the dreamer's soul, the result of his mental and physical state, which are unreliable; and (3) dreams which are sent by the devil to mislead or sadden the dreamer.[20]

---

14 Ibn Ḥajar, *Fatḥ al-bārī*, 16:327–338; Kinberg 1993, 285 note 16.

15 Goldziher, 1912. And, more recently, see: Lory 2003, 44–49. Interestingly, an opposite notion developed in Christianity, that Christ cannot be seen in a dream, and if he is, then that must be the act of the Devil. On the other hand, in a similar vein to the aforementioned hadith, the Devil cannot take the form of the Cross in a dream (and compared with a unique version of that hadith in which the Prophet states that "Satan cannot take my form, nor that of the Kaʿba"). On the Christian dictum, see Dagron 1985, 47; mentioned also in al-Bagdadi 2006, 127. For the version of the hadith which includes the Kaʿba see al-Zarkashī, *Iʿlām al-sājid*, 208.

16 Ibn Ḥajar, *Fatḥ al-bārī*, 16:277–293; Fahd 1966b; Sirriyeh 2015, 58–60.

17 Lamoreaux 2002.

18 See, e.g., Fahd 1966a; Kinberg 1985; Kinberg 2008; Kinberg 1999; Lamoreaux 2008.

19 Kinberg 1993.

20 Sirriyeh 2015, 59–60; Hermansen 2001, 73; Le Goff 1985.

The meaning of this typology is that dreams could indeed be messages from God, but could also be delusions of the soul or the ruses of the devil. Thus, dreams were viewed ambivalently and with suspicion. On the other hand, according to Muḥammad Ibn Sīrīn (d. 110/728), the most prominent classical authority of Islamic oneiric tradition, "whatever the deceased tells you in sleep is truth, for he stays in the world of truth."[21] Leah Kinberg rightfully claims that this saying emphasizes the authority reserved to dreams, no matter who the figure is seen in them: "Here the means of *dream*, and not the *Prophet*, creates authenticity."[22] Indeed, dreams in which deceased persons of different types appear and convey messages to the living are extremely numerous in the sources.[23] However, those dreams, while treated with respect, even reverence, did not solve the problem posed by the typology of dreams, since they could still be the result of such delusions. Thus, one kind of dream was considered more authoritative than others, as it was truthful by definition: dreams in which the Prophet appears. According to the hadith cited above, those were necessarily true. To the best of my knowledge, not a single voice was heard refuting this basic assumption, which has been a consensus among Sunni scholars throughout the ages.[24]

Modern academic scholars wrote extensively on the importance of such dreams for Islamic societies, and some, most notably Fritz Krenkow and Ignaz Goldziher, pointed out what they regarded as the absurdities this belief could lead to. As Krenkow wrote over a century ago, "Time after time we encounter in works of biography and history accounts where persons who are eager to give special weight to their own statements, disputed by others, claim to have seen the Prophet in a dream and to have received the authority for their statements from him."[25] Goldziher, on his part, accepted that "[i]t is no uncommon thing in Islamic literature to find both theological doubts and questions of practical controversy solved by the decision of the Prophet, who appears in a dream,"[26] and added that "the appeal to this form of decision passed among this superficial folk as the weightiest argument."[27] However, Goldziher added that the *ʿulamāʾ* (religious scholars) were aware

21 Kinberg 1993, 288.

22 Kinberg 1993, 288.

23 Romanov 2012.

24 I focus on Sunni views on dreams, though Shīʿī scholars have postulated similar views regarding the epistemic value of dreams in general, and dreams featuring the Prophet in particular. Unsurprisingly, a notable exception is that Shīʿī scholars considered the appearance of the imams in dreams as equivalent to that of the Prophet, thus adjusting the hadiths mentioned above to include them as well. See Sindawi 2008.

25 Krenkow 1912, 77.

26 Goldziher 1912, 503.

27 Goldziher 1912, 505.

of the unbearable lightness in which anyone could have turned to such dreams to strengthen his opinion: "Earnest voices were, indeed, upraised in disapproval of legal decisions being based on such visionary arguments, especially when they sanctioned practices which were in contradiction to the *Sunna*."[28]

Although he did not develop this thought much further, Goldziher was on point, not just in noticing the objection some scholars had to employing dreams as a legitimizing tool, but also in singling out possible contradictions to the Sunna as the litmus test set by the *'ulamā'* for whether such dreams should be accepted and what were the limits of their usage. We will return to this issue below, but first, let us consider the relation—and possible tensions—between dreams, time, tradition, and authority.

3 Tradition, Time, and the Challenge of Dreams

In her essay "What is Authority?" Hannah Arendt discusses the notion of authority, which was prevalent in the West since Antiquity and collapsed around the turn of the twentieth century, as the consequence of the secularization process that undermined religion and tradition, which, in her perception, are closely interconnected to authority.[29] Arendt's analysis provides a particularly useful model for understanding religious authority as a temporal structure, which, as I will demonstrate below, is as relevant to the Islamic context as it is to Western Christianity. For Arendt, beginning with the Romans, tradition, religion, and authority formed a trinity, the strength of which "lay in the binding force of an authoritative beginning to which 'religious' bonds tied men back through tradition."[30] For the Romans, this "authoritative beginning" was the foundation of Rome. This primary event was sanctified and preserved through tradition, which handed down "from one generation to the next the testimony of the ancestors, who first had witnessed and created the sacred founding and then augmented it by their authority throughout the centuries."[31]

The Roman perception of authority, embedded as it was in religion and tradition, was rooted in the ancestral tradition (*mos maiorum*), thereby forming the binding, authoritative example of the ancestors (*auctoritas maiorum*). In this perception, authority has an inherent temporal quality, as summed by Arendt:

28 Goldziher 1912, 505–506.
29 Arendt 1968.
30 Arendt 1968, 125.
31 Arendt 1968, 124.

> Thus precedents, the deeds of the ancestors and the usage that grew out of them, were always binding. Anything that happened was transformed into an example, and the *auctoritas maiorum* became identical with authoritative models for actual behavior [. . .] Contrary to our concept of growth, where one grows into the future, the Romans felt that growth was directed toward the past. If one wants to relate this attitude to the hierarchical order established by authority and to visualize this hierarchy in the familiar image of the pyramid, it is as though the peak of the pyramid did not reach into the height of a sky above (or, as in Christianity, beyond) the earth, but into the depth of an earthly past.[32]

As already implied in the previous passage, this trinity of authority-tradition-religion was later adopted by the Church, which translated the founding of Rome as the sanctified "authoritative beginning" to the mission of Jesus, and the *auctoritas maiorum* as the example of the Church Fathers. Applying Arendt's analysis of the perception of authority in the Roman-Christian West to the study of parallel Islamic formulations is an *etic* perspective.[33] However, if we translate Arendt's temporal logic of authority into an Islamic *emic* notion of tradition and authority, we could see how the very distance from the founding moment becomes the condition of religious authority itself: here, the "authoritative beginning" would be the moment of revelation and the prophetic career of Muḥammad, and the authoritative example of the ancestors would relate to the righteous ancestors (*al-salaf al-ṣāliḥ*).[34]

Sunni *'ulamā'* would always address the growing distance between their time and that of the righteous ancestors, and the resulting moral deterioration of the Islamic community. However, while the *'ulamā'* bemoan the temporal separation from the moment of foundation, their authority was built and depended upon this very same separation. One may even argue that this authority grows in correlation with the temporal growth of that separation. After all, the *'ulamā'* presented themselves as "heirs of the prophets," and in the absence of prophethood—which was sealed with the mission of Muḥammad—this self-designation carried great significance.[35] The *'ulamā'* were those who possess knowledge, that is, religious knowledge or, more precisely, they were the carriers of the tradition, the Sunna of the Prophet.[36] Thus, they had the authority to interpret and implement its pre-

---

32 Arendt 1968, 123–124.

33 To think of just one caveat in this *etic* endeavor, the word "authority", which is etymologically derived from the Latin *auctoritas* (Arendt 1968, 121–122), could be translated into Arabic in several different ways. One such word, *wilāya* (from the root *w-l-y*), represents authority as emanating from proximity, that is to the divine. This implies a very different perception of the sources of authority. See: Cornell 1998, xvii–xxi.

34 And we might add that this perception of authority would fit well with Rabbinic Judaism as well, where the "authoritative beginning" would revert to the revelation at Mount Sinai.

35 Friedmann 1989, 83–93.

36 Rosenthal 2007, 44.

scriptions for the community. This authority was founded on the knowledge passed down over the generations, from teacher to student. That this continuous chain of transmitters was of utmost importance for the self-definition of the Sunni *ʿulamāʾ* is exemplified by the insistence on maintaining, at least, an aura of direct master-disciple transmission, even in later periods, when the traditions had already been canonized and written down in books.[37] Thus, the resemblance to Arendt's paradigm of what is authority is, I believe, well-founded.

Meanwhile, dreams, although their epistemic authority was well-established within Islamic tradition, had the potential to disrupt the very structure upon which this tradition, and the authority of the *ʿulamāʾ*, were founded. Dreams, in fact, posed a challenge to the authority of the *ʿulamāʾ* on different aspects.[38] In Arendt's terms, dreams can invert the established hierarchy of the past by pulling the peak of the pyramid back into the present. The personal, subjective, and intuitive nature of dreaming stood in opposition to the learned, collective, restrictive, and institutionalized approach of the *ʿulamāʾ* to what constituted acceptable knowledge (*ʿilm*).[39] This is evident when we compare dreams and hadith. Both are considered highly within the Islamic tradition, and both fill the vacuum created by the cessation of prophecy.[40] Moreover, since both became extremely important legitimizing devices, they aroused suspicions and reservations as to their authenticity. But while the *ʿulamāʾ* developed a sophisticated and vast body of scholarship of hadith criticism—vouchsafing the accuracy of the content of the reports (*matn*), the credibility of the transmitters (*rāwī*; pl. *ruwāh*), and the chains of transmission (*isnād*; pl. *asānīd*)—this enterprise was almost irrelevant to verifying the authenticity of dreams.[41]

There are many parallels between the *ʿulamāʾ*'s approach to hadith and dreams. First, the awareness of the possibility that both could be forged. Regarding hadith, this concern is clearly echoed in a saying attributed to the Prophet: "He who lies in my name intentionally, let him take his place in Hell."[42] This saying parallels another saying attributed to the Prophet, this time relating to dreams: "He who lies about his dream will have to tie a knot in a small barley corn on the day of judge-

37 Davidson 2020. Drawing again the comparison to Rabbinic Judaism, where the Rabbis' authority was grounded, among others, on the Torah in the Mouth, which "was constructed as the embodiment of a generations-long series of transmissions that linked contemporary tradents and performers to ancient founders." Jaffee 2001, 10.

38 This is true of other monotheistic elites as well. See: Shulman, Stroumsa 1999, 5.

39 I focus on the intuitive dimension of dreams as a challenge to the *ʿulamāʾ* in another article, Amir 2025.

40 Ibn Abī al-Dunyā, *Morality*, 47.

41 Kinberg, 1993, 292.

42 Al-Bukhārī, *Ṣaḥīḥ*, 4:3461.

ment."[43] Another saying combines the Prophet's warning against lying in his name with his statement that seeing him in a dream means a true dream: "Whoever sees me in a dream, then surely he has seen me, for Satan cannot impersonate me. And whoever tells a lie against me (intentionally), then (surely) let him occupy his seat in Hell-fire."[44]

Another parallel between the *ʿulamāʾ*s endeavors to keep hadith and dream narrations in check is the scrupulous study of the personalities of the transmitters, who must be deemed trustworthy. The science known as *ʿilm al-rijāl* (lit. "Science of Men"), in which the biographies of hadith transmitters are scrutinized to verify their reliability, is a vast genre of Islamic literature. The notion that the biographies of such narrators must be verified was applied—at least in principle—to narrators of dreams as well. As in *isnād* criticism, authentic, true, and thus reliable dreams were said to be given only to pious and righteous Muslims.[45] This supposedly assured a measure of control over the judgment whether a dream is acceptable or not to the same persons who had the authority to decide who exactly is a righteous or pious Muslim.

And yet, a significant difference remains between hadith and dreams, one closely related to time. As Leah Kinberg wrote, "Dream-tellers did not have to be concerned about chains of transmitters to support their sayings, since through the medium of dream any gap of time or space could be bridged and no intermediaries of any kind were needed."[46] While, from around the fifth/eleventh century, after the canonization of the major hadith collections, it became increasingly difficult to invent new hadiths, dreams could still be fabricated. The dreamer had no need to devise a chain of transmitters.[47] He only had to say that he saw the Prophet declaring something, and, at least in theory, that should have been enough.[48] It is in this way that dreams could collapse time, bridge the temporal gap between the sacred

43 Al-Bukhārī, *Ṣaḥīḥ*, 9:7042.
44 Al-Bukhārī, *Ṣaḥīḥ*, 1:110.
45 Kinberg 1993, 291–292.
46 Kinberg 1993, 292.
47 Although there are instances of dreams being recounted through a chain of transmission, as hadith.
48 There is another interesting connection between dreams and hadith: could a person hear a hadith in a dream—thus making redundant the *isnād*—and this would make him an authoritative transmitter of that hadith? While generally the answer of the Sunni *ʿulamāʾ* was negative, there are quite a few instances in which Muslim scholars claimed to have heard a hadith in a dream. See, e.g., Ibn Qutayba, *Kitāb taʿbīr al-ruʾyā*, 57. ʿAbd al-Ghanī al-Nābulsī (d. 1143/1731) authored a short treatise on the question: is it permissible to receive an *ijāza* (a license to teach certain works) in a dream? In short, his answer is affirmative. See: al-Nābulsī, *Rawḍ al-anām*. Another common dream narrative has the dreamer receiving confirmation (or negation) to the reliability of a certain ha-

time of foundation and the present. As Nile Green wrote: "Visions and dreams were a crucial means of connecting with past time and the major figures with whom it was peopled."[49]

To summarize the conundrum of dreams in Islamic tradition, on the one hand, dreams were firmly established, both ontologically and epistemologically, within the tradition as a continuous mode of communication with the Prophet and revelation; thus, they could play a crucial role in filling the void left by the cessation of prophecy. Indeed, in the discourse of the *ʿulamāʾ* we find repeatedly dream narrations as a means to enhance the legitimacy and authority of various ideas, practices, and persons. On the other hand, and somewhat paradoxically, it is because dreams could bridge the gap between the "authoritative beginning" and the present, a gap that the *ʿulamāʾ* simultaneously bemoaned and derived their authority from, that dreams posed a challenge to that authority, and thus had to be restrained. In the next section, we will see how this conundrum was solved through a restrictive approach to the epistemic validity of dreams.

4 Controlling the Dream: The *fuqahāʾ*s Solution to the Challenge

The *fuqahāʾ* never dismissed the possibility of receiving divine communications through dreams, nor did they challenge the principle that if people see the Prophet in their dream, then they are assured of the veracity of the dream. However, the possibility that anyone could have claimed to have seen the Prophet in his dream and received direct guidance from him on matters of religion, and especially on matters of religious practice and creed, was unbearable for the *fuqahāʾ*, who saw themselves as "arbiters of epistemology."[50] To paraphrase Vincent Cornell's apt statement, the *ʿulamāʾ* did not just see themselves as "those who know what one is supposed to know,"[51] but, perhaps even more crucially, those who know *how* one can attain this knowledge. In other words, they were the guardians of the

dith transmitter or even regarding the content of a certain hadith. See: Kinberg 1993, Brown 2009, 110–111.

49 Green 2003, 288. Compare with Yehoshua Frenkel's comment: "Dreams were regarded as the locus in which past, present and future converged. In the mind of the dreamer, an event taking place in the present brings together the past and the future. Often the past took on the guise of the Prophet, and the latter's prediction of what would occur indicated the future." Frenkel 2008, 214.

50 Cornell 1999, 214.

51 Cornell 1999, 214.

proper temporal mediation of knowledge: revelation had to pass through established chains of transmission and interpretation, rather than through spontaneous encounters in dreams, which were detached from normative temporality. From the perspective of the *ʿulamāʾ*, dreams—and for that matter, any other subjective or intuitive mode of apprehension—could not be considered an acceptable mode for acquiring knowledge. The *fuqahāʾ* thus developed a restrictive approach to the authority of messages received in dreams. This is especially relevant to those dreams featuring the appearance of the Prophet, since other dreams could always be dismissed as possibly originating in the delusions of the soul or the enticement of the devil.

The general principle established by the *fuqahāʾ* regarding dreams of the Prophet was that they cannot lead to any new rulings or alterations in the Divine Law, the *sharīʿa*. The first argument was that, as Qurʾān 5:3 claims: "Today I have perfected your religion for you," meaning that the Islamic religion was completed during the life of the Prophet, and no further revelations will take place after him. Thus, it would be impossible for the Prophet to appear in a dream and add new rules or change existing ones: he could not re-enter historical time through a dream to legislate anew.[52] Furthermore, and the second argument, as the prolific thirteenth-century Shāfiʿī jurist, Muḥyī al-Dīn al-Nawawī (d. 676/1277) writes, although if one sees the Prophet, then the content of his dream must be true, the dreamer must not adhere to any statements the Prophet might utter which relate to legal rulings. This is for two reasons: first, the dreamer is held, in legal terms, to be in a state of inadequate apprehension.[53] And, second, the Prophet declared that Satan cannot take his form, thus ascertaining the visual reality of the dream, but he did not say anything about hearing him.[54]

Ultimately, the decisive criterion for evaluating dream visions of the Prophet was clear: if his message conforms with the accepted norms and rulings of the law, then it was in fact a true dream and should be seen as good-tiding and an ominous sign.[55] We could argue that this criterion was also one of temporal conformity: the dream's message had to align with the already established rules transmitted from the Prophet's historical moment in time. If the message given in the dream con-

---

52 Ibn Badrān, *al-Madkhal*, 297.

53 Al-Nawawī, *Rawḍat al-ṭālibīn*, 5:361.

54 Ibn Ḥajar, *Fatḥ al-bārī*, 16:334; Ibn al-Ḥājj al-ʿAbdarī, *al-Madkhal*, 4:303.

55 This approach could be, again, compared with that of hadith criticism, where hadiths which did not bear legal implications were treated more leniently. As Goldziher wrote: "Many theologians were less strict with ḥadīths which did not belong to the category of the law but offered pious tales, edifying maxims and ethical teachings in the name of the Prophet." Ignaz Goldziher 1971, 2:145. And see Kinberg 1993, 292; Brown 2009, 110–111.

tradicts the established principles of the law, then this is not a true dream. As the fourteenth-century Mālikī scholar, Abū Isḥāq al-Shāṭibī (d. 790/1388), writes:

> Sometimes, a certain person will say: I saw the Prophet in a dream, and he told me [to do] this, and ordered me [to do] that. And [that person] will then practice this, or neglect it, abandoning the boundaries set by the *sharīʿa*. This is an error, because rules cannot be based on dreams alone—except for dreams of prophets. Rather, they must first be juxtaposed with the rules we possess in the *sharīʿa*. If they correspond with [the *sharīʿa*], one follows them, and if not—one abandons them. [The dream] is only beneficial as good tidings or warning. As for acquiring rules from it—no.[56]

In this way, the jurists reasserted temporal distance as a criterion of truth. The dream's authority had to be tested against the fixed corpus of revelation and its juristic interpretation, both of which anchored knowledge in a completed past. Thus, they transformed the dream from a potential candidate for collapsing time (a disruptive challenge to their authority) into a reaffirmation of temporal hierarchy: Revelation belonged to the Prophet's age, while interpretation to theirs. It is noteworthy that the *fuqahāʾ*s attitude to the authoritative value of dreams is comparable to that of their Christian and Rabbinic counterparts. The approach of these two other monotheistic religious establishments to dreams as a source of knowledge and a mode of continuous revelation was also rooted in their scriptures and, in particular, their religious traditions. Both accepted that dreams could represent divine communication, thus revealing truthful messages hidden from sensual perception. But both, as in Islam, also developed a suspicious view of dreams as an alternative mode of attaining knowledge that could challenge the authority of the religious elites.[57] In a nutshell, the solution that both the Church and the Rabbinic elite arrived at was that dreams could indeed communicate divine messages but could not be taken as legal evidence. The ultimate way to distinguish between true and false dreams is the test of conformity: to scriptures, and to the orthodox teachings of the Church or the Rabbis.[58] Like their Muslim counterparts, they distinguished between the temporal closure of revelation and the timeless openness of divine communication.

---

56 Al-Shāṭibī, *al-Iʿtiṣām*, 2:93. Compare with: Ibn al-Ḥājj al-ʿAbdarī, *al-Madkhal*, 4:302.

57 Strathern 2019, 86.

58 For Christianity see: Keskiaho 2015, 130; Morreira 2000, 8–9; Le Goff 1985, 210–213. On Judaism: Kanarfogel 2012, 116.

5 Concluding Remarks

In a tradition that valued the unseen no less than the visually perceptible, dreams were ascribed with great epistemic authority. The numerous dream narrations found in the sources—legitimizing and giving authority to persons, institutions, and ideals of every walk of life—offer us, in the words of Nadia al-Bagdadi, "a discourse on the visual and visuality without material visual representation."[59] Dreams also have a strong temporal dimension: through them, the dreamer can attain access to ancestors and other important personalities of the past, and at times be given insights into the future by them. By offering believers a direct channel of communication with the prophetic past *and* the unseen realities, which was well-founded in the hadith, dreams created a dilemma for the religious establishment, since their temporal fluidity made them both indispensable and dangerous. On the one hand, their epistemic authority was an integral part of the Tradition, one that was impossible (if ever desired) to be dispensed with. On the other hand, they posed a threat to the common notions of tradition and, thus, to the authority of the religious establishment. The solution to the problem was to retain the epistemic authority of dreams while restraining it, ensuring that it would not be used to create changes to the Divine Law, which the religious scholars considered their exclusive field of authority.[60] The jurists' solution was not just epistemic but also temporal: to recognize the inherent truth of dreams—or, at least, some of them—while re-inscribing them within the completed past of revelation, ensuring that no dream could disrupt established legislation in the ever-unfolding present. In this way, the jurists transformed the dream from a timeless incursion into a sign of temporal harmony—an echo of revelation rather than a candidate for its renewal. Both the challenges posed by dreams to the *'ulamā'* and their solutions bear remarkable parallels to similar dynamics that Christian and Rabbinic Jewish religious establishments faced. Thus, dreams offer another glimpse into the shared world of the three monotheistic traditions that emerged from Late Antiquity.

---

59 Al-Bagdadi 2006, 119.

60 As Caillois writes: "Its [i.e., the dream's] weakness is that the first impostor who comes along can, at leisure, preempt a very precious investiture that rises from the heart of an inaccessible secret, that of a consciousness gone to sleep. One ought to be able to control, to record, the images of the dream. In fact—even though suspect by nature, fleeting, fantastic, and absolutely unverifiable—it tends to become institutionalized whenever it contributes to the basis of practical policy, its use regulated, and its area of competency carefully outlined." Caillois 1966, 31.

Bibliography

al-Bagdadi, Nadia (2006), "The Other Eye: Sight and Insight in Arabic Classical Dream Literature." *The Medieval History Journal* 9.1, 115–141.

al-Bukhārī, Muḥammad b. Ismāʿīl, *al-Jāmiʿ al-Ṣaḥīḥ*, edited by Muḥammad Zuhayr b. Nāṣir al-Nāṣir, 9 vols. Beirut: Dār Ṭawq al-Najāh, 2001.

al-Ghazālī, Abū Ḥāmid Muḥammad b. Muḥammad, *Iḥyāʾ ʿulūm al-dīn*, 4 vols., Beirut: Dār al-maʿrifa, 1982.

al-Nābulsī, ʿAbd al-Ghanī, *Rawḍ al-anām fī bayān al-ijāza fī al-manām*, edited by Muḥammad b. Muḥammad Khayr Haykal. Damascus: Dār ḍiyāʾ al-Shām, 2021.

al-Nawawī, Muḥyī al-Dīn Abū Zakariyyā Yaḥyā, *Rawḍat al-ṭālibīn*, edited by ʿĀdil Aḥmad ʿAbd al-Mawjūd and ʿAlī Muḥammad Muʿawwad, 12 vols. Riyadh: Dār ʿālam al-kutub, 2003.

al-Shāṭibī, Abū Isḥāq Ibrāhīm b. Mūsā, *al-Iʿtiṣām*, edited by Muḥammad b. ʿAbd al-Raḥmān al-Shuqayr, Saʿd b. ʿAbd Allāh Āl Ḥumayyid and Hishām b. Ismāʿīl al-Ṣīnī, 3 vols. Riyadh: Dār Ibn al-Jawzī, 2008.

al-Zarkashī, Muḥammad b. ʿAbd Allāh, *Iʿlām al-sājid bi-aḥkām al-masājid*, edited by Abū al-Wafāʾ Muṣṭafā al-Marāghī. Cairo: al-Majlis al-aʿlā li-l-shuʾūn al-islāmiyya, 1996.

Amir, Or (2025), "'Is fiqh now determined based on Dreams?!' The Debate Over the Legal Value of Dreams and the Question of Religious Authority in Sunni Islam." *Islamic Law and Society* 32.3, 173–202.

Arendt, Hannah (1968), "What is Authority?" In *Between Past and Future*. New York: Penguin Books, 91–141.

Böwering, Gerhard (1997), "The Concept of Time in Islam," *Proceedings of the American Philosophical Society* 141.1, 55–66.

Brown, Jonathan A. C. (2007), *The Canonization of al-Bukhārī and Muslim: The Formation and Function of the Sunnī Ḥadīth Canon*. Leiden: Brill.

Brown, Jonathan A. C. (2009), *Hadith: Muhammad's Legacy in the Medieval and Modern World*. Oxford: Oneworld.

Caillois, Roger (1966), "Logical and Philosophical Problems of the Dream." In *The Dream and Human Societies*, edited by Gustave E. von Grunebaum and Roger Caillois. Berkeley/Los Angeles: University of California Press, 23–52.

Cornell, Vincent J. (1998), *Realm of the Saint: Power and Authority in Moroccan Sufism*. Austin: University of Texas Press.

Cornell, Vincent J. (1999), "Faqīh Versus Faqīr in Marinid Morocco: Epistemological Dimensions of a Polemic." In *Islamic Mysticism Contested: Thirteen Centuries of Controversies and Polemics*, edited by Frederick De Jong and Bernd Radtke. Leiden: Brill, 207–224.

Dagron, Gilbert (1985), "Rêver de dieu et parler de soi. Le rêve et son interprétation d'après les sources byzantines." In *I Sogni nel Medioevo. Seminario internazionale, Roma, 2–4 ottobre 1983*, edited by Tullio Gregory. Rome: Edizioni dell' Ateneo, 37–55.

Davidson, Garrett A. (2020), *Carrying on the Tradition: A Social and Intellectual History of Hadith Transmission across a Thousand Years*. Leiden: Brill.

Fahd, Toufic (1966a), "The Dream in Medieval Islamic Society." In *The Dream and Human Societies*, edited by Gustave E. von Grunebaum and Roger Caillois. Berkeley/Los Angeles: University of California Press, 351–363.

Fahd, Toufic (1966b), *La Divination arabe: études religieuses, sociologiques et folkloriques sur le milieu natif d'Islam*. Leiden: Brill.

Frenkel, Yehoshua (2008), "Dream Accounts in the Chronicles of the Mamluk Period." In *Dreaming Across Boundaries: The Interpretation of Dreams in Islamic Lands*, edited by Louise Marlow. Boston: Ilex Foundation; Washington, D.C.: Center for Hellenic Studies, 2008, 202–220.

Friedmann, Yohanan (1989), *Prophecy Continuous: Aspects of Aḥmadī Religious Thought and Its Medieval Background.* Berkeley: University of California Press.

Goldziher, Ignaz (1912), "The Appearance of the Prophet in Dreams." *Journal of the Royal Asiatic Society* 44.2, 503–506.

Goldziher, Ignaz (1971), *Muslim Studies*, edited and translated by Christa R. Barber and Samuel M. Stern, 2 vols. London: George Allen and Unwin.

Green, Nile (2003), "The Religious and Cultural Roles of Dreams and Visions in Islam." *Journal of the Royal Asiatic Society*, 13.3, 287–313.

Hermansen, Marcia (2001), "Dreams and Dreaming in Islam." In *Dreams: A Reader on Religious, Cultural, and Psychological Dimensions of Dreaming*, edited by Kelly Bulkeley. New York: Palgrave, 73–91.

Ibn Abī al-Dunyā, *Morality in the Guise of Dreams: A Critical Edition of Kitāb al-Manām*, with introduction, edited and translated by Leah Kinberg. Leiden: Brill, 1994.

Ibn ʿAjība, Abū al-ʿAbbās Aḥmad b. Muḥammad, *al-Baḥr al-madīd fī tafsīr al-Qurʾān al-majīd*, edited by Aḥmad ʿAbd Allāh al-Qurashī Raslān, 5 vols. Cairo: Ḥasan ʿAbbās Zakī, 2000.

Ibn al-Ḥājj al-ʿAbdarī, Muḥammad b. Muḥammad, *al-Madkhal*, 4 vols. Beirut: Dār al-Kitāb al-ʿArabī, 1972.

Ibn Badrān, ʿAbd al-Qādir b. Aḥmad, al-*Madkhal ilā madhhab al-imām Aḥmad*, edited by ʿAbd Allāh b. ʿAbd al-Muḥsin al-Turkī. Beirut: Muʾassasat al-risāla, 1980.

Ibn Ḥajar al-ʿAsqalānī, Aḥmad b. ʿAlī, *Fatḥ al-bārī bi-sharḥ Ṣaḥīḥ al-Bukhārī*, edited by Naẓar Muḥammad al-Faryābī, 19 vols. Riyadh: Dār Ṭayyiba, 2005.

Ibn Qutayba al-Dīnawarī, Abū Muḥammad ʿAbd Allāh, *Kitāb taʿbīr al-ruʾyā*, edited by Ibrāhīm Ṣāliḥ. Damascus: Dār al-bashāʾir, 2001.

Jaffee, Martin S. (2001), *Torah in the Mouth: Writing and Oral Tradition in Palestinian Judaism. 200 BCE – 400 CE*, Oxford: Oxford University Press.

Kanarfogel, Ephraim (2012), "Dreams as a Determinant of Jewish Law and Practice in Northern Europe during the High Middle Ages." In *Studies in Medieval Jewish Intellectual and Social History: Festschrift in Honor of Robert Chazan*, edited by Lawrence H. Schiffman and Elliot R. Wolfson, Leiden: Brill, 111–143.

Keskiaho, Jesse (2015), *Dreams and Visions in the Early Middle Ages: The Reception and Use of Patristic Ideas, 400–900.* Cambridge: Cambridge University Press.

Kinberg, Leah (1985), "The Legitimization of the Madhāhib through Dreams." *Arabica* 32.1, 47–79.

Kinberg, Leah (1993), "Literal Dreams and Prophetic Ḥadīṯs in Classical Islam — a Comparison of Two Ways of Legitimation." *Der Islam* 70, 279–300.

Kinberg, Leah (1999), "Dreams as a Means to Evaluate Ḥadīth." *Jerusalem Studies in Arabic and Islam* 23, 79–99.

Kinberg, Leah (2008), "Qurʾān and Ḥadīth: A Struggle for Supremacy as Reflected in Dream Narratives." In *Dreaming Across Boundaries: The Interpretation of Dreams in Islamic Lands*, edited by Louise Marlow. Boston: Ilex Foundation; Washington, D.C.: Center for Hellenic Studies, 25–49.

Krenkow, Fritz (1912), "The Tarikh-Baghdad (Vol. XXVII) of the Khatib Abu Bakr Ahmad B. ʿAli b. Thabit al-Baghdadi: Short Account of the Biographies." *Journal of the Royal Asiatic Society* 44.1, 31–79.

Lamoreaux, John C. (2002), *The Early Muslim Tradition of Dream Interpretation*. New York: SUNY Press.

Lamoreaux, John C. (2008), "An Early Muslim Autobiographical Dream Narrative: Abū Jaʿfar al-Qāyinī and His Dream of the Prophet Muhammad." In *Dreaming Across Boundaries: The Interpretation of Dreams in Islamic Lands*, edited by Louise Marlow. Boston: Ilex Foundation; Washington, D.C.: Center for Hellenic Studies, 78–98.

Lazarus-Yafeh, Hava (1975), *Studies in al-Ghazzali*. Jerusalem: The Magnes Press.

Le Goff, Jacques (1985), *The Medieval Imagination*, translated by Arthur Goldhammer. Chicago: University of Chicago Press.

Lory, Pierre (2003), *Le Rêve et ses interpretations en Islam*, Paris: Albin Michel.

Montgomery Watt, William (1953), *The Faith and Practice of al-Ghazālī*. London: George Allen and Unwin.

Morreira, Isabel (2000), *Dreams, Visions, and Spiritual Authority in Merovingian Gaul*. Ithaca: Cornell University Press.

Ormsby, Eric L. (1984), *Theodicy in Islamic Thought: The Dispute over al-Ghazālī's "Best of All Possible Worlds."* Princeton: Princeton University Press.

Romanov, Maxim (2012), "Dreaming Ḥanbalites: Dream-Tales in Prosopographical Dictionaries." In *Dreams and Visions in Islamic Societies*, edited by Özgen Felek and Alexander D. Knysh. Albany: SUNY Press, 31–50.

Rosenthal, Franz (2007), *Knowledge Triumphant: The Concept of Knowledge in Medieval Islam*. Leiden: Brill.

Shulman, David, and Guy G. Stroumsa (1999), "Introduction." In *Dream Cultures: Explorations in the Comparative History of Dreaming*, edited by David Shulman and Guy G. Stroumsa. New York: Oxford University Press, 3–13.

Sindawi, Khalid (2008), "The Image of ʿAlī b. Abī Ṭālib in the Dreams of Visitors to His Tomb." In *Dreaming Across Boundaries: The Interpretation of Dreams in Islamic Lands*, edited by Louise Marlow. Boston: Ilex Foundation; Washington, D.C.: Center for Hellenic Studies, 179–201.

Sirriyeh, Elizabeth (2015), *Dreams and Visions in the World of Islam: A History of Muslim Dreaming and Foreknowing*. London: I.B. Tauris.

Strathern, Alan (2019), *Unearthly Powers: Religious and Political Change in World History*. Cambridge: Cambridge University Press.

Yehonatan Yahav

Vision and Time in Ibn Qutayba's Traditionist Islam

Seeing the Unseen through the Eyes of History and Belief

1 *Naẓar* and the Instantaneous Perception of the Mind

The faculty of vision, exemplified by the capacity to "see with one's own eyes", serves as a powerful and seemingly universal vehicle in the human pursuit of knowledge and truth. Yet counterbalancing this self-evident truism is its equally common, though less conspicuous, opposite: the realm of the invisible. In the Greek philosophical tradition, this tension manifests itself in the sensory world of *physics* and the concept of the *metaphysical domain*, which is accessible only through the intellect. Within classic Platonic dualism, the invisible, metaphysical reality is considered to possess greater epistemic value than the visible, sensory world. Nevertheless, the epistemic power accorded to visual experience is preserved through concepts such as the Greek *theoria* (literally, "seeing"), the allegory of the Platonic cave, the bright light and shadows, and the Platonic idea of Forms, connecting the notion of physical shapes and images with the metaphysical realm. Thus, while Plato and Aristotle advocate for the superiority of intellectual knowledge over sensory knowledge, both implicitly recognize the epistemic allure of vision and its semantic resonance within the language of thought.[1]

Early *falāsifa* such as al-Kindī (d. 256/873) and later figures such as Ibn Rushd (Averroes) (d. 595/ 1198) articulate the Platonic and Aristotelian relationship between sight and knowledge in ways that foreground an inherent tension: on the one hand, sensory sight may mislead, as in the case of dreams, reflections, or illu-

1 For an in-depth survey of the centrality of visual seeing to Platonic and Aristotelian epistemology, see Martin Heidegger's reading of Aristotle's *Metaphysics* in McNeill 1999, 1–13. Samer Akkach's edited volume on *naẓar* (Akkach 2021a) includes essential insights on the term, including a discussion of the meaning in the realms of *falsafa* and *kalām*, for example, by Hirtenstein 2021. Nevertheless, his focus remains predominantly on the Sufi conception of *naẓar* rather than the philosophical and *kalām* understanding of the term.

sions, yet on the other, it provides the seer with an immediate sense of certitude that is often analogized to the ultimate faculty of intellectual grasping or knowing.[2]

A comparable emphasis on vision also appears among the *mutakallimūn*, or *ahl al-kalām*, who frequently relied on speculative reasoning (often likewise referred to as *naẓar*) in a religious deliberation. For many of them, visual perception served as a model for the clarity and decisiveness of rational argumentation. In both *falsafa* and *kalām*, therefore, the "seeing of the mind" and its associated visual imagery function as crucial vehicles of epistemology, highlighting the visual dimension of cognition, imagination, and intellectual certainty.[3]

ʿAbd Allāh Ibn Qutayba (d. 276/889) was a prominent *adīb*, a master of *adab* literary style, and religious scholar who lived at the height of the state-sanctioned Greek-to-Arabic translation movement. He worked predominantly in Baghdad, the heart of the Abbasid empire. Well acquainted with Arabic translations of select Aristotelian texts and other adaptations of Greek philosophical and scientific works, he also demonstrated familiarity with Persian and Indian literature, as well as Arabic renditions of the Jewish Torah and Christian Gospel, which he frequently cited in his writings. Alongside his literary and philological pursuits, Ibn Qutayba aligned himself both theologically and politically with the *ahl al-ḥadīth*, a traditionist group advocating the primacy of *ḥadīth* (initially transmitted as an oral tradition) alongside the Qurʾān as the primary source for legal and theological inference. As a result, Ibn Qutayba's writings, composed in the style of *adab*, are thematically entwined with his religious and political vision, encompassing works on theology, jurisprudence (*fiqh*), exegesis, and intra-Muslim polemics.[4]

In Ibn Qutayba's writings, one encounters the intellectual energy of a broad cultural, political, and religious vision. Composed in the mid-third century A.H. / ninth century C.E., a time of political upheaval in the still-expanding Abbasid Caliphate, his work addresses both inherited and contemporary sectarian tensions, encompassing theological, political, and ethnic dimensions. Through this engagement, Ibn Qutayba strives to articulate a cohesive religious and political identity amid the multi-religious and multicultural fabric of the Abbasid empire. In many respects, his oeuvre represents an early articulation of a comprehensive Sunni orthodox *raison d'être*, one that centers on the Qurʾān, *ḥadīth*, broad communal agreement (*ijmāʿ*), and traditions. Ibn Qutayba's version of this proto-Sunni project is marked

2 For a discussion of al-Kindī and Averroes' articulation of the relation between the intelligible truths and the "visible" ones, see Jolivet 2003, 53–62.

3 For a comprehensive discussion of the various optical theories held by the *mutakallimūn* and their ontological consequences, including I Abū al-Hudhayl's (d. 235 / 841) seeing (God) with the heart, see van Ess 2003, 1–13.

4 Lecomte 1965, 1971; Lecomte 1962.

by a vehement rejection of speculative reasoning in theology, law, and epistemology, opposing rival currents such as *kalām*, *ra'y*, and *falsafa*, respectively. Within this context, Ibn Qutayba's *adab* and religious writings should be understood as constituting a comprehensive scholarly and theological alternative to *kalām* and *falsafa*, particularly with regard to the realm of *dīn*. This alternative emphasizes Arabic philology, the study of Arab heritage as articulated in the *adab* tradition, and the integration of linguistic and philological (*lugha*) methods in interpreting *ḥadīth*.[5]

It is within this conceptual framework that I propose to examine Ibn Qutayba's treatment of temporality in relation to visuality as two modes of measuring epistemic certainty. Ibn Qutayba contrasts what he perceives as the strongly persuasive visual underpinnings of *falsafa* with the epistemic force of cultural transmission, the discursive movement of ideas and narratives over time. This emphasis on the historical and collective dimension of knowledge, in which longevity serves to bolster veracity, is perhaps unsurprising within the context of the *ahl al-ḥadīth*. Yet Ibn Qutayba's approach extends beyond the pursuit of discrete, authenticated prophetic reports preserved through flawless chains of transmission. Drawing on his *adab* sensibilities, he broadens epistemic authority to include the collective semiotic structures embedded in societies, their language, and culture.

As previously noted, Ibn Qutayba interprets *naẓar* as an intellectual act of the mind which is closely connected to visuality. In one particular example, he describes visuality as the strongest kind of certain knowledge (*yaqīn*). This appears in part of Ibn Qutayba's defense of a Qur'ān verse discussing Abraham's alleged doubt over God's ability to revive the dead (Q 2:260):

> The interpretation (*ta'wīl*) of Abraham's saying, "but just to put my heart at rest"[6] is: (that) he [Abraham] may be assured by the certainty of *naẓar*. Certain knowledge (*yaqīn*) is of two kinds: one is the assurance of hearing (*sam'*), and the other is the assurance of eyesight (*baṣar*). And the certainty of eyesight is greater than the other two. Therefore, the Messenger of God said: 'The hearer' (*al-mukhbar*) is unlike 'the seer' (*al-mu'āyin*).[7]

In this example, Ibn Qutayba introduces *naẓar* as clearly encompassing both intellectual reflection and sensory vision, two modes of perception that, in his view, converge in the production of epistemic certainty (*yaqīn*). This certainty, he explains in this example, ultimately resides in the *qalb* (heart), the seat of emotional sensibility, rational insight, and belief.[8]

---

5 Yahav 2024.

6 Q 2:260, all translations of the Qur'ān, are based on M.A.S. Abdel Haleem's translation.

7 Ibn Qutayba, *Ta'wīl Mukhtalif*, 160.

8 Gardet 1978; the use of *naẓar* here may be further explained by Samer Akkach's analysis of the term in similar texts. Most notably, his differentiation between *ru'ya* and *naẓar* in which the first

However, Ibn Qutayba's epistemology does not culminate in assurance and conviction. Although he draws on elements of the philosophical tradition, namely the notion of "seeing something in the mind" and its association with the intellectual or rational aspect of *naẓar*, he simultaneously turns this concept into the focal point of his critique, challenging its claim to ultimate epistemic authority. For Ibn Qutayba, the act of intellectual "seeing" remains bound to human limitation; it cannot, on its own, yield certainty, especially in the realm of religion (*dīn*).

2 Ibn Qutayba's Critique of *Naẓar* through the Invocation of the Unseen

In his theological and polemic work *Ta'wīl Mukhtalif al-Ḥadīth*, Ibn Qutayba responds to criticisms of *aḥadīth*, prophetic traditions, that are denounced by his interlocutors as contradictory, fanciful, and, in certain instances, conflicting with *naẓar*. While he addresses each critique with careful deliberation, he also engages in occasional polemic strategies aimed at undermining the legitimacy of his interlocutors by casting doubt on their religiosity and commitment to Islam. One key aspect of his criticism is the recurring allegation that the rationalist reproach, i.e., the *ḥadīth*'s contradiction with *naẓar*, conceals a deeper, more subversive challenge to religious authority. Ibn Qutayba repeatedly contends that such critics reject knowledge that cannot be verified by direct sensory perception, thereby suggesting that they be considered outside the borders of the Muslim community and as a threat to the very foundations of religious knowledge (*dīn*). *Naẓar*, in this context, is treated by Ibn Qutayba as a source of assurance that conflates rational thought and visual perception.

For Ibn Qutayba, the "seeing of the mind" may be understood in two complementary ways: first, as the imagination's capacity to render ideas into mental images; and second, as the more abstract, intellectual act of reflective reasoning, which is strongly related to the undertaking of seeing. Consequently, one of the issues which Ibn Qutayba presents repeatedly as a point of contention between his religious (*dīnī*) epistemology and that of the *falāsifa* is the realm of the unseen (*'ālam al-ghayb*).

---

complies with the sensory aspect of seeing with the eyes, while *naẓar* pertains to the intention or will of seeing something, which is a broader, at times more intellectual, intermediary of eyesight, Akkach 2021b; On *naẓar* see also De Boer and Daiber 2021, 57–62.

In this context, Ibn Qutayba reiterates that belonging to any religious tradition entails a commitment to transmitted reports concerning the unseen, as well as a tacit adherence to a shared narrative or lore. While the term "folklore," which seems fitting in this context, may carry fictitious or mythical connotations in modern usage, Ibn Qutayba's treatment of cultural lore reflects a rather literal dimension of folklore, as a repository of collective narratives and meaning, which he envisages as essential to religious identity. Ibn Qutayba introduces the epistemic importance of time and temporality, vis-à-vis the "immediacy" of visual and contemplative information as part of this critique.

The veracity of this shared wisdom is measured by its consistency and pervasiveness within the community over time. To counter the immediacy of vision and the intellectual perception associated with *naẓar*, Ibn Qutayba repeatedly invokes the realm of the unseen (*ʿālam al-ghayb*), which he at times treats as the ultimate measure of genuine religious fidelity. As an example, here is Ibn Qutayba's discussion of the *al-ʿayn*, the notion of the evil-eye (a powerful folkloric concept) and its contested ability to affect people at a distance:

> They (the interlocutors) said: 'You narrated about the Prophet that He said: 'The evil eye almost preceded (*kādati al-ʿaynu tasbiqu al-qadara*) the decree of fate'[9]. The two sons of Jaʿfar Ibn Abī Ṭālib[10] came to the prophet, [and] they were thin. He [the prophet] said: 'Why do I see them so thin?' [The people] answered, the evil eye is rapidly getting to them.' He said: 'Use incantations on them' (*ʿistarqū lahumā*). [The interlocutors continue:] But He [the Prophet Muḥammad] has forbidden the use of incantations in more than one *ḥadīth*. They also said: 'How can the evil eye work from a distance and make people ill?' This cannot be established by imagination (*wahm*) or verified by reflective reason (*naẓar*). Abū Muḥammad [Ibn Qutayba] said: 'We say that it *is* imaginable and intelligible from the point of view (*jiha*) of religion (*diyāna*) as well as from the point of view (*jiha*) of philosophy, to which they agree and to which they relate [all] things.[11]

---

9 Ibn Qutayba, *Taʾwīl Mukhtalif*, 473. It is a widely accepted folkloric belief that the evil eye, instigated by someone's malevolent gaze or thought, causes a 'break' in the normal process of a person's life or his divine decreed fate. The evil eye affects the person faster than the casual chain of events instigated by fate. This is also described in *Ṣaḥīḥ Muslim*, vol. 7, 13, which narrates that The Prophet said: "The evil eye is true, if anything (*wa-law kāna shay'un*) would precede (*sābaqa*) the decree of fate (al-*qadar*) it would be the evil eye. . .". In both instances, the prophet does state unequivocally that the evil eye is indeed "faster" than *qadar* but uses the words "*kāda*" (almost) or "*law*" presumably to bypass any contradictions that may arise with the orthodox belief in divine predetermined fate, while at the same time mitigating folkloric beliefs. On the evil eye in Muslim scripture and folklore, see Marçais 1960; also Abu-Rabia 2005.

10 He is the older brother of ʿAlī Ibn Abī Ṭālib, the Prophet Muḥammad's cousin and son-in-law.

11 Ibn Qutayba, *Taʾwīl Mukhtalif*, 314. Compare the *ḥadīth* with Al-Tibrīzī, *Mishkāt al-Maṣābīḥ*, Vol. 2, 1285. A similar version of this *ḥadīth* appears in *Muwaṭṭaʾ* Mālik, vol. 2, 939.

Building on his distinction between religious and philosophical epistemic approaches, Ibn Qutayba defends the veracity of the belief in magic based on Qur'ānic and other literary sources. Finally, he reaches his conclusion:

> They (i.e., his interlocutors) believed that magic is a trick (*ḥīla*) by which one person may be turned away from another or by which a husband may be separated from his wife, as [it is with] talismans and lies (*kidhb*). They said: these [include] incantations, potions which, when given to men for drinking, cause them to avoid women and change their character as well as make their beard and hair shed. They believed that Pharaoh's sorcerers made Moses imagine and not truly see [the magic]. They said, this is like if we take copper and empty it into a vessel in the shape of a snake, then we set it in a hot place; it will coil and wiggle like a snake. God's words are a proof of this: through their sorcery, their ropes and staffs seemed to him to be moving."[12] Hence, it is causing imagination (*takhyīl*) and thus nothing of it is real.[13]

The very example Ibn Qutayba employs here functions as a form of critique, precisely because it highlights the inherent limitations of sight as a source of knowledge, namely, its potential to mislead. Thus, Ibn Qutayba, via his opponents' argument, implicitly underscores the fact that the supposed empirical certainty derived from vision is, at its core, grounded in a priori belief or a conceptual predisposition. Visual inference does not operate in a vacuum; it is always shaped by underlying assumptions about what is real, credible, or possible. He then continues, focusing his critique on this predisposition:

> . . .We say that whoever takes this position opposes the Muslims, the Jews, the Christians, and all the people of revealed books and contradicts all nations, the Hindus, the greatest believers in magic, the Byzantines, the Arabs, in the time of the *jāhiliyya* and of Islam. He denies the Qur'ān, stubbornly resisting it with no [convincing] interpretation (*ta'wīl*). Because God Almighty told his apostle: "Say [Prophet], 'I seek refuge with the Lord of daybreak, the harm in the night when darkness gathers, the harm in witches when they blow on knots.'[14] Therefore, He taught us that the witches blow on knots that they make, as do the enchanters and spellbinders spit.[15]

Ibn Qutayba then ends a long account of traditions dealing with sorcery and magic with the following statement:

> [. . .] We do not believe this thing through *qiyās* (logical inference) or through rational contemplation (*ḥujjat al-'aql*), rather we believe in it by the power of the Qur'ān and the reports of the prophets (*the ḥadīth*), and the trustworthy [reports] confirmed by all nations (*tawāṭu'*

---

12 Q 20:66.

13 Ibn Qutayba, *Ta'wīl Mukhtalif*, 473–474.

14 Q 113:1–4.

15 Ibn Qutayba, *Ta'wīl Mukhtalif*, 261.

> *al-umam*)[16] of all ages. This is true [in the eyes of all] beside the group that does not believe in anything save those things which are necessitated by *naẓar* (rational reflection) and established through *qiyās* (logical inference) among those things which they have observed and seen (*shāhadū wa-rā'aw*).[17]

As previously noted, Ibn Qutayba performs several layered moves in this example. First, by combining language and scenarios related to vision and rational inference, he draws the philosophical conception of *naẓar* closer to its intellectual reflection, aligning it with its sensory and visual connotations. Second, he tacitly demonstrates that sensory perception itself is prone to error and grounded in an a priori predisposition. Finally, Ibn Qutayba criticizes this stance as fundamentally irreligious, insofar as it entails the a priori rejection of the unseen (*ʿālam al-ghayb*), a principle which he claims is shared by all recognized religious communities.

3 Knowledge and Truth as a Collective and Temporal Undertaking

Ibn Qutayba reiterates his critique of those who apply *naẓar*-driven scrutiny to religious texts and traditions at multiple points throughout *Ta'wīl Mukhtalif al-Ḥadīth* in which he portrays this *naẓar*-gaze upon *dīn* as animated by a misguided sense of epistemic superiority, one that is fundamentally alien to the structure of large-scale, tradition-based belief systems.[18] This approach is further reinforced by Ibn Qutayba's

16 See the discussion of the term *tawāṭu' al-umam* below, pages 59–63.

17 Ibn Qutayba, *Ta'wīl Mukhtalif*, 269.

18 See for example: "And we say that the Prophet, peace and blessings be upon him, and others as well, knew that a she-camel gives birth to a camel, and that it is not possible for a she-devil to give birth to a camel, nor for a she-camel to give birth to a devil. Rather, the Prophet taught us that [the camel] was originally created from the same breed from which the devils were created. According to this view, it is conceivable (*yajūzu*) that they originally came from the jinn livestock (*naʿam al-jinn*), rather than from the jinns themselves. That is why it was said: 'from the environs of the devils', meaning, from their vicinity. This thing cannot be denied unless one rejects the very [existence] of demons and devils and believes only in what his eyes see and that which he perceives through the senses alone. *He [therefore] belongs to the group of unbelievers [zanādiqa] and philosophers called the dahriyya and not to the Muslims.*" (Ibn Qutayba, *Ta'wīl Mukhtalif*, 204–205).

"There are those who submit the issues of religion to the evidence of the senses [*ʿalā mā shahada*]. For them the beast is unable to talk, the bird unable to praise, a geographic area [*al-buqʿa min biqāʿ al-arḍ*] unable to complain to another [*lā tashkū*] and the fly unable to distinguish the place of the medicine and that of the poison, criticizing the *ḥadīth* regarding things he does not understand. These kinds of persons ask, 'How is one qirāt (a measurement of value in weight) like

understanding of language and meaning as embedded within the semiotic structures shared by societies and religious communities. For him, sense-making is not a personal rational act, but one that operates within the boundaries of a collective tradition-bound linguistic and interpretive framework. One of the more revealing examples of this approach may be found in Ibn Qutayba's *Ta'wīl Mushkil al-Qur'ān*, a relatively early work that predates *Ta'wīl Mukhtalif al-Ḥadīth* and is similarly polemical in tone and structure.[19] In *Ta'wīl Mushkil al-Qur'ān*, Ibn Qutayba devotes a substantial section of the book to the linguistic phenomenon of *majāz* (transgressive or metaphoric language) in the Qur'ān, focusing in particular on rebutting the dichotomy, advanced by Muʿtazilite theologians and philosophically inclined scholars, which rigidly separates real (*ḥaqīqa*) from metaphorical or transgressive (*majāz*) meaning. This stance is succinctly articulated in the following passage, which concludes the theoretical prelude to the *majāz* section, before Ibn Qutayba proceeds to categorize and exemplify a range of linguistic phenomena, including *mutashābih* (allegorical language), *al-maqlūb* (inversions or syntactic transpositions), *al-ḥadhf* (ellipsis or omission), and *al-ikhtiṣār* (concise expression or abbreviation).

> Regarding those who allege [*majāz*] on the Qur'ān, they consider it to be false. Since the wall does not wish,[20] and the village does not ask,[21] this comes from the worst of their ignorance and the best indication of their shortsightedness and their lack of understanding. If *majāz* were false (*kidhb*), then every verb which was associated with an inanimate object would be

uḥud?' And how does *bayt al-maqdis* talk? And how does the devil eat with his left hand and drink with it as well? And what is this left of his? And how did Adam and Moses meet to discuss the issue of destiny (*qadar*) even though they are separated by centuries? Where then could they have argued? *[Whoever asks these questions] parts ways with Islam. He is [in fact] a Muʿaṭṭil, but he utilizes this and similar senseless and polemical sayings, and rejections of reports and traditions [about the Prophet]*, contradicting what the Messenger of God had delivered and the ways of the finest of his companions and followers. Whoever declares a part of what the Messenger of God had said to be false is equal to him who declared all of it to be false.

If he [the criticizer] wanted to convert from Islam to another religion that does not believe in these similar things, he would not find a fitting relocation. Because the Jews, the Christians, the Zoroastrians, the Sabeans, and the idol worshipers all believe in similar things, and you will find this written in their books. I do not know of anyone who denies this, except a group called the *dahriyya*, and they were followed by a group from the *ahl al-kalām* and the *jahmiyya*." (Ibn Qutayba, *Ta'wīl Mukhtalif*, 334–335).

19 Ibn Qutayba, *Ta'wīl Mushkil al-Qur'ān*.

20 Q 18:77: "So they moved on until they came to the people of a town. They asked them for food, but the people refused to give them hospitality. There they found a wall ready to collapse (lit. *yurīdu 'an yanqadda*), so the man set it right. Moses protested, 'If you wanted, you could have demanded a fee for this.'

21 Q 12:82: "Ask [the people of] the land (lit. "*wa-'is'ali al-qaryata. . .*") where we were and the caravan we travelled with. We are certainly telling the truth."

> void [of meaning] (*bāṭil*) so that most of our speech would be untruthful. Since we say, 'the legume has grown' and 'the tree rose' ('*ṭālat al-shajaratu*'), 'the fruit ripened', 'the mountain stood', and 'the price went down'.[22]

In order to fully grasp Ibn Qutayba's approach to *majāz* in the Qur'ān, it is necessary to backtrack to an earlier point in *Ta'wīl Mushkil al-Qur'ān*, where he illustrates the absurdity of applying rationalist interpretive methods to the language of *ḥadīth*. In the following passage, he addresses the criticism of magic and sorcery which appears in Q 2:102 in which the devils are said to have 'taught people witchcraft', exemplified by the story of the two angels Hārūt and Mārūt:

> Do you imagine that the two [angels] were teaching people talismans, falsehoods, or how to administer poisons?
>
> It is through such reasoning (*naẓar*) that they denied the punishment of the grave, the questioning [of the deceased] by the two angels, the living provision of martyrs with their Lord, the harmful effects of the evil eye, the efficacy of protective incantations and charms, the whisperings of *jinn*, the agitation caused by Satan, and the wailing of the *ghūl*.[23] But when they observed the widespread agreement (*tawāṭu'*) among the Arabs regarding such phenomena, and the frequency with which poets mentioned them. . . [Ibn Qutayba then quotes several examples from renowned Arab poets] they sought an excuse, saying: 'The cause of what people claim to see and hear is their isolation and unruliness in deserts and wilderness. One who is alone, reflects, becomes delusional, feels anxious, and imagines things, seeing what cannot be seen and hearing what cannot be heard.'

Ibn Qutayba continues by citing poetry and paraphrasing what he takes to be *naẓar*-based objections to the unseen world. The key term in this passage is *tawāṭu'*, which in this context refers to widespread consensus or collective agreement among a group over time.

Ibn Qutayba employs the term *tawāṭu'* repeatedly throughout his works, particularly when addressing issues of tradition, transmitted reports (*akhbār*), and the meanings of words and expressions.[24] In most cases, Ibn Qutayba's use of *tawāṭu'*

---

22 Ibn Qutayba, *Ta'wīl Mushkil al-Qur'ān*, 85.

23 "A fabulous being believed by the ancient Arabs to inhabit desert places and, assuming different forms, to lead travelers astray (sometimes, like the Bedouins, lighting fires on the hills the more easily to attract them), to fall upon them unawares and devour them." (MacDonald and Pellat 1965).

24 The use of the term *tawāṭu'* here draws special attention due to its dual and opposing meaning in medieval Arabic literature. On the one hand, the word means an agreement on a narrative or vision, which is proof of its veracity. For example, the term appears in a famous *ḥadīth* describing the vision of *laylat al-qadr* (the night of decree during Ramadan) in which it describes an agreement between the Prophet's companions' dreams. In the *ḥadīth* the Prophet Muḥammad says: "*arā ru'yākum qad tawāṭa'at*", "I see that your visions agree" (*Ṣaḥīḥ Muslim*, vol. 3, 170; *Ṣaḥīḥ al-Bukhārī*, vol. 3, 46), leading to its acceptance as truthful proof of *laylat al-qadr*'s timeframe. In Avicenna's

signifies not conspiracy or collusion, the common meaning in Modern Arabic and one which was employed in Ibn Qutayba's time as well, but rather the epistemic authority of communal consensus, especially when grounded in linguistic and cultural continuity.[25] It is especially telling that Ibn Qutayba draws upon Arab *lore* as a source of validation. For him, it is through the poetry, idioms, and proverbial expressions of the Arabian tribes that the true meanings of words, and indeed the semiotic architecture of the Arabic language, are revealed. As part of Ibn Qutayba's broader intellectual project which may be described as reconstructing interpretation (which one can find in the term he chooses to use for interpretation, *ta'wīl*, i.e., the return to the *awwal*, "the prime" – meaning) of religious texts and traditions on the philologic study of Arab culture and language, carried out more broadly in his *adab* work, he is also propagating a special reverence of the Arab culture and "nature". This exaltation of Arabism is made explicit in his treatise *Fī Faḍl al-ʿArab* ("On the Excellence of the Arabs"), which serves as a defense of Arab supremacy in various fields and characteristics. Ibn Qutayba then turns to the Arab *tawāṭu'*, as well as to faith in the revealed words of the Qur'ān to make his point:

> And we do not deny that such things as they mention may indeed occur in the wilderness, but that does not negate the truth of what is heard and seen.
>
> The Arabs in their entirety, with their insight and intelligence, could not have collectively agreed (*tawāṭa'at*) upon illusion and conjecture. Not all can be said to have been produced

writing on language and metaphysics, *fī sabīl al-tawāṭu'* is a form of univocal meaning in which a name (a universal) carries one clear meaning and predicates one type of referent. De Haan 2015, 266–270. On the other hand, the term is used to describe a falsehood based on premediated collusion between parties to spread a false narrative, probably stemming from the phrase *al-tawāṭu'alā al-kidhb*, "conspiring to lie". This meaning is found in the field of *ḥadīth* study or criticism, a falsehood that may be countered by *tawātur*, the broad authentication of the *ḥadīth* usually based on the many successive reports and independent transmitters. See, for example, Ibn Taymiyya in: Ibn Taymiyya, *Dar' Taʿāruḍ al-ʿAql wa-al-Naql*, vol. 1, 360–362.

25 See the use of the term by Yaḥyā Ibn ʿAdī (d. 974), the Iraqi Christian philosopher and translator who wrote, among other things, polemics in Arabic: "Among the evident proofs is that the pure Gospel is accepted by many peoples whose countries are far from each other and who have different religions and diverse ambitions. It is not possible for ones such as them to collude (*lā yajūzu ʿalā amthaliha al-ṭawāṭu'*) nor is it thinkable that they would agree with one another." (translation by Sam Noble: https://www.tertullian.org/fathers/sbath_15_yahya_ibn_adi_01.htm [last accessed on January 8, 2026]), for the Arabic original, see Sbath 1929, 168.

> by fear or cowardness. Consider Abū al-Bilād al-Ṭahawī[26] and Ta'abbaṭa Sharran,[27] two of the rebellious spirits of the Arabs, almost like human demons, both of whom described the *ghūl*, depicted her features, and even wrestled with her.
>
> Or take Abū Ayyūb al-Anṣārī, who captured her. And 'Umar, may God be pleased with him, who wrestled with a *jinn*. Reports on this subject are too numerous to be fully encompassed. So, whoever believes in Muḥammad, peace and blessings be upon him, and in the truth of what he brought, must also believe in all of this and open his heart to it. But whoever denies it, because he only believes in that which is proven by rational deduction (*naẓar*) or by analogy (*qiyās*) with what he has personally seen among the inanimate and living things, what remains for the Muslims? And what, then, is left for the heretics (*mulḥidīn*)?[28]

As stated earlier, the verb *tawāṭa'a* is central to Ibn Qutayba's argument in this section. He elaborates on its significance through examples drawn from the Arab literary canon, demonstrating the authority of this continued communal consensus by citing the works of canonical Arab poets. Ibn Qutayba insists that the Arabs could not all have "agreed" on such matters unless they were in some sense real. The reasoning appears circular at first glance, yet it is precisely this circularity that defines his epistemology: the very fact of ongoing communal agreement constitutes proof of reality. The argument then culminates in an appeal to common religious sensibility and to the inescapability of faith in the unseen for those who consider themselves members of a religious community. Taken together, these elements form Ibn Qutayba's critique of *naẓar*-based reasoning; for Ibn Qutayba, the first premise of religious knowledge is not individual speculation but a volitional commitment to belonging within a community. To this end, he invokes two key verbs that construct communal epistemology: *āmana* (to believe) and *tawāṭa'a* (to agree by consensus).

This position must be situated within the broader context of Ibn Qutayba's *adab* training and his conception of language (*'ilm al-lugha*) as a culturally rooted phenomenon. For him, the meaning of words (*ma'ānī*) is a discursive linguistic entity created within the collective use of a speech community. Ibn Qutayba's focus is on the Arabic language and its historical and cultural foundations, which he considers indispensable to the project of interpreting religious texts. As long as the community agrees on their usage, through various acts of communication, these *ma'ānī*

---

26 An Arab poet, nicknamed Abū al-Ghūl and mentioned in Ibn Qutayba's book on "Poetry and Poets" (Ibn Qutayba, *al-Shi'r wa-al-Shu'arā'*, 259). He and others tell of his sighting and physical struggle with a *ghoul*.

27 This pre-Islamic poet and acclaimed warrior is known as Thābit Ibn Jābir Ibn Sufyān, and the stories around his character also include encounters with the *ghūl*. Arazi 2000. Also mentioned in Ibn Qutayba's *al-Shi'r wa-al-Shu'arā'*, 179–181.

28 Ibn Qutayba, *Ta'wīl Mushkil al-Qur'ān*, 79.

cannot be "false" or "unreal," but signify what is truly meant, and are therefore valid carriers of truth.

Thus, the verb *tawāṭa'a* underscores a fundamental aspect of language and meaning, its inherently collaborative nature within a community of speakers. Interestingly, in this context, *tawāṭa'a* stands in near opposition to its modern sense of ad hoc collusion or conspiracy. For Ibn Qutayba, the imbuing of meaning in *ma'ānī* across generations is what renders them real and authentic: their truth emerges through continuous and shared usage over time. This temporal dimension ensures that certain *ma'ānī* are not the products of individual interests, desires, or momentary inspiration, but rather the result of an organic, impersonal evolution of speech unfolding across generations. The persistence and stability of meaning across generations serve as a form of testimony to its veracity. Moreover, as entities that drive both daily communication and belief, they play a constitutive role in shaping collective identity. Their truth is, in this sense, discursive if not circular: they are deemed true because they function as axioms of community itself. By sustaining shared meaning, they reinforce the very bonds they presuppose, becoming indispensable both to the coherence of the tradition and to the epistemological framework that undergirds it.

The aspect of temporal continuity becomes even more apparent in other instances where *tawāṭa'a* is used. In *Ta'wīl Mukhtalif al-Ḥadīth*, Ibn Qutayba writes:

> We say that if their rejection of this *ḥadīth* is due to their disbelief in the creation of demons and devils [. . .] they are denying the truth of the Qur'ān and the widely established reports (*tawāṭa'at 'alayhi al-akhbār*) from the Messenger of God, and [denying] the previous prophets, God's books, and the past nations (*al-'umam al-khāliyya*).[29] Because God Almighty told us in his book that the devils make the sky a place for listening and that they throw [around] the stars.[30]

In this example, Ibn Qutayba invokes an even broader form of agreement, reports corroborated by the Prophet Muḥammad, the Qur'ān, and the accounts of past nations, all of whom, he argues, affirmed belief in these supernatural beings. This reference to the "ancient peoples," and to the accumulation of reports and narra-

---

29 The *umam al-khāliyya* motif has been discussed by John Wansbrough in *Quranic Studies* (2004, 3–4), where he identifies it as an exegetical theme found in the works of commentators such as Muqātil Ibn Sulaymān. He relates it to a broader literary topos, comparable to the *ubi sunt* motif in Wisdom Literature, which reflects on the fate of those who came before. In Qur'ānic exegesis, the theme typically appears in narratives concerned with divine retribution and destruction. See also Stewart 2024, 58–61.

30 Ibn Qutayba, *Ta'wīl Mukhtalif*, 194; The throwing of stars is a paraphrasing of Q 72:8–9 "[Earlier] we tried to reach heaven [for news], only to find it filled with stern guards and shooting stars. We used to take up positions there for eavesdropping, but whoever dares eavesdrop now will find a flare lying in wait for them."

tives that mutually reinforce one another across time, recurs throughout his writings, particularly in discussions of the supernatural. For Ibn Qutayba, the persistence of such accounts over the long *durée* functions as a transhistorical testimony to their truth. Finally, we return to the passage quoted above in which Ibn Qutayba defends the traditions on magic and sorcery by invoking the *tawāṭuʾ* throughout the ages (*tawāṭuʾ al-umam fī kul zamān*): "We do not believe (*lam nuʿmin*) this thing through inference (*qiyās*) or through rational logic (*ḥujjat al-ʿaql*), rather we believe in it by the power of the Qurʾān and the reports of the prophets and the trustworthy [traditions] confirmed by all nations of all ages ("*tawāṭuʾ al-umam fī kul zamān ʿalayhi*")."[31]

This passage is particularly revealing in that the *tawāṭuʾ* of past nations across history serves, for Ibn Qutayba, to corroborate and vindicate the reports of the prophets and even what is mentioned in the Qurʾān. This does not mean that the agreement of cultures throughout time, here concerning belief in sorcery and the supernatural, constitutes more substantial evidence than prophetic or Qurʾānic testimony. Rather, Ibn Qutayba emphasizes the element of belief (*lam nuʿmin*): the internal conviction that things are true. This conviction arises from timeless, cross-cultural narratives transmitted from generation to generation, narratives that themselves reinforce faith through their persistence and universality. Ultimately, Ibn Qutayba juxtaposes this form of conviction with that sought through rational argumentation, namely syllogistic inference or analogy (*qiyās*) and the proof of reason (*ḥujjat al-ʿaql*). In doing so, he asserts that true assurance stems not from personal speculative reasoning but from the enduring and collective structures of meaning embedded in human language and history.

Ibn Qutayba's defense of revelation and Prophetic tradition against the critique of reason (*naẓar*) operates on several levels. First, in his critique of *naẓar*, Ibn Qutayba illuminates the intricate interplay between vision, philosophical reasoning, and their shared dependence on a visual mode of conviction. Second, he demonstrates that veracity and certainty do not emerge from the intellect in isolation but from a discursive network of belonging—anchored in shared language, collective memory, and inherited meaning. Such conviction, for Ibn Qutayba, cannot exist in the timeless vacuum of logical abstraction; it is cultivated historically, through the successive transmission of cultures, peoples, and their narratives, reports, and words. In this sense, belief is not the product of detached speculation but of participation in an ongoing linguistic and communal tradition that sustains both meaning and faith. It is via time, human communication, and activity that the "real" and "meaningful" is revealed.

31 See above, page 62; Ibn Qutayba, *Taʾwīl Mukhtalif*, 270.

Bibliography

Abdel Haleem, M. A. S. (2004), *The Qur'ān.* Oxford: Oxford University Press.

Abu-Rabia, Aref (2005), "The Evil Eye and Cultural Beliefs among the Bedouin Tribes of the Negev." *Folklore* 116.3, 241–254.

Akkach, Samer, ed. (2021a), *Naẓar: Vision, Belief, and Perception in Islamic Cultures.* Leiden: Brill.

Akkach, Samer (2021b), "Naẓar: The Seen, the Unseen, and the Unseeable." In *Naẓar: Vision, Belief, and Perception in Islamic Cultures*, edited by Samer Akkach. Leiden: Brill, 12–32.

al-Bukhārī, Muḥammad b. Ismāʿīl, *al-Jāmiʿ al-Ṣaḥīḥ*, edited by Muḥammad Zuhayr b. Nāṣir al-Nāṣir. Beirut: Dār Ṭawq al-Najāh, 2001.

al-Khaṭīb al-Tibrīzī, Muḥammad b. ʿAbd Allāh, *Mishkāt al-Maṣābīḥ*, edited by Muḥammad Nāṣir al-Dīn al-Albānī. Beirut: al-Maktab al-Islāmī, 1979.

Arazi, Albert (2000), "Taʾabbaṭa Sharran." In *Encyclopaedia of Islam*, 2nd ed. Leiden: Brill. https://referenceworks.brillonline.com/entries/encyclopaedia-of-islam-2/taabbata-sharran-SIM_7313 (last accessed on October 30, 2025).

De Boer, Tjitze, and Hans Daiber (2021), "Naẓar." In *From the Greeks to the Arabs and Beyond. Volume 2: Islamic Philosophy.* Leiden: Brill, 57–62.

De Haan, Daniel D. (2015), "The Doctrine of the Analogy of Being in Avicenna's Metaphysics of the Healing." *The Review of Metaphysics* 69, 261–286.

Gardet, Louis and Jean-Claude Vadet (1978), "Ḳalb." In *Encyclopaedia of Islam*, 2nd ed. Leiden: Brill. https://referenceworks.brillonline.com/entries/encyclopaedia-of-islam-2/kalb-SIM_4025 (last accessed on October 30, 2025).

Goldstein, Miriam (2019), "Ibn Qutayba and the Rise of the Conceptions of Authorship in the Classical ʿAbbasid Period." *Jerusalem Studies in Arabic and Islam* 45, 37–71.

Goldziher, Ignaz (1962), "Dahriyya." In *Encyclopaedia of Islam*, 2nd ed. Leiden: Brill. https://referenceworks.brillonline.com/entries/encyclopaedia-of-islam-2/dahriyya-SIM_1682 (last accessed on October 30, 2025).

Heinrichs, Wolfhart (1984), "On the Genesis of the Ḥaqīqa–Majāz Dichotomy." *Studia Islamica* 59, 111–140.

Hirtenstein, Stephen (2021), "Human Looking, Divine Gaze: Naẓar in Islamic Spirituality." In *Naẓar: Vision, Belief, and Perception in Islamic Cultures*, edited by Samer Akkach. Leiden: Brill, 63–87.

Huseini, Ishaq Musa (1950), *The Life and Works of Ibn Qutayba.* Beirut: The American Press.

Ibn Qutayba, ʿAbd Allāh b. Muslim. *al-Shiʿr wa-al-Shuʿarāʾ*, edited by Mufīd Qamīḥa. Beirut: Dār al-Kutub al-ʿIlmiyya, 1985.

Ibn Qutayba, ʿAbd Allāh b. Muslim. *Faḍl al-ʿArab wa-al-Tanbīh ʿalā ʿUlūmihā (The Excellence of the Arabs)*, edited by James E. Montgomery and Peter Webb; translated by Sarah Bowen Savant and Peter Webb. New York: New York University Press, 2017.

Ibn Qutayba, ʿAbd Allāh b. Muslim. *Taʾwīl Mukhtalif al-Ḥadīth.* Beirut: al-Maktaba al-Islāmiyya, Muʾassasat al-Ishrāq, 1999.

Ibn Qutayba, ʿAbd Allāh b. Muslim. *Taʾwīl Mushkil al-Qurʾān*, edited by Ibrāhīm Shams al-Dīn. Beirut: Dār al-Kutub al-ʿIlmiyya, 1971.

Ibn Taymiyya, Taqī al-Dīn Aḥmad b. ʿAbd al-Ḥalīm. *Darʾ Taʿāruḍ al-ʿAql wa-al-Naql*, edited by Rashād Sālim. Riyadh: Jāmiʿat al-Imām Muḥammad b. Saʿūd al-Islāmiyya, 1991.

Jolivet, Jean (2003), "Les yeux des chauves-souris." In *Autour du regard: Mélanges Gimaret*, edited by Éric Chaumont et al. Leuven: Peeters Press, 53–62.

Lecomte, Gérard (1965), *Ibn Qutayba: L'homme, son œuvre, ses idées.* Damascus: Presses de l'Ifpo.

Lecomte, Gérard (1962), *Le traité des divergences du ḥadīth d'Ibn Qutayba.* Damascus: Presses de l'Ifpo.
Lecomte, Gérard (1971), "Ibn Ḳutayba." In *Encyclopaedia of Islam,* 2nd ed. Leiden: Brill. https://referenceworks.brillonline.com/entries/encyclopaedia-of-islam-2/ibn-kutayba-SIM_3335 (last accessed on October 30, 2025).
Lowry, Joseph E. (2004), "The Legal Hermeneutics of al-Shāfiʿī and Ibn Qutayba: A Reconsideration." *Islamic Law and Society* 11.1, 1–41.
MacDonald, Duncan B., and Charles Pellat (1965), "Ghūl." In *Encyclopaedia of Islam,* 2nd ed. Leiden: Brill. https://referenceworks.brillonline.com/entries/encyclopaedia-of-islam-2/ghul-SIM_2411 (last accessed on October 30, 2025).
Mālik b. Anas. *al-Muwaṭṭaʾ*, edited by Muḥammad Fuʾād ʿAbd al-Bāqī. Beirut: Dār Iḥyāʾ al-turāth al-ʿArabī, 1985.
Marçais, Philippe (1960), "ʿAyn." In *Encyclopaedia of Islam,* 2nd ed. Leiden: Brill. https://referenceworks.brillonline.com/entries/encyclopaedia-of-islam-2/ayn-SIM_0883 (last accessed on October 30, 2025).
McNeill, William (1999), *The Glance of the Eye: Heidegger, Aristotle, and the Ends of Theory.* Albany: State University of New York Press.
Muslim b. al-Ḥajjāj al-Qushayrī, Abū al-Ḥusayn, *al-Jāmiʿ al-Ṣaḥīḥ*, edited by Muḥammad Dhihnī Afandī et al. Istanbul: Dār al-Ṭibāʿa al-ʿĀmira, 1915–1916.
Sbath, Paul (1929), *Vingt Traités Philosophiques Et Apologétiques D'auteurs Arabes Chrétiens Du IXe Au XIVe Siècle.* Cairo: H. Friedrich et co.
Soravia, Bruna (2004), "Ibn Qutayba en al-Andalus: La préface à l'*Adab al-Kātib* dans le commentaire d'Ibn al-Sīd al-Baṭalyawsī." *al-Qanṭara* 25.2, 539–565.
Stewart, Devin J. (2024), "Signs for Those Who Can Decipher Them: Ancient Ruins in the Qurʾān." In Behind the Story: Ethical Readings of Qurʾānic Narratives, edited by Samer Rashwani. Leiden: Brill, 44–92.
Van Ess, Josef van (2003), "Schauen und Sehen als ontologisches Problem in der frühen islamischen Theologie." In *Autour du regard: Mélanges Gimaret*, edited by Éric Chaumont et al. Leuven: Peeters Press, 1–13.
Wansbrough, John (2004), *Quranic Studies: Sources and Methods of Scriptural Interpretation.* Amherst, NY: Prometheus Books.
Yahav, Yehonatan (2024), *Ibn Qutayba al-Dīnawarī and the Relationship between Adab and Theology in his Work.* PhD dissertation, The Hebrew University of Jerusalem.

Part II: **Poetic and Qurʾānic Temporalities**

Hannelies Koloska

Creating Time through Memory and Vision

The Companions of the Cave in the Qur'ān and Their Pictorial Afterlife

1 Introduction

"*On the Day they see it, it will seem they lingered an evening, or its morning.*" (Q 79:46). This verse, which concludes sūrat al-Nāziʿāt, refers to the moment when final judgment will appear, and when those who denied resurrection will perceive the entire span between death and resurrection as no more than a single night or morning. It resumes the polemical exchange introduced earlier (vv. 10–12), where the opponents express doubt about the resurrection of the dead. It concludes the counterargument to their demand for precise chronological predictions of the world's end (v. 43) by reaffirming the Prophet's specific role as warner (v. 45), a role that explicitly excludes any claim to exact temporal knowledge (v. 44). It reiterates the suddenness with which the end will occur. Yet the verse does more than emphasize eschatological surprise. It also reveals how the passage of time is perceived at the moment of awakening from death. What had seemed to be a long absence to human perception is, upon awakening, experienced as only a brief interval. The verse thus links consciousness and perception directly to temporal awareness. Similar reflections on the brevity of life and the differing perception of time between humans and God are familiar from biblical traditions (e.g., Psalm 90:4), yet the Qur'ān situates this perception within a concrete eschatological scene: The *Hour* itself is seen, and the elapsed time is felt as momentary.

Contemporary scholarship, particularly in non-Muslim academic traditions, focuses on philological and contextual analyses of time-related vocabulary and concepts in the Qur'ān. Studies have illuminated the significance of terms such as *ajal* ("appointed term"), *as-sāʿa* ("the Hour"), or *al-ākhira* ("the Hereafter"), tracing their connections to pre-Islamic poetry or inscriptions, Christian apocalyptic traditions, or Greco-Roman thought.[1] Yet this term-centered approach often overlooks how time in the Qur'ān is not simply named or measured, but generated through literary practices. What happens when we shift our attention from time as a conceptual category to time as a mode of and in narration?

1 For example, Tamer 2008, El-Masri 2020, Karic 2023, or Sinai 2023.

https://doi.org/10.1515/9783112240038-005

I would like to argue that the Qur'ān does not merely describe time through terminology, it actively constructs temporal consciousness through its literary forms and sensory evocation.[2] It invites the audience to construct a particular sense of time through its language, structure, and imagery. Memory thereby emerges as the central mechanism of temporal experience, as a means by which the past is made present again. The Qur'ān repeatedly names itself *dhikr*, "reminder," situating time in acts of remembering. Memory is hence not abstract or disembodied; it is mediated mainly through the senses—most notably through hearing and vision. Thus, the Qur'ān establishes time not just as a theological category, but produces it as an affective, embodied experience.

This understanding resonates with Shahzad Bashir's conceptualization of Islamic temporality, which provides a productive framework for examining how perception, memory, and narration intersect in the Qur'ānic text.[3] Bashir conceives of "past" and "future" not as fixed temporal concepts but as relational constructs that emerge through human acts of positioning. Such positionings are attempts to orient oneself toward what cannot be directly sensed.[4] What he calls the "horizon" marks the "vantage point" from which individuals imagine and engage pasts and futures, and which shifts with every act of interpretation. Time, then, is not only indexed by words but generated by a form of subjectivity. My contention is that in the Qur'ān, this vantage point is structured around the concept of remembrance *(dhikr, tadhkira)*, which renders past and future events temporally accessible and experientially immediate. Stories from the past are invoked as if they are immediately present. Scenes from the afterlife are rendered visible, as though the listener were witnessing them.[5] The audience is instructed to watch and behold signs in nature (e.g., Q 51:21), to observe the end of previous generations (e.g., Q 6:11), or to see and taste the punishment of hell (Q 44:43–49).[6] In the following, I will trace how such temporal consciousness emerges through literary texture.

Methodologically, the Qur'ān is treated as a literary-theological text whose meaning arises in the interplay between textual form and interpretive horizon.[7] This approach is attentive to the Qur'ān's dialogical relationship with its audiences—past and present. The horizon of meaning for the Qur'ān's first audience

2 Berndt 2014, 48–67.

3 Bashir 2022, chapter: "Time".

4 Gadamer argued similarly that the past is approached through the act of interpretative positioning, and hence one's horizon is the lens through which meaning is constructed, Gadamer 2006, 297–301.

5 Lange 2015, 37–48, al-Azmeh 1995.

6 Koloska 2024, 1–3.

7 Abu Zaid 2005, 13–14.

included local cultural memory, biblical and late antique traditions, and Arabic poetic conventions.[8] For later interpretive communities, it also encompassed accumulative commentary, evolving theological commitments, and changing historical contexts. Understanding the Qur'ān's establishment of memory-based temporality thus requires a study of its literary strategies and the interpretative options it offers. Hence, the article proceeds in two stages. First, it surveys the Qur'ānic interplay of remembrance and vision. Second, it turns to a close reading of the narrative of the Companions of the Cave (Q 18:9–26), a passage in which past, present, and future are interwoven into a multilayered text. Through this case study, I want to show how the Qur'ānic text offers a sensory-based experience of time through literary and rhetorical means. I will countercheck the literary analysis with the exegetical works of aṭ-Ṭabarī (d. 310 AH / 923 CE), and of al-Zamakhsharī (d. 538 AH / 1144 CE). Al-Zamakhsharī's *al-Kashshāf* is particularly suited to this study because of its strong engagement with the Qur'ān's rhetorical form and linguistic precision, which aligns with this article's focus on time as a literary experience. Finally, an outlook examines how these temporal and perceptual dynamics are reimagined in later Islamic visual culture, where the Qur'ānic theology of time is translated into image.

2 A Temporal Framework: Not History but Memory

The Qur'ān does not present a sustained historical or chronological narrative, unlike, for example, the Biblical scriptures. There is no Genesis-to-Apocalypse arc, nor a biographical sketch of the life of the Prophet. The Qur'ānic text avoids historicizing tendencies and operates with a conception of time that is moral and eschatological rather than historical.[9] It evokes events not to locate them in temporal sequence, but to embed them in the consciousness of the audience as remembered truths and as moral examples. In other words, it constructs memory and not history.[10] This plays out through distinct yet interconnected levels of memory and remembrance. At the most fundamental level, *dhikr* or *tadhkira* is a divine reminder: the Qur'ān designates itself as a reminder that shall reactivate knowledge already embedded within human consciousness.[11] This is evident in passages such as Q 68:52: "*But truly it [the Qur'ānic revelation] is nothing other than a Reminder (dhikr) for the inhabitants of*

8 Neuwirth 2019, 105–138.

9 Neuwirth 2014, 104, and Ghaffar 2025, 181.

10 Böwering 1997, Neuwirth 2019, 113–114, Kermani 2015, 4–5.

11 Sells 2018.

all worlds". This represents memory as an ontological reality rather than a mental faculty. At a second level, there is memory of collectives, where the experiences of past messengers and their communities are presented not as distant historical events but as perpetually accessible and recurring moral exemplars.[12] The imperatives in Q 38:41: "*Remember (udhkur) Our servant Job*", or in Q 46:21: "*Remember (udhkur) one of ʿAd's brethren*" activate a collapse of temporal distance into moral proximity. At a third level operates collective memory, where the community around the Prophet is addressed through its shared past, as in Q 8:26: "*Remember (udhkurū) when you were few*". It summons the early Muslim community's experiences as living memory. Finally, there is individual remembrance, the personal and immediate accepting or rejecting response to divine signs, such as Q 25:73: "*Who, when reminded (alladhīna idhā dhukirū) of their Lord's signs, do not turn a deaf ear and a blind eye to them*". Each level permeates the others, creating what Shahzad Bashir identifies as a "temporal horizon" that situates the audience simultaneously within divine eternity, prophetic precedent, communal heritage, and personal encounter.

Nonetheless, the Qurʾānic text acknowledges temporal structures, not just the sequence of night and day, but also of past events, present imperatives, and future judgment. However, its rhetorical strategy is to collapse this structure into a simultaneity.[13] Narratives about earlier prophets are recounted to serve theological and moral purposes, shifting focus depending on the context in which they are retold and frequently moving between narration and direct address to the audience. Eschatological scenes are placed alongside exhortations to act, and natural cycles are described for their mnemonic power: "*So will you not remember?*" (Q 37:155). As Michael Sells has shown, the meanings of *dhikr* and *tadhkira* evolve across the Qurʾānic corpus, yet consistently center on memory as a mode of divine-human interaction.[14] The polyvalent notion of memory—cognitive, ethical, and ritual—is, thus, central to the Qurʾānic understanding of time.

3 A Sensory Framework: Visualizing Memory

Memory can be defined as an abstract concept, but in personal experience, it is rooted in sensory encounters—the sound of a voice, the sight of a place, or the smell of an object. The Qurʾān, in emphasizing memory, draws on this sensory foundation. It constructs and activates memory through what can be heard and seen,

12 Stewart 2024, 55–58.
13 Brown 1983, 167–168.
14 Sells 2018.

what can be made visible, and ultimately, what can be imagined. Since the past and future lie beyond immediate sensory perception, they must be accessed through acts of imagination or recollection. The Qurʾānic text does not entrust this process solely to the intellect. Rather, it scaffolds the imagination through recurring sensory cues. Of the five traditional senses, the Qurʾān places remarkably little emphasis on touch, taste, or smell—the senses often most closely associated with the longevity of individual memory.[15] Instead, it foregrounds two senses with distinct epistemological and ethical valence: hearing and seeing.[16] The Qurʾān repeatedly presents these faculties, along with the heart, as the instruments by which knowledge can be obtained and as the loci of comprehension. Moreover, they are created to perceive divine communication, and humans will be held accountable for their use, as in Q 90:8–10 that asks rhetorically: *"Have We not made for him a pair of eyes, and a tongue, and a pair of lips, and point out to him the two clear paths?"*; or in Q 16:78: *"It is God who brought you forth from your mothers' wombs when you knew nothing; and He made for you hearing, sight, and hearts, so that you may be thankful."* A sharp eschatological emphasis is displayed in Q 17:36: *"Do not pursue that of which you have no knowledge. The hearing, the sight, and the heart—each of those shall be questioned."* In Q 18:100–101 the consequence of disregarding the Qurʾānic message and its inherent memorial character is described: *"On that Day We shall present Hell plainly to the disbelievers, those whose eyes were veiled from My reminder, and who could not bear to hear."* Hence, the senses are not merely physiological faculties; they are instruments of epistemic and moral significance. They do not simply gather impressions—they store, they remember, and ultimately they testify. This theological weight of the senses is made fully explicit in the eschatological scene of Q 41:20–22, where bodily faculties become witnesses:

> Their ears, eyes, and skins will, when they reach it [the fire], testify against them for their misdeeds. They will say to their skins, 'Why did you testify against us?' and their skins will reply, 'God, who gave speech to everything, has given us speech—it was He who created you the first time and to Him you have been returned—yet you did not try to hide yourselves from your ears, eyes, and skin to prevent them from testifying against you. You thought that God did not know about much of what you were doing.[17]

In this depiction of the afterlife, the senses are sites of recording and, eventually, autonomous narrators of the truth. The language of testimony (*shahāda*) given to ears, eyes, and skin reframes sensory experience as embedded memory. What one sees, hears, or feels remains inscribed and reemerges in the ultimate moment of

15 Lange 2022, 24.

16 Koloska 2024, 10–20.

17 Translations of longer Qurʾānic passages are based on Abdel Haleem 2004.

judgment. Memory, then, is distributed across the body and grounded in its sensory engagements with the world. Among these faculties, hearing seemingly occupies a privileged place in the Qur'ān. While the verses reference sight, speech, and touch, it is through hearing that revelation is primarily received, remembered, and enacted.[18] The Qur'ān is first and foremost an oral text: God *says*, the Prophet *speaks*, the believers hear. Thus, hearing the verses (*āyāt)* is the original source of memory. However, sight plays an equally important role in the Qur'ānic epistemology of memory. The audience is repeatedly commanded to look, to observe, to consider what is visible: the natural world, the ruins of past civilizations, cosmological phenomena. Seeing is framed not as a passive act of visual reception, but as a prerequisite to recognizing and acknowledging divine signs (*āyāt*). In Q 32:27, the rhetorical question "*Have they not seen that We drive water to barren land. . .?*" demands that the audience not merely look at natural phenomena but also interpret them as divine action. Similarly, Q 6:11 urges: "*Roam the land, then observe how was the consequence for those who denied the truth.*" Here, sight becomes the vehicle for historical memory, as an immediate and moral lesson inscribed in the landscape.

The Qur'ān thus constructs a sensory pedagogy of memory. *Seeing* and *hearing* become tools to access both the remembered past and the anticipated future. Through hearing the verses (*āyāt*) and seeing the signs (*āyāt*), the audience is set into a temporal horizon in which past events, present observation and audition, and future expectations converge.[19]

4 Comparative Horizons: Memory, Senses, and Time in Late Antiquity

The Qur'ān shares with its emphasis on hearing and seeing in the broader late antique interest in embodied memory and sensory instruction, but it shifts the focus from ritual reenactment to ethical hearing and seeing. While Christian and Jewish traditions engage the full range of sensory experience—taste, touch, smell, sight, and sound—the Qur'ān emphasizes above all hearing and sight. Since early on, memory has been activated among Christian communities through multisensory liturgy, particularly in the Eucharist.[20] The directive: "*Do this in remembrance of me*" (Luke 22:19) underscores memory not as passive recollection but as re-expe-

18 Kermani 2015, 138–140.
19 Stewart 2024, 61–68.
20 Caseau 1999, 101–110.

riencing by the tasting of bread and wine. In Jewish tradition, embodied memory likewise takes form in rites such as the Passover Seder, where storytelling, ritual foods, and symbolic gestures merge to reactivate the memory of the Exodus.[21] Moreover, pilgrimage to sacred sites played a vital role in the sensory formation of memory. Moving through sacred landscapes allowed Christian or Jewish believers to transform physical into spiritual proximity, so that the visual encounter with a sacred site was not only commemorative but participatory.[22] Guy Stroumsa has noted that in the religious transformations of Late Antiquity, the spiritualization and interiorization of religion often led to a de-historicization of narrations in favor of a symbolic paradigm.[23] The Qur'ān participates in this shift, not by abandoning history, but by transforming its function: the past becomes archetype, not origin; an example, not a precedent. As a result, the Qur'ān's engagement with time is foremost typological and eschatological. The sensory faculties function as doorways into this moral temporality. What distinguishes the Qur'ān is not the use of the senses per se, but its theological investment in the ethical function of sensory perception, since the body records and the senses testify.

5 Memory and Vision and the Companions of the Cave

Sūrat al-Kahf (Q 18) occupies a unique place within the Qur'ānic corpus for its incorporation of narrative elements of late antique storytelling.[24] Among these, the legend of the Companions of the Cave (*aṣḥāb al-kahf*) is perhaps the most emblematic. Recounted in verses 9 to 26, it engages with the Christian legend of the Seven Sleepers of Ephesus—a story of persecution, miraculous survival, and resurrection that was widely transmitted in Syriac, Greek, and Latin from the 6th century CE onwards.[25] The Qur'ānic narrative, however, does not merely recount the story. Rather, it reworks the legend in its own theological and rhetorical framework, wherein memory, witnessing, and temporality are woven together to engage the reader as a participating spectator.

---

21 Yerushalmi 1996, 1–26.
22 Frank 2000, 13–16, Neis 2013, 225–226.
23 Stroumsa 2009, 1–10.
24 Koloska 2015, 21–22.
25 Koloska 2015, 76–81.

6 Narrative Structure

Through a layered narrative that interlaces storytelling, commentary, and exhortation, the narrative demonstrates how Qur'ānic memory functions to recall the past and also to frame present ethical orientation and future hope. The narrative begins with a rhetorical challenge to the audience: "*Do you assume the Companions of the Cave and al-Raqīm were one of Our wondrous signs?*" (Q 18:9) It introduces the story as a known event, the question functions as a reminder: The story is not presented as a new miraculous spectacle to be marveled at, but as a theological prompt.[26] Accordingly, the narrative does not proceed with a chronological retelling of events. Instead, it shifts directly to a decisive moment of the story and its moral orientation: the youths taking refuge in the cave and praying, "*Our Lord, grant us mercy from Yourself and guide us rightly through our ordeal*" (Q 18:10). This moment of supplication is immediately followed by divine intervention—God causes them to sleep for many years, suspending them in time and transforming them into a subject of debate (Q 18:11). What follows is a more linear recollection of selected events such as the reason of their flight into the cave, with particular emphasis on the nature of their prolonged sleep therein, which becomes the narrative centerpiece: "*You would have thought them awake, though they were asleep. We turned them to the right and to the left, while their dog lay at the threshold with its forelegs outstretched. Would you see them, you would have turned and fled, filled with fear.*" (Q 18:18) The tension between sleep and wakefulness, perception and misrecognition are at the heart of this verse. Upon their awakening, the youths are unaware of how much time has passed, initiating a reflection on their knowledge of time. The following verses do not present a resolution to the story but its transformation into commentary and instruction. God alone knows the exact number of the sleepers (v. 22), and the Prophet is reminded not to speak of future intentions without invoking divine will: "*Do not say of anything, 'I will do it tomorrow,' without adding, 'If God wills.'*" (Q 18:23–24). Even the duration of their sleep is not definitively fixed, but enveloped in divine knowledge: "*They stayed in their cave three hundred years, some adding nine more. Say, 'God knows best how long they stayed'*" (Q 18:25–26).

26 See Ṭabarī, *Jāmiʿ al-bayān*, 155, who paraphrases the verse: What I have created of the heavens and the earth and the wonders therein is even more wondrous than the affair of the Companions of the Cave, and My proof through all of that is established.

7 The Role of Material Memory

As already mentioned above, the introductory verse functions as more than a rhetorical question, it reactivates the memory of the audience: "*Or do you think that the Companions of the Cave and al-Raqīm were, among Our signs, a wonder?*" (v. 9). The verse encapsulates a Qurʾānic strategy of memory-making: not the introduction of novelty, but the revitalization and reevaluation of remembered knowledge. The invocation of "*al-Raqīm*" contributes to this memorial structure. Though the exact referent remains debated, most classical and modern interpreters have read "*al-Raqīm*" as referring to a written record, possibly the lead tablets described in the Christian hagiographic tradition of the Seven Sleepers as the written records of their fate.[27] If so, the Qurʾānic mention of "*al-raqīm*" signifies a physical trace that preserves memory through inscription. Hence, the story is remembered twofold, as an event and as a material trace. Al-Zamakhsharī, not resolving the ambiguity of *al-raqīm*, draws attention to the linguistic and rhetorical function of the verse in relation to the previous verses that state the divine power of creation and destruction. He interprets *ʿajaban* ("wondrous") either as a descriptive verbal noun emphasizing the astonishing nature of the event, or as indicating that it is a source of wonder among God's signs.[28] Hence, the interpretive plurality of *raqīm* and of the nature and source of amazement marks the verse as a site of layered recollection, inviting the audience not only to recall a familiar story but to reconsider its meaning within the broader theological and epistemological framework of the Qurʾān.

The motif of material remembrance resurfaces at the narrative's conclusion, where groups debate how to commemorate the Companions: "*Let us build over them a structure (bunyan); their Lord knows best about them. Others propose, 'We will surely build a place of worship (masjid) over them*'" (Q 18:21). This tension between commemoration and sacralization mirrors a broader late antique and following Islamic debate around saint veneration, pilgrimage, and spatial memory.[29] The cave of the Seven Sleepers in Ephesus became, as early as the 5th century, a locus of pilgrimage among Early Christians, but sources indicate that the story and the space of veneration started travelling very soon. In later times, several places under Muslim rule were dedicated to the memory of the Companions of the Cave.[30] However, the interpretation of the dispute in Islamic tradition shares a different understanding of the material reference, where the discussion is understood as

27 Koloska 2015, 61–62.
28 Zamakhsharī, *Kashshāf*, 705.
29 Bursi 2021, 481–483.
30 Koloska 2017, 371–74, Zimmermann 2019.

a contest between non-Muslims—building a structure, and Muslims—building a mosque. Al-Ṭabarī reports that the associators (*mushrikūn*) insisted on building a structure over the youth: "for they are the sons of our ancestors, and we will worship God therein. But the Muslims said: We have more right to them, they are ours, we will build a place of worship (*masjid*) over them and pray therein and worship God."[31] The memorial of the sleepers becomes a materialized identity marker, and the act of building becomes an assertion of collective religious conviction. Zamakhsharī's interpretation provides a wider frame, emphasizing the functional dimensions of sacred architecture. He reminds the reader how the proposed structures serve specific devotional and preservation purposes. The building proposal represents a protective imperative: "so that people would not intrude upon them, being protective of their burial place and preserving it", which he compares to how an enclosure protected the Prophet's burial place. The mosque proposal, however, articulates a more spiritual economy: "where Muslims would pray and seek blessings from their place."[32] His interpretation transforms the commemoration contest from a question of material ownership into one of appropriate religious stewardship, where the rightful claimants propose the most theologically sound utilization of a sacred space.

8 Sensory Experience and the Imagination of Time

The narrative's power lies in its ability to collapse the temporal distance between past, present, and future. Through rhetorical involvement, description, and direct address, the audience is made to feel as though they are witnessing the event, which already foreshadows the future. Hence, the audience is invited to see in Q 18:17: "*And you would see the sun, when it rose, inclining away from their cave on the right, and when it set, passing away from them on the left, while they were [lying] within an open space thereof.*" This verse describes a cosmological observation, but it also crafts an experiential vision. The reader or listener is drawn into this moment as a witness. Even more striking is the way the state of the sleepers is described, Q 18:18: "*And you would think them awake, while they were asleep. And We turned them to the right and to the left, while their dog stretched its forelegs at the entrance. Would you see them, you would have turned and fled, filled with fear.*" Here, the interplay of

31 Ṭabarī, *Jāmiʿ al-bayān*, 217.
32 Zamakhsharī, *Kashshāf*, 711.

sight, emotion, and time is further exposed: what appears as wakefulness is in fact sleep, and yet within this sleep is divine action – God turns their bodies from side to side. The audience is not merely told about an event; they are invited to visualize and feel it.

Al-Zamakhsharī's interpretation of the verse engages with the linguistic and perceptual paradoxes embedded in the narrative. He begins by noting the ambiguity of the visual scene: "It is said: their eyes were open while they slept, so anyone looking at them would assume they were awake. Another opinion is: it was due to their frequent turning over during sleep."[33] Zamakhsharī's emphasis on grammatical variants enhances the effect of an ambiguous moment of sight. The reading *yuqallibuhum* ("He turns them") centers on God's action; in another, *taqallubihim* ("their turning") becomes a scene to be visualized, as if the reader is witnessing a continuous present: "as if it were said: you see and observe their turning".[34] He hence creates a performative story, pulling the audience into a state of temporal and perceptual tension. His attention also turns to the theological limits of seeing; he relates a tradition about the first Umayyad ruler Muʿāwiya, who wished to uncover the sleepers' cave but was warned by Ibn ʿAbbās. When Muʿāwiya persisted and sent men to investigate, they were killed.[35] This anecdote positions the act of seeing as a transgressive desire and dependent on divine permission. Furthermore, Al-Zamakhsharī's comments contribute a crucial dimension to the interplay of time and movement: "They turned twice a year, or once on the Day of ʿĀshūrā'"—introducing a rhythm of time, which is disconnected from natural human expectations and oriented towards sacred times.[36]

---

33 Zamakhsharī, *Kashshāf*, 708.

34 Zamakhsharī, *Kashshāf*, 709: "As if it were saying: 'you would see and witness their turning over.'"

35 Zamakhsharī, *Kashshāf*, 709: "It is reported that Muʿāwiya once went on a campaign against the Byzantines and passed by the cave. He said: 'If only it were unveiled for us so we could look at them.' Ibn ʿAbbās, may God be pleased with him, replied: 'That is not for you to do. God has already prevented one better than you from doing so, saying: 'Had you looked upon them, you would surely have turned away from them in flight". But Muʿāwiya said: 'I will not rest until I know their reality.' So he sent some people and said to them: 'Go and look.' They did so, but when they entered the cave, God sent upon them a wind that burned them.

36 Zamakhsharī, *Kashshāf*.

9 Perceiving Time: Memory, Duration, and Divine Knowledge

The entire narrative of the Companions of the Cave functions as a sustained reflection on time—its perception, its measurement, and its theological meaning. Hence, Muslim commentaries would view the narrative as demonstrating how God transcends human temporal limitations. The text presents time as a horizon open to divine action and human contemplation. The pivotal moment occurs in Q 18:12, when it explains why the sleepers were awakened: "*Then We raised them up so that We might make clear which of the two parties was better at calculating the time they had stayed.*" Time itself becomes a subject that tests human cognition and interpretive skill. Although the identification of both "parties" is contested,[37] one could argue that they are part of the narrative: the sleepers themselves, who later speculate about how long they have slept, and those outside the cave who will eventually discover them and debate their significance. Time is not an objective quantity here but a matter of dispute. When the companions awaken, their first impulse is not existential wonder but a practical question: "*They said, 'How long have we remained [here]?' They said, 'We have remained a day or part of a day'*" (Q 18:19). The phrase, which is used at different occasions in the Qur'ān to describe the time span between death and resurrection,[38] illustrates the experiential aspect of time measurement, what they experience as a brief rest, spans centuries. The narrative withholds immediate clarification and instead embeds the uncertainty into the story, drawing attention to the contrast between subjective perception and divine reality. Only at the end of the story do we find a numerical designation: *"And they remained in their cave for three hundred years, and some add nine."* (Q 18:25). Yet even this statement is surrounded by ambiguity. The addition of *wa-azdādū tisʿan* "some add nine" points toward speculation, not resolution. And the following verse reinscribes divine control over temporal knowledge: "*Say: God knows best how long they stayed*" (Q 18:26). Al-Zamakhsharī cites Qatāda's view that the numbers may be the reported speech of the "People of the Scriptures", while the divine command *"Say: God knows best how long they remained"* operates as a rebuttal.[39]

37 Ṭabarī, *Jāmiʿ al-bayān*, 176–177, he refers to groups among Muslims, non-Muslims, and groups among the companions.

38 E.g., Q 20:102–104, Q 23:112–115, 17:52, see Koloska 2015, 68–69.

39 Zamakhsharī, *Kashshāf*, 716.

10 Expecting Time—Future Events

Hence, the verses suspend the listener between different registers of time: human and divine, measurable and ineffable, and also historical and eschatological. The sleepers' temporal dislocation becomes a parable for future resurrection itself, Q 18:21: "*In this way We brought them to people's attention so that they might know that God's promise [of resurrection] is true and that there is no doubt about the Hour, [though] people argue among themselves.*" Through this verse, the story is bound to the later interpretation, the immediate audience, and extended forward toward the future. In verses 18:23–24, the question of future time and human agency is directly addressed. These verses mark a turning point from narrative to instruction, drawing out implications for how, firstly, the Messenger, and ultimately all believers, should speak about, imagine, and inhabit the future: "*And do not say about anything, 'I will do that tomorrow,' without adding, 'If God wills.' And remember your Lord when you forget and say, 'May my Lord guide me to what is nearer to right guidance.'*" The verses are apparently simple: they instruct not to make firm declarations about future actions without invoking God's will (*in yashā' Allāh*). Beneath this religious etiquette, a theology of time can be deduced: time is not possessed and cannot be properly perceived. The only way to orient oneself toward what is to come is through remembrance of God (*udhkur rabbaka idha nāsīta*). The verse deepens the dynamic between forgetfulness and *dhikr*; human beings are not only limited in their grasp of the future, but they are also prone to forget even their own present commitments and obligations. Zamakhsharī's interpretation of these verses extends this theology of time by showing how language itself becomes a field of temporal discipline. For him, the emphasis "*except if God wills*" is grammatically linked to the prohibition, not to the intended action. He shifts the focus to the act of speaking itself, suggesting that time begins not with doing, but with utterance. He explores the verse's implication that remembrance (*dhikr*) retroactively changes the moment of forgetfulness. Drawing from reports that allow for the phrase *in shā' Allāh* to be added even long after the initial intention, he affirms that divine time accommodates human delay. Moreover, Zamakhsharī interprets the closing prayer "*May my Lord guide me to that which is nearer to right guidance*" as an acknowledgment that even one's original intention might not have been the most virtuous.[40] Thus, remembrance becomes both memory and aspiration.

---

40 Zamakhsharī, *Kashshāf*, 715.

11 Outlook: From Text to Image

We have seen that the Qur'ānic text constructs a dynamic sense of time through the interplay of memory, imagination, and sensory experience. The story of the Companions of the Cave is perhaps an especially vivid example, but it is by no means exceptional; similar narrative patterns appear elsewhere in the Qur'ān. Looking outward, and in the literal sense of a look-out, I would like to turn to one visual depiction of this story in later Islamic miniature painting. In my view, these images enact on a pictorial level what the Qur'ān achieves textually: they translate the collapse of temporal distance and the intertwining of observation and remembrance into visual form.[41] Illustrated book production in the Islamic world began to flourish in the late 12th and 13th centuries CE, particularly under the ʿAbbāsid and Ilkhanid dynasties, when manuscripts, such as scientific treatises, histories, and *qiṣaṣ al-anbiyāʾ* (Stories of the Prophets), started to be illuminated with depictions or pictorial scenes. Among the recurring images was the story of the Companions of the Cave, whose compositional structure remained stable, showing the reclining youths sheltered in the cave.[42] One type of miniature expands this established composition by including figures gathered around the cave, such as the one presented here from the *Falnāmah.*[43] The story of the Companions of the Cave appears in such manuscripts, where its themes of sleep, awakening, and divine revelation are reimagined as visual meditations on fate, time, and the hidden workings of the divine.

---

41 The juxtaposition of several scenes of a narrative in one painting, as well as the use of multiple viewpoints, which leads to a temporal layering, was already stressed by Demirel and Dündar 2019.

42 Milstein, Rührdanz, and Schmitz 1999.

43 On the *Falnāma*, see Afshar 1999. The term *fal-nāma* ("book of omens") broadly designates manuals of divination, most often used for bibliomancy—consulting a sacred or poetic text for divine guidance. While early examples include Qur'ānic and poetic *fal-nāmas*, the most celebrated are the illustrated Safavid manuscripts of the sixteenth and seventeenth centuries, which paired verses and oracles with vivid miniature paintings of prophets, saints, and cosmological scenes. These pictorial *fal-nāmas*, as Afshar notes, reflect a syncretic tradition that combined Qur'ānic imagery, *qiṣaṣ al-anbiyāʾ* (Stories of the Prophets), and astrological symbolism, transforming acts of divination into meditations on fate, time, and divine agency.

Fig. 1: The Seven Sleepers, folio from the Falnāmah (Book of Omens), attributed to Iran, Qazvin, 1550s. Ink, opaque watercolor, and gold on paper. The Metropolitan Museum of Art, New York, Rogers Fund, 1935 (35.64.3), https://www.metmuseum.org/de/art/collection/search/449026 (last accessed on January 8, 2026).

In this miniature (Fig. 1), the seven sleepers lie side by side inside a shadowed cave, and their dog lies stretched across the entrance. Around the cave rise stylized rock formations. Outside, several figures surround the cave: a mounted ruler in ornate garments, soldiers, and attendants. They gesture toward the cave and toward each other, indicating their astonishment at the sight of the sleepers. Positioned slightly apart, a dark-skinned man wearing a white turban raises his hand upward toward the sky rather than toward the sleepers while addressing the ruler. This figure, interpreted as a vizier or religious counselor, with his gesture, may allude to the Qur'ānic verse (Q 18:9), “Do you think that the Companions of the Cave and al-Raqīm were one of Our wondrous signs?”, directing attention away from the miraculous bodies toward the divine source of the event. The miniature captures the central elements of the Qurʾānic account: the cave, the miraculous sleep, and the wonder surrounding the sleepers. While the Qurʾān dwells on the dialogue that unfolds after their awakening, the uncertainty about how long they remained, the debate over their number, and the manner of their commemoration, the painting concentrates on the miracle itself: the suspended sleep and the moment of their rediscovery, so to speak, when the hidden treasure of the cave becomes visible. In Dirk Westerkamp's terms, the scene's *Bildinhaltszeit,*[44] that is the temporal structure inherent to the pictorial content itself, is multilayered and independent of narrative sequence. Here, the coexistence of the sleepers' centuries-long repose, the moment of their rediscovery, and the gesture pointing toward divine eternity creates a layered temporality in which past, present, and transcendent timelessness unfold simultaneously. Moreover, the artist organizes the composition not around a single perspectival focus but through multiple vantage points: the viewer looks simultaneously into the cave and at the reclining youths, and across the cave and the upper plane where the ruler and his interpreter approach. Furthermore, the viewer's gaze is guided by the different figures, what they are looking at, and by their gestures.

This multiplicity of viewpoints parallels the Qurʾānic construction of narration, commentary, and command, and thus its construction of time, where past, present, and future coexist within a single perceptual horizon. The viewer becomes a co-participant in the scene, and the verse's prediction is fulfilled for the observer: “so that they might know that God's promise is true” (Q 18:21). In this way, the act of beholding becomes, through the very mode of depiction, a form of visual testimony to the Qurʾānic statement that “this is among God's signs (*āyāt*)” (Q 18:17). The painting thus functions as a visual *tadhkira*, a reminder that fuses recollection with vision. Through its layered perspectives, temporal simultaneity, and participatory gaze, the *Falnāmah* painting exemplifies how later Islamic art internalized the Qurʾānic theology of time by rendering simultaneity visible through spatial composition.

And yet, my interpretation remains one among others, and it must remain open to the ambiguities embedded in the picture. Art historians, such as Massumeh Farhad and Serpil Bağcı, remind us that the Falnāmah paintings were designed for divinatory use and thus invited multiple, even contradictory, readings.[45] In this context, the image requires the observer to bring along theological, communal, and moral knowledge: to recognize the reclining youths as God's protected believers or

44 Westerkamp 2022, 14.
45 Farhad and Bağcı 2009.

maybe the awaited Mahdi, the dark-skinned figure as Satan or an evil guide, and the mounted ruler as Daqyānūs (Decius), the persecuting king, or the later Christian king who discovers the sleepers, a shift that inverts the polarity of good and evil and turns the scene into one of miraculous recognition rather than persecution. This ambiguity invites the viewer to move between temporal planes: the time of the Qur'ānic revelation, the times when meanings were attached to the story, and the time of its pictorial reenactment. In this sense, the image not only materializes Qur'ānic time creation, as I assume, but also tests our capacity to discern and to imagine multiple horizons of temporal perception and interpretation.

Bibliography

Abdel Haleem, Muhammad A. S. (2004), *The Qur'ān*. Oxford: Oxford University Press.

Abu Zaid, Nasr (2005), *Rethinking the Qur'ān. Towards a Humanistic Hermeneutics*. Philadelphia: Humanistic University Press.

Afshar, Iraj (1999), "Fāl-Nāmā." *Encyclopaedia Iranica Online*. https://www.iranicaonline.org/articles/fal-nama (last accessed on October 30, 2025).

al-Azmeh, Aziz (1995), "Rhetoric for the Senses: A Consideration of Muslim Paradise Narratives." *Journal of Arabic Literature* 26.3, 215–231.

Bashir, Shahzad (2022), *A New Vision for Islamic Pasts and Futures*. Cambridge, MA and London: The MIT Press. https://islamic-pasts-futures.org (last accessed on October 30, 2025).

Berndt, Frauke (2014), "Literarische Bildlichkeit und Rhetorik." In *Handbuch Literatur und visuelle Kultur*, edited by Claudia Benthien and Brigitte Weingart. Berlin: De Gruyter, 48–67.

Böwering, Gerhard (1997), "The Concept of Time in Islam." *Proceedings of the American Philosophical Society*, 141.1, 55–66.

Brown, Norman O. (1983), "The Apocalypse of Islam." *Social Text* 8, 167–168.

Bursi, Adam (2021), "Fluid Boundaries: Christian Sacred Space and Islamic Relics in an Early Ḥadīth." *Medieval Encounters* 27, 481–483.

Caseau, Béatrice (1999), "Christian Bodies: The Senses and Early Byzantine Christianity." In *Desire and Denial in Byzantium*, edited by Liz James. Aldershot: Ashgate, 101–110.

Demirel, Emre, and Zeynel Dündar (2019), "The Dialectic of Time and Space in Miniature Art: An Analysis of Kamāl ud-Dīn Behzād's Works." In *Zeitgeist*, edited by Nihat Ülner, Erkan Zengin et al. Berlin/Bern: Peter Lang, 47–62.

El-Masri, Ghassan (2020), *Semantics of Qur'ānic Language: al-Āḫira*. Leiden: Brill.

Farhad, Massumeh, and Serpil Bağcı (2009), "Freer Gallery of Art and Arthur M. Sackler Gallery." In *Falnama: The Book of Omens*, edited by Massumeh Farhad and Serpil Bağcı. Washington, D.C.: Arthur M. Sackler Gallery/Smithsonian Institution, 160–161, 260.

Frank, Georgia (2000), *Memory of the Eyes: Pilgrims to Living Saints in Christian Late Antiquity*. Berkeley: University of California Press.

Gadamer, Hans-Georg (2006), *Truth and Method*. Translated by Joel Weinsheimer and Donald G. Marshall. London/Oxford: Continuum.

Ghaffar, Zishan (2025), "Muhammad as a Prophet of Late Antiquity: The Anti-Apocalyptic Nature of Muhammad's Prophetic Wisdom." In *Theology of Prophecy in Dialogue: A Jewish-Christian-Muslim Encounter*, edited by Zishan Ghaffar and Klaus von Stosch. Leiden: Brill/Schöningh, 161–184.

Karic, Enes (2023), "Time in the Qurʾān: An Introductory Overview." *American Journal of Islam and Society* 40.1–2, 172–212.

Kermani, Navid (2015), *God is Beautiful: The Aesthetic Experience of the Quran*, translated by Tony Crawford. Oxford: Wiley.

Koloska, Hannelies (2015), *Offenbarung, Ästhetik und Koranexegese. Zwei Studien zu Sure 18 (al-Kahf)*. Wiesbaden: Harrassowitz.

Koloska, Hannelies (2017), "Ephesos und seine schlafenden Märtyrer in islamischer Tradition." In *Ephesos. Die antike Metropole im Spannungsfeld von Religion und Bildung*, edited by Tobias Georges. Tübingen: Mohr Siebeck, 361–375.

Koloska, Hannelies (2024), "Senses in the Qurʾān." In *Islamic Sensory History. Volume 2: 600–1500*, edited by Christian Lange and Adam Bursi. Leiden: Brill, 3–26.

Lange, Christian (2015), *Paradise and Hell in Islamic Traditions*. Cambridge: Cambridge University Press.

Lange, Christian (2022), "Qurʾānic Anosmia." In *Non Sola Scriptura: Essays on the Qurʾān and Islam in Honour of William A. Graham*, edited by Bruce Fudge et al. New York/London: Routledge, 23–43.

Milstein, Rachel, Karin Rührdanz, and Barbara Schmitz (1999), *Stories of the Prophets: Illustrated Manuscripts of Qiṣaṣ al-anbiyāʾ*. Costa Mesa: Mazda.

Neis, Raphael R. (2013), "Pilgrimage Itineraries: Seeing the Past through Rabbinic Eyes." *Jewish Studies Quarterly* 20.3, 224–256.

Neuwirth, Angelika (2019), "The Qurʾān and History." In *The Qurʾān and Late Antiquity: A Shared Heritage*, edited by Angelika Neuwirth. Oxford/New York: Oxford Academic, 105–138.

Neuwirth, Angelika (2014), *Scripture, Poetry, and the Making of a Community: Reading the Qurʾān as a Literary Text*. Oxford: Oxford University Press.

Sells, Michael (2018), "Memory." *Encyclopaedia of the Qurʾān Online*. https://doi.org/10.1163/1875-3922_q3_EQSIM_00276.

Sinai, Nicolai (2023), "Ajal." In *Key Terms of the Qurʾān: A Critical Dictionary*, edited by Nicolai Sinai. Princeton/Oxford: Princeton University Press, 26–30.

Stewart, Devin J. (2024), "Signs for Those Who Can Decipher Them: Ancient Ruins in the Qurʾān." In *Behind the Story: Ethical Readings of Qurʾānic Narratives*, edited by Samer Rashwani, Leiden: Brill, 44–92.

Stroumsa, Guy G. (2009), *The End of Sacrifice: Religious Transformations in Late Antiquity*. Chicago: University of Chicago Press.

al-Ṭabarī, Abū Jaʿfar Muḥammad b. Jarīr. *Jāmiʿ al-bayān ʿan taʾwīl āy al-Qurʾān*, edited by Maḥmūd Muḥammad Shākir, vol. 15. Mecca: Dār al-Tarbiyya wa-l-Turāth, n.d.

Tamer, Georges (2008), *Zeit und Gott*. Berlin/New York: De Gruyter.

Westerkamp, Dirk (2022), Schrift, Bild, Handlung. Hamburg: Felix Meiner Verlag.

Yerushalmi, Yosef Hayim (1996), *Zakhor: Jewish History and Jewish Memory*. Seattle: University of Washington Press.

al-Zamakhsharī, Maḥmūd b. ʿUmar. *al-Kashshāf ʿan ḥaqāʾiq ghawāmiḍ al-Tanzīl wa-ʿuyūn al-aqāwīl fī wujūh al-taʾwīl*, edited by Muṣṭafā Ḥusayn Aḥmad, vol. 2, Beirut: Dār al-Kitāb al-ʿArabī, 1987.

Zimmermann, Norbert (2019), "The Seven Sleepers of Ephesos: From the First Community Cemetery to a Place of Pilgrimage." In *Ephesos from Late Antiquity until the Late Middle Ages*, edited by Sabine Ladstätter and Paul Magdalino. Vienna: Österreichisches Archäologisches Institut, 257–271.

Ula Aweida

The Vision of Time in Ṭarafa ibn al-ʿAbd's *Muʿallaqa*

Mortality, Presence, and the Poetics of Temporality

1 Time in Ancient Arabic Poetry: A Conceptual Introduction

From the earliest stages of Arabic poetry, time (*al-zaman*) constituted one of the most prominent semantic fields through which the existential reflections of the ancient Arabs were articulated. Time was not merely conceived as an external framework by which events are measured but as an active force weaving destiny and summoning the great questions of life, death, and immortality. Pre-Islamic poets expressed an acute awareness of the volatility of *al-dahr* (fate/time) and the swiftness of mortality; their verses are laden with nostalgia, loss, and fear of the unknown. Thus, time became a fundamental structure for poetic expression. Emotions in this conception are at once bodily events and interior experiences of being. It is through feelings that we participate in the world, and emotions, so to speak, become the record of our existence within this world.[1]

Such a vision reveals that time in pre-Islamic poetry is not neutral or physical, but a symbolic force embodied in the ruins (*aṭlāl*), memory, fate (*al-dahr*), and death. This symbolic force is apprehended above all through vision: the poet's gaze upon ruins, traces, or fading marks transforms the external scene into an inner recognition of temporality. In this way, the awareness of time is mediated by vision, which transforms absence into presence and renders memory perceptible. The poet's awareness of time thus calls forth contrasting stances, including courage and hesitation, joy and grief,[2] to transform time into a concept charged with the meaning of life and death, happiness and sorrow, and the continuous transition between these states.[3]

This vision also resonates with religious and cultural attestations. The Qurʾān cites the pre-Islamic perception of *al-dahr* as a coercive force,[4] Q 45:24: "Moreover, they 'who reject resurrection' have said: There is nothing but our life in this world:

1 Macquarrie 1972, 121–122.
2 al-Ṣāʾigh n.d., 179.
3 al-Ṣāʾigh n.d., 179.
4 al-Ṣāʾigh n.d., 179–180.

we die 'once'. And we live 'once'. Therefore, nothing destroys us but 'the passage of' time".[5] Time, in this worldview, was organically bound to human beings and served as a medium through which praise or blame was articulated. *Al-dahr* thus assumed social dimensions, insofar as it was understood in relation to human actions, experiences, and responsibility.[6] Time was the container and humanity its substance.[7] Ibn al-Muqaffa' (d. 759 CE) later underscored this formative relationship when he wrote "Time is people."[8] Thus, time became deeply ingrained in the linguistic and cultural consciousness of the Arabs. The human being in pre-Islamic poetry was never outside of time but always shaped by and within it.

This problem of temporality in pre-Islamic poetry has already been addressed by several major scholars. Suzanne Stetkevych has emphasized the ritual structure of the *qaṣīda*, interpreting its progression from loss to journey as a symbolic negotiation with time and mortality.[9] James Montgomery has explored the ontology of *al-dahr* as an active force pressing upon the poetic self and shaping early Arabic reflections on existence.[10] More recently, Ghassan al-Masrī has examined how Qur'ānic discourse reconfigures pre-Islamic conceptions of temporality, fate, and divine agency, drawing extensively on pre-Islamic poetry and semantic-linguistic evidence.[11]

Beyond these scholarly engagements, this conception converges with later philosophical explorations of humanity's relation to temporality. Existential questions are treated through both poetry and philosophy, not only in the Arabic tradition but across cultures, where each serves as a medium to articulate being.[12] Poetry expresses possibility and what may be, not necessarily what already is, whereas philosophy articulates actuality and the being that is presently realized. Yet, human existence cannot be reduced to either pole; it unfolds through both, i.e., from possibility into actuality.[13] Poetry and philosophy thus strive, each in its own manner, to illuminate the darkness woven by time around human destiny.

Within this broader cross-cultural horizon, modern philosophy also engaged deeply with temporality. Heidegger, for instance, emphasized the human being as a creature "in-time" that is open to being and living existence self-consciously. Human life is a project directed toward its possibilities, not a static given; exist-

---

5 Hammad 2009, 872.
6 al-Ṣā'igh n.d., 190.
7 al-Ṣā'igh n.d., 190.
8 Ṣafwat n.d., 3:49.
9 Stetkevych 1993, 3–54.
10 Montgomery 2022.
11 El Masri 2020, especially chapters 3, 4, and 6.
12 Badawī 1947, 107.
13 Badawī 1947, 107.

ence is always oriented towards its ultimate potential.[14] Whereas the philosopher approaches this question conceptually, the pre-Islamic poet embodied temporal tension through imagery and metaphor. Ṭarafa ibn al-ʿAbd, for instance, articulates this awareness in his verse:

لَعَمْرُكَ إِنَّ المَوْتَ مَا أَخْطَأَ الفَتَى   لَكَالطِّوَلِ المُرْخَى وثِنْيَاهُ باليَدِ[15]

By your sweet life though death may miss a lad for the nonce
he's like a loosened lasso, whose loops are firmly in hand.[16]

And Labīd ibn Rabīʿa[17] proclaims:

ألا كُلُّ شيءٍ ما خَلا اللهَ باطِلُ   وكلُّ نَعيمٍ لا مَحالةَ زائِلُ[18]

Behold, everything apart from God is vain
and every pleasure is destined to decay.[19]

ʿUbayd ibn al-Abraṣ,[20] with stark brevity, captures life's fragility:

ما تَبْتَغي مِنْ بَعْدِ هذا عِيشَةً   إلا الخُلودَ ولَنْ تنالَ خلودَا[21]

What life beyond this could you desire;
save immortality? Yet that you shall not gain.

---

14 Heidegger 2001, 36–40.
15 Ṭarafa ibn al-ʿAbd, *Dīwān*, 26; On Ṭarafa ibn al-ʿAbd, see below.
16 Arberry 1957, 87.
17 Labīd b. Rabīʿa (b. ca. 545 or 565 CE, d. ca. 40/660–1) was one of the greatest pre-Islamic and early Islamic poets. He is renowned for his vivid depictions of nature, particularly in the *aṭlāl* (deserted campsite) and *raḥīl* (journey) sections of his *qaṣīdas*. Labīd also developed the onager topos, portraying the wild ass both as a mirror of the she-camel and as a symbol of hardship. In his later poetry, he turned his focus to the theme of the passage of time, though he also composed invective, as well as self- and tribal panegyric. For his biography and works, see: Labīd ibn Rabīʿa al-ʿĀmirī, *Dīwān*, 5–15; Imhof 2018.
18 Labīd ibn Rabīʿa al-ʿĀmirī, *Dīwān*, 132.
19 Unless otherwise indicated, all translations from Arabic poetry into English are my own. For Ṭarafa's *Muʿallaqa*, I have relied on Arberry 1957; verses not included in his translation are rendered by me.
20 A pre-Islamic poet who lived during the first half of the sixth century CE, he was a notable leader among his tribe and served as its poet. He was distinguished by sound judgment and keen insight. It is said that most of his poetry was composed in his later years, when he recalled his youth and reflected on questions of existence and destiny. The exact date of his birth remains unknown, and he is reported to have died around 554 CE.
ʿUbayd b. al-Abraṣ, *Dīwān*, 7–13; Weipert 2007.
21 ʿUbayd b. al-Abraṣ, *Dīwān*, 49.

These verses express an acute consciousness of mortality. Death is not an incidental event but the very essence of human experience and an inescapable destiny. Its shadow infiltrates every moment of life. Time, in this poetic vision, is marked by perpetual motion, ceaseless change,[22] and the absence of certainty. It grants no existential stability to the self but leaves it in continual flux and exposure.

Time in literature is, therefore, human time—our awareness of temporality as part of the fabric of human life. This awareness arises only through lived experiences, within the "lifeworld" that embodies the sum of all these experiences. For the pre-Islamic poet, time was subjective, psychological, distinct from its general, objective sense measurable through the "objective structure of temporal relations in nature."[23] It did not submit to abstract rationality and instead was governed by the logic of the senses, feeling, emotion, and will. This is a qualitative time in which subject and object merge, which some call "subjective relativity."[24] In this sense, time in pre-Islamic poetry is psychological time, colored by emotions, especially anxiety and fear, the defining features of life in the Arabian Peninsula.[25] The poet's sense of temporality arose from daily lived experience, imbued with profound unease at the passing of days.[26]

In pre-Islamic Arabia, one of the most salient manifestations of temporal awareness was the coupling of time with destiny, whether individual or collective. In pre-Islamic poetry, this coupling was among the most profound conceptions of temporality. The poet dwelt upon his personal fate,[27] making time synonymous with destiny, and turning it into a haunting preoccupation. Through verse, he presented multiple stances toward the issues of fate, death, and annihilation.[28]

Because time was inseparable from the poet's personal experience, it became a source of reflection as intellectual experience crystallized through inner feelings and was shaped by surrounding circumstances and opaque realities.[29] Here, the role of environment in shaping poetic consciousness is revealed, as many scholars have noted. Yūsuf Khulayf, for instance, stressed that Arabic poetry is not merely an aesthetic expression but the echo of its geographical, social, and psychological

22 Change is considered one of the fundamental characteristics of time in pre-Islamic poetic consciousness, and it is most often perceived in its negative dimension—that is, as a decline for the worse. Shaḥāda 1995, 66.

23 Meyerhoff 1960, 4–5.

24 al-Ghayḍāwī 2001, 1:261.

25 Fūghālī 2008, 53.

26 Fūghālī 2008, 63.

27 al-Ghayḍāwī 2001, 1:254.

28 al-Ghayḍāwī 2001, 1:255.

29 Fūghālī 2008, 89.

milieu.[30] The human factor operates as the driving force behind all human activity, while the geographical factor constitutes the fixed determinant that imposes its necessity upon the activity.[31]

Thus, the harsh desert environment with its perpetual mobility, tribal conflicts, and absence of stability played the most decisive role in shaping the poet's temporal awareness and intensifying his sense of death.[32] Therefore, pre-Islamic poetry not only captures a passing temporal moment but also evokes time as the arena of existential struggle and a medium to reflect the finitude of life and the inevitability of mortality. The desert, with its vast openness to the unknown, remained the mirror of this existential temporality. In one of its symbolic registers, it even signified the "dwelling place of the dead," pointing to what lies beyond life itself.[33] Yet this raises a crucial question: how does what the poet sees, hears, and feels manifest as a reflection of time? Is the desert itself, in its openness and uncertainty, the very image of time, while the ruins and traces stand as markers of destiny and inscribed moments of temporality?

2 The Vision of Time in Ṭarafa's *Muʿallaqa*

Ṭarafa ibn al-ʿAbd (543–569 CE) is one of the foremost poets of the *Muʿallaqāt*. Orphaned at an early age, he turned to amusement, indulgence, and wine. He was marginalized when he refused to conform to the expectations of his tribe. His upbringing within a turbulent pre-Islamic milieu that was marked by conflict and instability left a profound imprint on his poetic consciousness, particularly his conception of time. He experienced firsthand the fragility of life and the fickleness of

---

30 Khulayf 1981, 107–108. Victor Cousin argued that geography predetermines the nature of human beings and their role in history. He stated: "Give me the map of a country—its configuration, climate, winds, its entire physical geography; give me its natural products, its plants, its animals, etc., and I pledge to foretell in advance what the human being of this land will be and the role he will play in history." Quoted in Plekhanov 1977, 25. Plekhanov, however, criticized Cousin's view, describing it as a form of "strange conceit," an exaggerated and unrealistic stance, since geographical influence is not always direct or deterministic. Plekhanov 1977, 25.

31 Khulayf 1981, 107; he states: In every problem of history, two fundamental factors are at work: the human being and the geographical environment. The human factor represents the dynamic driving force in all human activity, whereas the geographical factor constitutes the fixed force that directs this activity, continuously exerting its influence and imposing its necessity upon its orientations and domains. Khulayf 1981, 107.

32 ʿAbd al-Salām 1991, 9–30.

33 As well as the desert (*bādiya*) and the barren wilderness (*qafrāʾ*). Ḥannūn 1986, 175–176.

fate, which manifested in his poetry as an acute awareness of time and a shifting force, torn between the delights of living and the inevitability of annihilation.[34] In Ṭarafa's poetry, time occupies a central position. It is not a mere backdrop to events or an external framework but an existential force that dominates the structure of awareness and experience. His vision of time is characterized by a blend of frivolity, rebellion, and philosophical reflection, oscillating between the pleasures of the fleeting moment and the dread of inevitable extinction. From this arises the tone of irony, bitterness, and protest that distinguishes his verse, endowing it with a reflective quality that intertwines the personal with the cosmic-existential. This study analyzes the representations of time in Ṭarafa's *Muʿallaqa* through three main axes:

2.1 Between Permanence and Transformation

2.1.1 The Ruins (*aṭlāl*): Absent Presence and Temporal Transformation

Ṭarafa's *Muʿallaqa* begins with the traditional theme familiar in the openings of pre-Islamic odes, i.e., the poet's pause before the deserted and ruined dwellings. What is foregrounded here, however, is not merely the individual's separation from a "social structure" but the disappearance of the community itself, which vanished and dissolved. The poet's desolation projected onto the ruined scene is expressed within a dialectic of nature and culture; the incursion of nature into the site contrasts with the retreat and disappearance of culture. This semantic line runs throughout the twenty-one verses constituting the *nasīb*.[35]

The *ṭalal* prelude[36] in pre-Islamic poetry is one of the most prominent manifestations of temporal awareness.[37] Standing before the ruins and observing them is a meditative act that recalls the past in the immediacy of the present through a spatial medium that remains fixed in the face of temporal movement and transformation. This act, however, does not merely evoke nostalgia for what has passed; it establishes a deeper existential dimension, making the ruins a threshold through which the poet contemplates human destiny and the fragility of existence. The

34 Ṭarafa ibn al-ʿAbd, *Dīwān*, 3–9; Nūr al-Dīn 1990, 31–40; Arberry 1957, 67–89; Montgomery 2012; cf. al-Ghalāyīnī 1998, 109–127.
35 Stetkevych 1993, 18.
36 The conventional opening of the pre-Islamic *qaṣīda* in which the poet pauses before the traces of a deserted campsite, conventionally recalling the absent beloved and evoking temporality through the imagery of ruins.
37 Shaḥāda 1995, 76.

dilapidated dwellings assume a symbolic role, re-presenting the past in the present and exposing an underlying anxiety about mortality and change. Anxiety and tension are therefore confined to the present moment because they gesture toward nothingness—experienced not as a stable entity but as the fleeting instant called *al-ʾān* (now).[38]

The experience of time in pre-Islamic poetry is recursive rather than sequential. Through recollection and visual description, the poet transforms loss into renewed presence, so that what has passed re-enters the present through the act of seeing. In this sense, the *ṭalal* functions as a poetic device that makes the absent visible and suspends time between memory and perception.

The *ṭalal* scene gathers multiple temporal dimensions where the past, as the locus of joy and hope, confronts the present marked by painful desolation; presence intersects with absence, continuity with rupture.[39] The very opening of the ode is thus constructed upon temporal antinomies that begin from the "now"—a moment charged with the dynamism of poetic consciousness in its apprehension of self and existence. Yet this apprehension is fraught with deep tension, for the *ṭalal* functions as a symbol overflowing with intertwined meanings: it signifies a temporal rupture between past and present while at the same time representing a collective self that no longer exists, leaving poetic consciousness uncertain of its fate.[40] Hence, the erotic prelude or *ṭalal* scene is far more than a conventional introduction; it is a symbolic form that conveys the atmosphere in which the poet lives and shapes the very texture of his poetic experience.[41] The ruins encapsulate memory, past, and present, the emotions of both individual and community, and the meanings of life, endurance, and death, alongside other symbols with wide-ranging human resonance.

In this sense, the *ṭalal* prelude embodies the duality of presence and absence and the moment of transition from past to future: it stores the past as the direct opposite of the present and as the intimate counterpart of the hoped-for future. The past is ever-present in the *ṭalal* opening, though always marked by extinction, while the present only discloses its essence through the shock of that luminous past.[42] Within this dialectic, time and space converge: space, represented by the ruins, appears to resist obliteration, whereas time emerges as the relentless force that reshapes all things through decay and disappearance, asserting its supremacy over tangible existence. The ruins thus stand as a complex symbol of life and death, of trace and absence, casting a mournful hue over the present moment, suffused

38 Shaḥāda 1995, 76.

39 al-Dukhaylī 2011, 128.

40 al-Jihād 2007, 144–145.

41 al-Bahbītī 1970, 100.

42 al-Yūsuf 2001, 95.

with longing and reflection on mutability. Their defining feature is decay—a comprehensive term encompassing erasure, effacement, desolation, erosion, and anonymity[43]—qualities imposed by time as the principal agent of ruination.

This interaction between the sensory and temporal is vividly illustrated in the opening verse of Ṭarafa's *Muʿallaqa*:

لِخَولَةَ أَطلالٌ بِبُرْقَةِ ثَهمَدِ   تلوحُ كَباقي الوَشمِ في ظاهِرِ اليدِ[44]

> There are traces yet of Khaula in the stony tract of Thahmad
> apparent like the tattoo-marks seen on the back of a hand.[45]

In this opening image, Ṭarafa employs a striking sensory simile—the fading tattoo—to capture the tension between endurance and decay. The tattoo, designed to be permanent, nevertheless fades with time; likewise, the ruins endure outwardly even as they erode from within. The present-tense verb *talūḥu* ("appear") sustains this sense of continuity, keeping the ruins vividly before the poet's eyes and turning them into living signs of disappearance. They do not simply evoke nostalgia but transform the present into a field of perception where loss itself becomes visible. In this image, time is not an instant of erasure but a slow, perceptible process that leaves behind the pale shadows of what once was. The ruins thus stand as a temporal vessel in which persistence and decline, memory and matter, are intertwined—a visible protest against oblivion and a testament to human presence amid the vast desolation of the desert.[46]

The imagery of the ruins thus encompasses the language of eternal persistence through the expression "apparent like the tattoo-marks seen on the back of a hand," alluding to the problem of being and annihilation, of life and death. Elsewhere, the she-camel becomes a complementary symbol of timeless endurance, reinforcing this existential tension.[47]

Nature effaces what human hands once built; what was once inhabitable and flourishing becomes barren wilderness, exposing the transience of all that is cultural before the endurance of nature.[48] Yet this process is not merely material but visual: the poet sees time's work inscribed upon the landscape. The encroaching sands and eroded stones bear the visible marks of disappearance, turning the scene itself into an image of temporality. Within this setting, the *ṭalal* prelude ceases to

---

43 Jihād 2001, 139–140.
44 Ṭarafa ibn al-ʿAbd, *Dīwān*, 19.
45 Arberry 1957, 83.
46 ʿUmar al-Ṭālib 1989, 65.
47 Muṣliḥī 2000, 249.
48 Muṣliḥī 2000, 249.

be a mere rhetorical convention and becomes a philosophical space where time, fate, and transformation are apprehended through sight. The poet's gaze binds perception to reflection, transforming vision into a means of understanding impermanence. Time haunts this visual field, torn between the yearning to recover the past and the certainty of its loss.

Thus, the ruins, in this context, are not simply material remnants but existential symbols in which time overlaps and visions intersect. Places and traces are bound to human life in a fateful relation that links man to the land with an unbroken thread.[49] Poetry itself becomes a ritual of seeing and remembering—a way of fixing fragility, transforming loss into recurrence, and reconstituting emotion through the act of looking.

From this perspective, the ruins are past, yet they saturate the present with their memory; weeping over them becomes a form of re-production, a renewed encounter with a past that remains present.[50] Ṭarafa expresses this temporal awareness in the second verse of the *Muʿallaqa*:

وَقوفاً بِها صَحْبِي عَلَيَّ مَطِيَّهُمْ   يَقُولُونَ: لا تهلِكْ أسىً وتجلَّدِ[51]

There my companions halted their beasts awhile over me
saying, 'Don't perish of sorrow; bear it with fortitude!'[52]

The verse captures a moment of stillness and emotional tension: Ṭarafa halts before Khawla's ruins, overwhelmed by grief, while his companions pause beside him and urge restraint—"Do not perish of sorrow; bear it with fortitude." This brief interruption of movement, the act of *waqf*, transforms the forward motion of the journey into suspension. In this suspension, time momentarily ceases to follow a linear course; memory circles back upon itself as the present sight becomes saturated with the past. Each return to the ruins renews the encounter, so that loss is not left behind but continually re-experienced in the very act of pausing and seeing. Thus, what appears as a simple emotional paradox between individual grief and communal counsel discloses a deeper existential dilemma: time as a force that both arrests and reiterates, binding the poet's perception of being to the perpetual return of loss.

49 al-Qaysī 1980, 32–33.
50 Jumʿa 2002, 38.
51 Ṭarafa ibn al-ʿAbd, *Dīwān*, 19.
52 Arberry 1957, 83.

Al-Aʿlam al-Shantamarī drew attention to this interpretive dimension when he explained the poet's lament over the ruins in response to their transformation and decay, not merely as a fleeting emotional reaction—contrasted with his companions' call for endurance.[53] The surviving trace, with its fragility and fading, thus becomes a source of pain more than reassurance and a site for mourning absence more than preserving memory.

In this intricate scene, personal sentiment converges with a philosophical stance as sorrow becomes a manifestation of existential experience, rooted in the awareness of life's fragility and its perpetual subjection to the law of transformation imposed by time. This vision resonates with later European thinkers[54] who viewed time as a form that confers upon the nothingness manifest in things the semblance of vanishing permanence, and which consumes joy and delight that lies before us.[55]

Here emerges a sharp emotional paradox: the poet's grief before Khawla's ruins collides with the counsel of his companions urging endurance. Yet the verse discloses more than an emotional conflict: it renders time as a mode of perception rather than chronology. Time is experienced through absence—through what is no longer there yet still seen, felt, and remembered. In perceiving what has vanished, the poet transforms loss into visibility, turning disappearance into the very condition of temporality itself. Ṭarafa's poetic experience thus embodies time not as an abstraction but as a sensory and existential field inscribed through memory and longing.

2.1.2 The Journey: The Women's Caravan

In the traditional structure of the *qaṣīda*, the poet moves from the static contemplation of loss in the *nasīb*, where ruins embody absence and memory, to the forward momentum of the *raḥīl*, the journey section, where movement, endurance, and temporal progression replace lament. This transition marks a shift from the temporality of absence to that of motion—time no longer seen in ruins but embodied in travel. Temporal awareness in Ṭarafa ibn al-ʿAbd's *Muʿallaqa* extends beyond the *ṭalal* scene to encompass a dynamic, kinetic vision of time as a force of ceaseless motion. It emerges vividly in the scene of the women's caravan where spatial movement intersects with temporal transformation to create a symbolically charged image, as in his verses:

53 Ṭarafa ibn al-ʿAbd, *Dīwān, sharḥ al-Aʿlam al-Shantamarī*, 24.

54 Such as Heidegger, who saw time as the horizon in which being discloses itself through finitude and the transience of joy. Heidegger 2001, 279–311.

55 Badawī 1945, 215–216.

كَأَنَّ حُدوجَ المالِكيَّةِ غُدوَةً خَلايا سَفينٍ بِالنَواصِفِ مِن دَدِ
عَدَوليَّةٌ أَو مِن سَفينِ اِبنِ يامِنٍ يَجورُ بِها المَلّاحُ طَوراً وَيَهتَدي[56]

> The litters of the Máliki camels that morn in the broad
> watercourse of Wadi Dad were like great schooners
> From Adauli, or the vessels of Ibn-i Yámin
> their mariners steer now tack by back, now straight forward.[57]

In these two lines, spatial and temporal movement converge to suggest a shifting scene transformed by visual imagery into profound symbolism. The swaying litters borne by camels are likened to ships tossed on water, evoking time's instability where flux is the rule and restless movement the destiny of existence. The litters that quiver on the camels' back, resembling ships buffeted by winds, denote a metaphor for human fate and its perpetual vicissitudes. The sailor who "goes astray" (*yajūru*) at times and "finds his way" (*yahtadī*) at others embodies the human mind itself, wavering between confusion and guidance, between bewilderment and insight, adrift in the currents of time.

The comparison of departing caravans to great ships upon the sea is widespread in pre-Islamic poetry,[58] used chiefly to describe their enormity, movement, and speed.[59] Poets' acute sense of the journey's uncertain fate prompted them to choose images of ships cleaving the depths of the sea, for to be lost in the desert is no less perilous than to be lost in the sea's darkness.[60] The analogy between the she-camel and the ship has multiple facets, with some related to form and others to posture and movement. The camel's swaying gait on the sand mirrors the undulating flow of a ship across the sea, while the movement of the camel's neck resembles the heaving of a ship's prow or sail.[61]

This sense of flux and change is intensified through the pairing of the words *al-nawāṣif* and *Dad.* The first term designates spacious tracts of land and, by extension, the watercourses that cut through them—spaces marked by openness and movement.[62] *Dad*, meanwhile, refers to a specific locality *(Wādī Dad)*, yet the word

56 Ṭarafa ibn al-ʿAbd, *Dīwān*, 19.

57 Arberry 1957, 83. It should be observed that the translator rendered the verbs *yajūru* and *yahtadī* as a mere oscillation, tacking back and forth. However, the more accurate sense is that of erring and finding guidance. The semantic field of *jawr* denotes deviation or going astray, while *hudā* refers to guidance and right direction. Accordingly, the second hemistich is more precisely translated as: whose sailor at times goes astray and at times finds his way.

58 ʿAṭwān 1982, 12–14.

59 Abū Suwaylim 1983, 1:212–213.

60 Abū Suwaylim 1983, 1:214.

61 Abū Suwaylim 1983, 1:213–214.

62 Ibn Manẓūr, *Lisān al-ʿArab*, 8:586.

also connotes play and amusement in its lexical range,[63] adding undertones of rhythm and vitality. Their semantic resonance imparts to the image a quality of perpetual transformation, reinforcing the impression of time as a surging force that never rests, shaping appearances and propelling them into a whirlpool of motion and change.

Some scholars read symbolic dimensions into the imagery of the woman in her litter and the she-camel as well as that of the ship, interpreting them as early symbolic attempts to flee the destructive vision embodied in the *ṭalal*. In confronting the ruins, the poet finds himself in a complex existential situation where inner conflict crystallizes in the journey: a voyage by sea that signifies descent into the depths of the self, fraught with danger and unpredictability.[64]

From this perspective, the caravan becomes a symbolic representation of the journey of existence itself—with its movement, turbulence, and fluctuation, and its perpetual search for meaning and direction. In this sense, the journey functions as an aesthetic symbolization of the collective self's movement within the vast horizon of *dahr* (Time/Fate).[65] The journey is not a mere spatial transition but a temporal unfolding that reflects the anxieties of human experience and its awareness of finitude and constant change. The term *ghudwa* (early morning) acquires a layered temporal significance. It denotes a precise time of day, traditionally associated with beginnings and departures, and, in this context, it simultaneously intimates imminent passing, lending the image a tense dynamism.

The litters, moving like ships, signify not only a means of transport but also the existential passage between a fragile present and an uncertain future, between the consciousness of loss and the longing to transcend it.

This vision is deepened by the image of the sailor who errs at times and finds his way at others. This fluctuation not only describes nautical navigation; it mirrors the nature of time itself, which does not proceed in a straight line but is continually reconstituted from one instant to the next by the interplay of absence and presence that governs human destiny. The sailor thus becomes a symbolic embodiment of the human self, oscillating between the grasp of meaning and its loss and between certainty and bewilderment, amid all the shifting currents of time.

This sensory dramatization of temporality reaches its height in the following verse:

---

63 Ibn Manẓūr, *Lisān al-ʿArab*, 3:319.

64 Nāṣif 1981, 159.

65 al-Jihād 2007, 145.

يَشُقُّ حَبابَ الماءِ حَيزومُها بِها كَما قَسَمَ التُّرْبَ المُفايِلُ بِاليَدِ[66]

Their prows cleave the streaks of the rippling water
Just as a boy playing will scoop the sand into parcels.[67]

In this verse, time itself becomes palpable. The verb *yashuqqu* ("to cleave") not only describes the ship's movement, but it also materializes time as an active force that pierces matter and alters it. Time is no longer a neutral context through which events pass but is a penetrating power inscribed at the heart of human experience, leaving its mark upon both the world and self.

Thus, the journey in these verses unfolds as an extended metaphor for the existential dialectic of restless becoming, shifting between beginnings that vanish swiftly and unforeseen endings. While the sea may be read as the continuum of existence, the cutting prows mark successive moments: each trace carved upon the water lingers briefly before vanishing, embodying the rhythm of time as both continuity and disappearance. In this interplay, the caravan and the ship express not just physical movement, but an inner existential transformation measured by human awareness of time's motion and its ungraspable quality. There is no permanence save in change and no presence except as a shadow slipping into the stream of perpetual transformation.

2.1.3 The She-Camel: Time as a Force of Release and Transformation

Departure in the pre-Islamic ode is an ordeal—an existential test of the poet's mortal fate and an attempt to transcend death, or at least the fear of it by direct confrontation. Within the structure of the Arabic *qaṣīda*, the sharpness of departure manifests in the poet's solitude or his withdrawal into himself. Whereas the *nasīb* traditionally portrays him in the company of companions or absorbed in social relations, whether fulfilled or failed—with his beloved and her tribe, in the *raḥīl* he is alone. His only companion is his faithful mount, almost always the she-camel.[68]

Thus, in the architecture of the *qaṣīda*, the she-camel is inseparably linked to the journey, that liminal stage of transition within the ritual of passage, a stage of transition between two states. Beyond its poetic function, the she-camel is also ritually suited to the act of crossing itself, being the indispensable creature of survival in the hardship of the desert. By identifying himself with his camel, the poet

66 Ṭarafa ibn al-ʿAbd, *Dīwān*, 19.
67 Arberry 1957, 83.
68 Stetkevych 1993, 26.

symbolically guarantees his successful passage.[69] In this section of the poem, the poet, like the traveler in liminality, is not in a fixed place; rather, he traverses a desolate wilderness threatened by danger and hardship. Yet his mount, the she-camel, signals his ultimate success in the ordeal and his eventual return to the tribal homeland. On the one hand, she symbolizes the poet's will and resolve, and on the other, by virtue of being the economic and ritual foundation of tribal life, she symbolizes the tribe itself.[70]

In Ṭarafa's *Muʿallaqa*, the she-camel is not a conventional means of transport; she becomes a symbolic equivalent of time's motion, a tangible embodiment of transformation, a force that carries the poet from grief into action, from inertia into passage.[71] Ṭarafa renders this transformation vividly:

وإني لأمضي الهمَّ، عند احتضاره   بعوجاءَ مِرقالٍ تروح وتغتدي[72]

> Ah, but when grief assails me, straightway I ride it off
> mounted on my swift, lean-flanked camel, night day racing.[73]

In this verse, the she-camel becomes an existential practice of confronting grief. Riding her is the act that enables transcendence of sorrow at its peak. The epithets "long-bodied" (*ʿawjāʾ*) and "swift-paced" (*mirqāl*) highlight her strength and speed, making her a symbol of psychological and intellectual transformation as much as physical motion. The verbs in the present tense—*tarūḥu wa-taghtadī* (she departs in the evening and returns in the morning) impart a cyclical temporality, suggesting continuity and recurrence within the span of a single day so that spatial movement becomes an analogue of time itself that can be reshaped through human agency.

---

69 Stetkevych 1993, 27.
70 Stetkevych 1985, 64–65.
71 While Ṭarafa's use of the she-camel as a symbolic embodiment of time's motion is especially pronounced in his *Muʿallaqa*, the broader topos of the she-camel as more than a mere means of transport is well attested in pre-Islamic poetry. In Imruʾ al-Qays (d. 545 CE) *Muʿallaqa*, the camel functions as a measure of distance and speed, thereby marking the passage of time. Imruʾ al-Qays, *Dīwān*, 11–17; in Zuhayr b. Abī Sulmā (d. 609 CE), it figures as an image of endurance across long journeys, mirroring human confrontation with temporality. Zuhayr b. Abī Sulmā, *Dīwān*, 102–112; and in Labīd b. Rabīʿa (d. 661 CE), the camel embodies patience and continuity, yet simultaneously discloses the inevitability of decay. Labīd ibn Rabīʿa al-ʿĀmirī, *Dīwān*, 168–173. What distinguishes Ṭarafa is the explicit linkage between the she-camel's motion and the existential awareness of time as transformation.
72 Ṭarafa ibn al-ʿAbd, *Dīwān*, 20.
73 Arberry 1957, 83.

This symbolic dimension is deepened in the following verse:

أمونٍ كألواحِ الأَرانِ نصأتُها على لاحِبٍ كأنّهُ ظهرُ بُرجُدِ[74]

Sure-footed, like planks of a litter; I urge her on
down the bright highway, that back of a striped mantle.[75]

The epithet *amūn* (sturdy, firm in build)[76] evokes lightness of movement and speed, while *lāḥib* (a clear, level path)[77] suggests openness and the unimpeded flow of temporality. Time is thus embodied in the movement of the animal's body—sensed and perceived, not merely abstracted.[78]

Ṭarafa devotes more than thirty lines[79] to the meticulous description of his camel.[80] "It appears that the pre-Islamic poet's insistence on enumerating the physical and temperamental qualities of his mount, especially its gaits, derives from his concern with his own physical and psychological capacity for the journey of transition."[81] Yet, this profusion is not ornamental but integral to the poem's symbolic structure: the camel's physical vitality recasts the relation between self, time, and space. By her strength and vigor, she enacts the passage from heaviness to lightness, from latency to flow.

The camel thus represents the counter-state to grief born of fragmentation and change. Her image unfolds along two axes—propulsion and endurance, both infused with temporality and even with death itself. She sets out in the evening and returns in the morning, and she is likened to the planks of coffins for lords. Gradually, however, she begins to detach from the temporal frame to rise beyond it.[82]

---

74 Ṭarafa ibn al-ʿAbd, *Dīwān*, 20.

75 Arberry 1957, 83.

76 Ibn Manẓūr, *Lisān al-ʿArab*, 1:235.

77 Ibn Manẓūr, *Lisān al-ʿArab*, 8:42.

78 As for *al-irān*, it denotes a coffin for the dead. Ibn Manẓūr, *Lisān al-ʿArab*, 1:132; and *al-burjud* is a woolen garment, red in color; some also say it is a large striped cloak. Ibn Manẓūr, *Lisān al-ʿArab*, 1:371.

79 See the verses 11–40, 43–44; Ṭarafa ibn al-ʿAbd, *Dīwān*, 20–24.

80 Ṭarafa lingered long in his description of the she-camel. al-Jubūrī 1986, 366–368; al-ʿArīḍ 2000, 55–91.
In this study, the images of the she-camel as presented in the *Muʿallaqa* can be summarized in four scenes: The she-camel woven into the fabric of the beloved's journey; the she-camel as a refuge to which the poet turns to escape his sorrows; the camel as an expression of loneliness, disdain, and continuity; the she-camel as a symbol of challenge embodied in the poet himself. al-ʿArīḍ 2000, 74–84.

81 Stetkevych 1985, 65.

82 Abū Deeb 2000, 177–178; Muṣliḥī 2000, 252.

From this perspective, the sea journey and the camel form two parallel strategies to confront the ruins.[83] The poet turns to his camel after turning to the past, realizing that the past will not return; departure is his only recourse. In symbolic sequence, he moves from the present (the ruins) to the past (the caravan of women) and finally to the journey (the future).[84]

Thus, the camel occupies a third position in Ṭarafa's network of temporal images, alongside the ruins (symbol of the collapsed past) and the ship (symbol of wandering and fluctuation). The camel represents the ascending trajectory in his vision of time—from stillness to motion, from mourning to action, and from remembrance to transcendence. She embodies a philosophy that regards time not merely as an occasion for passive lament but as a field of action and transformation.

The ritual of passage consists of three stages: separation, severance from one's previous status in society; marginality or liminality, an in-between phase spent at the margins of society, exposed to danger and uncertainty; and reincorporation, reintegration into the community in a new form.[85]

Through the three motifs delineated by the poet—the ruins, the caravan/ship, and the she-camel—time in Ṭarafa ibn al-ʿAbd's *Muʿallaqa* emerges not as a neutral backdrop to events but as a dominant agent, manifest in the distance between trace and absence, stillness and motion, and memory and action. Taken together, these images disclose a reflective engagement with time: the ruins fix memory against erasure, the caravan and ship mark mobility and uncertainty, and the she-camel embodies the possibility of renewal.

This progression, from the ruins to the camel, is not a mere shift in theme but reflects a temporal structure unfolding from stillness to flow, from memory to action, and from contemplation to movement. The temporalities of the poem are not linear but interwoven and layered as images intersect, symbols overlap, and time itself becomes an existential field in which the self continually redefines itself.

Accordingly, the *ṭalal* discourse in Ṭarafa's *Muʿallaqa* articulates not merely elegy but a reflective engagement with time and existence. At the apex of this symbolic architecture, the she-camel emerges as a vehicle of release—not through denial of time but through confronting it by motion and participation, transforming it into an open horizon that surpasses grief.

---

83 Nāṣif 2000, 33–34.
84 Shaḥāda 1995, 193.
85 Stetkevych 1985, 59–60.

2.2 Between the Inevitability of Death and the Celebration of the Moment

2.2.1 Time (*al-dahr*) and Mortality: Existential Awareness of Transformation

Time in the *Muʿallaqa* of Ṭarafa emerges as a coercive existential force, not content with framing events but exercising absolute authority over human life, stripping away youth, health, and status, and driving the individual towards extinction. This force, often personified as *al-dahr*, is an unseen but active entity, reshaping human existence, moving it from fullness to depletion, and from presence to disappearance. Within this horizon, death not only appears as an incidental event but as the inevitable conclusion of time's trajectory, one that spares no one and disregards justice or merit.[86]

Thus, the duality of time and death in pre-Islamic poetry transcends transient emotion to articulate a profound existential vision where everything that exists, human or otherwise, becomes prey to the "supreme hunter" that is fate itself, embodied in *al-dahr*, from whose grasp none can escape.[87] Ṭarafa conveys this vision through sensory images imbued with symbolic force, intensifying the awareness of mortality and human impotence before the sovereignty of time.

He expresses a coherent philosophical stance on human destiny, grounded in acute awareness of death's inevitability and the universal equality it imposes, as in the verses:

أَرَى قَبْرَ نَحَّامٍ بَخِيلٍ وَمَالِهِ   كَقَبْرِ غَوِيٍّ فِي البَطَالَةِ مُفْسِدِ
تَرَى جُثْوَتَيْنِ مِن تُرَابٍ، عَلَيْهِمَا   صَفَائِحُ صُمٌّ مِن صَفِيحٍ مُنَضَّدِ[88]

> To my eyes the grave of the niggardly who's mean with his money
> is one with the wastrel's who's squandered his substance in idleness;
> All you can see is a couple of heaps of dust, and on them
> slabs of granite, flat stones piled shoulder to shoulder.[89]

Here, social distinctions and earthly privileges are effaced, the grave renders noble and base, wealthy and dissolute, all the same. Through this condensed imagery, the poet exposes the fragility of worldly glory before the power of death, reducing all to a single origin consisting of two mounds of dust beneath layered slabs. This unveil-

---

86 Stetkevych 1985, 59–60.
87 Montgomery 2022, xv.
88 Ṭarafa ibn al-ʿAbd, *Dīwān*, 26.
89 Arberry 1957, 87.

ing is mediated by vision in its two modes: the sensory act of seeing and the cognitive act of insight. Observation here becomes both the means and the metaphor of poetic knowledge, turning the act of looking into an instrument of reflection and revelation. Time is not a neutral succession but a force of erasure, disclosing the fragility of existence and reshaping fate. Death is thus given a revelatory function of stripping away the symbolic masks of humanity and placing man before his naked truth—a vision as severe as it is uncompromising.

Ṭarafa deepens this vision in the lines:

أَرَى المَوْتَ يَعْتَامُ الكِرَامَ وَيَصْطَفِي عَقِيلَةَ مَالِ الفَاحِشِ المُتَشَدِّدِ
أَرَى العَيْشَ كَنْزًا نَاقِصًا كُلَّ لَيْلَةٍ وَمَا تَنْقُصِ الأَيَّامُ وَالدَّهْرُ يَنْفَدِ[90]

I see Death [*al-mawt*] choose the generous folk, and takes for his own
the most prized belonging of the parsimonious skinflint
I see life is a treasure diminishing every night,
and all that the days and Time [*al-dahr*] diminish ceases at last.[91]

Death (*al-mawt*) here is a blind force, indifferent to honor or baseness, choosing the dearest as readily as the vilest. Life itself is condensed into a striking material image, a "diminishing treasure" dwindling night after night. This metaphor renders time as a power of daily depletion, irreversible and absolute. Time thus appears not as neutral movement but as a dominant force of loss, instilling in humanity a perpetual sense of erosion. This vision is linguistically anchored in Ṭarafa's repeated use of the verb *ʾarā* (I see), which frames temporality through an act of observation oscillating between the empirical and the contemplative. He sees death's arbitrary work in lived experience, yet at the same time, he sees, by discerning and reflecting, an abstract law that governs existence. Death chooses without criterion, while life erodes like a wasting hoard, an intense distillation of the dialectic of presence and dissolution. Within this framework, Ṭarafa's awareness goes beyond resignation, shaping a tension between the delight of the moment and the specter of extinction, and between wisdom and defiance, lending his poetry an existential tenor that is rare in its historical setting.

He crystallizes his philosophical vision of time and death in a powerful representational simile:

90 Ṭarafa ibn al-ʿAbd, *Dīwān*, 26.
91 Arberry 1957, 87.

لَعَمْرُكَ إِنَّ الْمَوْتَ مَا أَخْطَأَ الْفَتَى   لَكَالطِّوَلِ الْمُرْخَى وَثِنْيَاهُ بِالْيَدِ[92]
مَتَى مَـا يَشَأْ يَوْمًا يَقُـدْهُ لِحَتْفِهِ   وَمَـنْ يَكُ فِـي حَبْلِ الْمَنِيَّةِ يَنْقَدِ[93]

By your sweet life though Death may miss a lad for the nonce
he's like a loosened lasso, whose loops are firmly in hand[94]
Whenever he so wills, he leads a man to his doom
And whoso is bound by the cord of fate must yield.

In these lines, death becomes a concentrated sensory scene in which man appears as a beast tethered with a loosened rope in the hand of its master, time or fate. The animal seems free in appearance but is invisibly bound to its end. The slack rope conceals a latent force, ready at any moment to tighten and lead the creature to its doom. The verb *yaqudhu* (he leads) marks the moment of total control as death does not merely await, it "chooses," drawing man irresistibly to his fate.

This image embodies the interplay between apparent stillness and inevitable movement. Death does not arrive suddenly; it advances invisibly, biding its time, yet never failing to strike its target. The tension between slackness and compulsion enacts a shift from death as abstract presence to death as active domination.[95] The conditional construction: "whenever he so wills, he leads." converts possibility into immediate action, binding life to its unseen end by an inexorable cord.

The rope thus becomes a grand metaphor for time as an existential constraint by which life itself is bound and led toward annihilation. Yet this subjection is not devoid of consciousness. Ṭarafa does not present a purely defeatist vision; rather, amid the tragedy, he intimates a sharp awareness—recognition of inevitability does not entail surrender but the seizing of presence.

Thus, the tethered-rope image becomes a metaphor for existence itself, bound to its end: inevitable submission yet not without insight and dignity; a continual test of the self's ability to preserve meaning even as it is led to extinction.

Despite the overwhelming presence of time as a force of annihilation, Ṭarafa does not lapse into resignation. He preserves the spark of dignity even in the face of death. Looking directly into mortality, he does not beg for survival but demands remembrance befitting of his worth, as in verses:

92 Ṭarafa ibn al-ʿAbd, *Dīwān*, 26.

93 This verse is generally absent from the standard editions of Ṭarafa's *Muʿallaqa* but is recorded in al-Ghalāyīnī 1998, 131.

94 Arberry 1957, 87.

95 ʿAṣfūr 1992, 294–306.

فإنْ مُتُّ فانعيني بما أنا أهلُهُ   وشُقّي عليّ الجَيْبَ يا ابنة معْبَدِ
ولا تَجعَليني كامرىءٍ ليس همُّه   كهمي ولا يُغني غَنائي ومشهدي[96]

If I should die, cry me, sweet daughter of Maʿbad
as my deeds deserve, and rend the collar of your gown for me
Make me not out as a man whose zeal was not any way
like my zeal, who served not in battle and tumult as I have served.[97]

In these verses, the poet insists on securing his final image in collective memory, not as a mere mortal passing but as one of gravity and stature, unworthy of oblivion. This is an assertion of the self's value in the face of erasure, a symbolic victory over obliteration. The paradox lies in the combination of acknowledging death's sovereignty while insisting on symbolic immortality. This reveals a philosophical awareness that transcends pessimism, amounting to a form of "existential protest" wherein death is not denied but reinterpreted as a moment to affirm meaning rather than effacing it.

This awareness reaches its culmination in Ṭarafa's verse:

أرَى المَوْتَ أعْدَادَ النُّفُوسِ وَلا أرَى   بَعِيدًا غدًا، مَا أقْرَبَ اليَوْمَ مِنْ غَدِ[98]

I see Death numbered with all souls, and I see not
tomorrow as a far—how near today is to tomorrow.

Here collapses the illusion of temporal extension; the distance between today and tomorrow contracts into the sense of harrowing inevitability. Time becomes an unbroken stream that doesn't allow delay or reprieve; tomorrow dissolves into today, and the present is bound to its fate. Yet even in this stark awareness, the self does not falter but resists erasure in silence, clinging to the assertion of meaning. Again, Ṭarafa marks this awareness with the verb *ʾarā* (I see), turning perception into understanding. Observation here becomes the very medium through which time is rendered thinkable within lived experience.

Thus, Ṭarafa's poetry becomes a symbolic ritual in which time is re-presented not merely as an enemy to be resisted but as a force confronted with dignity and reinterpreted through poetry as a bearer of meaning. Time in his verse emerges as existential awareness poised at the edge between absurdity and celebration, between the specter of annihilation and the delight of presence, endowing his poetic experience with a singular distinctiveness within the corpus of pre-Islamic poetry. This awareness is anchored in the act of seeing (*ʾarā*): perception here

96 Ṭarafa ibn al-ʿAbd, *Dīwān*, 29.
97 Arberry 1957, 89.
98 Ṭarafa ibn al-ʿAbd, *Dīwān, sharḥ al-Aʿlam al-Shantamarī*, 58.

becomes embodied awareness, a mode through which being discloses itself in time, and thought arises from what is observed.

The poem, then, overflows with a vision of death's inevitability and its erasure of distinctions in existence, exposing the absurdity of value systems rooted in a superficial understanding of daily and social life. Ṭarafa's *Muʿallaqa* becomes a ritual of freedom—a rite of self-liberation from its tribal context, a labor of birth and rebirth, the bow taut in the moment of release.[99]

2.2.2 Death as a Temporal Pursuit: The Poet's Consciousness under Existential Siege

In a scene of striking density and dramatic tension, Ṭarafa depicts death as a stalking force that encircles man from every direction, enclosing his awareness in an existential anxiety from which there is no escape:

لَعَمْرُكَ مَا أَدْرِي وَإِنِّي لَوَاجِلٌ   أَفِي اليَوْمِ إِقْدَامُ الْمَنِيَّةِ أَوْ غَدِ
فَإِنْ تَكُ خَلْفِي لاَ يَفُتْهَا سَوَادِيَا   وَإِنْ تَكُ قُدَّامِي أَجِدْهَا بِمَرْصَدِ[100]

> By your life, I do not know—though fear is in my heart—
> whether Death assail today or tomorrow;
> If it is behind me, my shadow shall not escape it
> and if it is before me, I shall find it lying in wait.

In these two verses, death does not appear as an abstract concept or a deferred fate but as a lurking being, pursuing man from front and rear, ambushing him from every direction. Death here enacts an existential siege that leaves no outlet or hope of escape. Although the verses explicitly evoke death, what they ultimately disclose is the experience of time itself. Death here is not a terminal event but the very modality through which temporality becomes perceptible—an enclosing presence that surrounds man from all directions. The uncertainty between *al-yawm* (today) and *ghad* (tomorrow) signals not the fear of a specific end but the collapse of temporal distance: time and death converge into a single enclosing force. No longer a linear progression from present to future, time appears as a circular enclosure that absorbs both today and tomorrow into one encompassing present—a field of imminent threat from which there is no release. Ṭarafa's imagery thus articulates a pre-Islamic perception of temporality as both spatial and existential, binding human awareness to mortality in a state of perpetual anxiety and recognition.

---

99 Abū Deeb 2000, 190, 192–193.
100 al-Shaybānī, *Sharḥ al-Muʿallaqāt*, 82; al-Tabrīzī, *Sharḥ al-Qaṣāʾid*, 200.

The rhetorical image intensifies this sense of enclosure. The first line conveys anticipatory anxiety through a suspended question that yields no certainty. The second reveals the impossibility of escape: if death is behind me, it will not miss me, and if it is before me, my encounter with it is inevitable and near. The word *sawādīyā* (my shadow or my dark outline) with its visual and temporal resonances deepens this impression. It evokes not only darkness but a condition of obscurity and total exposure to danger so that existence itself seems like a narrow nocturnal passage lined with ambushes.

This scene enacts what Kamal Abu-Deeb termed the existential tension between the external and the internal. The external pursuit—death as a stalking force intersects with an inner closed circuit of recurring emotions of impotence and exposure, whose loops complete themselves within the self.[101] This dual structure renders time itself a negative agent, lying in wait for the self and gradually driving it towards an inescapable fate.

The representational skill here lies in the kinetic personification of death: it is not depicted merely as an end but as an active pursuer that encircles the creature and advances towards it with invisible steps. Time becomes a combative space where emotion is inseparable from geography, and the inner from the outer. Within this framework, anxiety and suffocation intensify as the movement of time merges with the hostile environment of ambush.

Yet after having drawn this dense image of temporal siege and inevitable annihilation, Ṭarafa does not abandon his reader to despair. He surprises them with a turn of awareness towards a resistant poetic stance in which the enjoyment of transient existence becomes a conscious act of defiance against extinction:

لَعَمرُكَ ما الأَيّامُ إِلّا مُعارَةٌ   فَما اسْتَطَعْتَ مِن مَعْرُوفِها فَتَزَوَّدِ[102]

By your life, the days are but a loan
so take from their goodness whatever you may.

Here emerges a new vision: the days are not permanent possessions but borrowed time, limited and certain to be reclaimed. Man must therefore draw from them—whether from virtue or from pleasure, for *ma'rūf*[103] connotes both the provisions of life before it expires. In this perspective, delight itself becomes a legitimate form of

101 Abū Deeb 1977, 222–223.

102 al-Shaybānī, *Sharḥ al-Mu'allaqāt*, 81; al-Tabrīzī, *Sharḥ al-Qaṣā'id*, 200; al-Tabrīzī notes that it is said to be composed by 'Adī ibn Zayd.

103 *Ma'rūf* lit. what is deemed good of deeds, what is recognized and familiar as virtuous. Cf. Ibn Manẓūr, *Lisān al-'Arab*, 6:197.

knowledge and provision, a conscious investment in existence before its inevitable repossession.

In this horizon, time in Ṭarafa's poetry unfolds as a fraught duality. On the one hand, there's a crushing force that strips man of stability and drives him towards extinction; on the other hand, there's a spur to rebellion and a call to celebrate life. Death, present as an inescapable inevitability, is confronted with an insistence on dignity, symbolic immortality, and the transformation of presence into an act of meaning.

This vision does not remain bound within the limits of pessimism or defeat; it surpasses them towards a coherent poetic philosophy in which contemplation of inevitability coexists with a hymn of defiance and sorrow intersects with flashes of celebration. For Ṭarafa, death is neither denied nor submitted to; it is encircled by precise poetic description and resisted through a will to preserve dignity and symbolic endurance. Even as he underscores time as a power of dissolution, Ṭarafa does not neglect to highlight the fleeting moments of enjoyment, as though seeking to wrest from the heart of nothingness a cause for joy.

This vision may be compared with Martin Heidegger's notion of *Sein zum Tode* (being-toward-death) wherein awareness of death grants the human being the possibility of realizing authentic existence, not as a passive surrender to fate but as a self-conscious recognition of finitude through which life may be grasped at its own terms.[104] Existence within time is thus a living confrontation with temporality, for we reckon with it and orient ourselves through acts of measurement and not the opposite. Time is experienced from within subjective life and reconfigured narratively as the interweaving of past, present, and future within a structure of consciousness and inner temporality.[105] Thus, Ṭarafa's poem becomes an existential discourse that weaves from the temporality of decline a spark of meaning, transforming the harshness of *al-dahr* into a moment of defiance and life.

3 The Celebration of the Present Moment: Between the Specter of Death and the Tenacity of Existence

Time in Ṭarafa's poetry is not depicted solely as a lethal force; it also emerges as a provisional, immediate space to be seized before it is confiscated by the hand of annihilation. Here, a striking duality takes shape within the structure of his poetic

104 Heidegger 2001, 279–311.

105 Ricoeur 1984, 1: 62–63; For more details, cf. Ricoeur 1984, 1:52–87.

consciousness. On the one hand, a sharp awareness of death's inevitability takes place, and on the other, an insistence on converting this awareness into an energy of action that grounds a sensual philosophy of life, countering dread with activity and mortality with joy.

This vision rests on an existential stance that refuses to surrender to nothingness, investing the limited temporality of presence as a final opportunity to affirm life. Implicitly, it intersects with the ancient Epicurean impulse to embrace pleasure, not out of frivolity or indulgence, but as an expression of acute awareness of human finitude and time's limitation.[106]

3.1 Awareness of Inevitability as a Drive to Live

Awareness of inevitability in Ṭarafa's *Muʿallaqa* is inscribed both in abstract reflection and in the very structure of the *qaṣīda*. The *nasīb* registers the acknowledgment of loss and mortality, dramatized in the dialogue with *al-lāʾim* (reproachful moralist), where Ṭarafa poses a rhetorical question that exposes the futility of counsel in the face of death's inevitability. In the *raḥīl* this awareness is reshaped into motion and endurance. The arduous journey, borne by the she-camel, embodies the continuation of life despite its destined end. Here, the poet's existential stance becomes fully enacted: verses that speak of irrigating the soul, clinging to wine, or affirming valor emerge in this forward momentum, where the confrontation with mortality turns into the affirmation of living.

This stance is encapsulated in Ṭarafa's rhetorical challenge to *al-lāʾim* (the reproacher), which exposes the futility of counsel in the face of the impossibility of granting immortality:

ألا أيُّهذا اللّائمي أحضُرَ الوغى وأن أشهدَ اللذّات، هل أنتَ مُخلِدي؟
فإنْ كنتَ لا تسطيعُ دَفْعَ منيّتي فدعْني أبادرْها بما مَلَكَتْ يدي[107]

> So now then, you who revile me because I attend the wars
> and partake in all pleasures, can you keep me alive forever?
> If you can't avert from me the fate that surely awaits me
> then pray leave me to hasten it on with what money I've got.[108]

The poet does not deny the sovereignty of death, but he confronts it through an existential act that restores value to the moment. Here, the awareness of mortal-

106 White 2021, 453–454.
107 Ṭarafa ibn al-ʿAbd, *Dīwān*, 25.
108 Arberry 1957, 86.

ity is reconfigured within an active temporal framework that views the present as the only domain for action and meaning. This vision achieves heightened sensory intensity in his verse:

فَذَرْنِي أُرْوِي هَامَتِي فِي حَيَاتِهَا   مَخَافَةَ شُرْبٍ فِي الحَيَاةِ مُصَرَّدِ[109]

> So permit me to drench my head while there's still life in it,
> for I tremble at the thought of the scant draught I'll get when I'm dead.[110]

In this image, the "soul" (*hāma*)[111] becomes a metaphor for the self. The verb *arwī* (I drink deeply) likewise transcends its literal sense of quenching thirst to denote the longing for complete participation in life's fullness. The poet fears that death will overtake him before he tastes his allotted share of delight. This reflects an acute sensitivity to the limits of time and implicitly calls for transforming the awareness of mortality into an existential motive for investing in life's fleeting present.

This once more recalls Heidegger's notion of *Sein-zum-Tode* (being-toward-death), where awareness of death constitutes the very condition for authentic existence, not as passive submission to fate but as a conscious possession of life in the face of temporality.[112]

3.2 The Pursuit of Pleasure: Delight as an Existential Act of Resistance

Ṭarafa's existential stance is defined by his inclination to seize life's pleasures out of fear of losing them and despair at their impermanence; for in the attainment of pleasure lies a victory over death, which in the pre-Islamic imagination is the end of existence.[113] Death, in this regard, is the very source and foundation of all meaning; it is what impels human consciousness to establish its efficacy in life, precisely because human temporality is finite in it. Hence, man cannot remain bound to the conditions of mere survival or enclosed within the self.[114]

---

109 Ṭarafa ibn al-ʿAbd, *Dīwān, sharḥ al-Aʿlam al-Shantamarī*, 48.

110 Arberry 1957, 86.

111 The word هَامَة *(hāma)* has several related meanings in classical Arabic; Literal: head, skull; Figurative: soul, self; and Mythical *hāma* refers to a bird that emerges from the skull of a murdered man. Ibn Manẓūr, *Lisān al-ʿArab*, 9:164–165.

112 Cf. Heidegger 2001, 279–311.

113 Muṣliḥī 2000, 239.

114 al-Jihād 2007, 151.

It is worth noting that the pre-Islamic responses to death took shape in three primary modes: action, devotion to pleasure, and the sense of absurdity.[115] Wine-drinking, delight in women, and valor in horsemanship exemplify these strategies. What is particularly striking is that in Ṭarafa's vision, even *furūsiyya* (chivalric valor) is reframed as one of life's pleasures, an innovation compared to earlier pre-Islamic conventions.[116]

This orientation is exemplified in his verses:

ولَولا ثلاثٌ هُنَّ مِنْ عيشةِ الفتى   وَجَدِّكَ لم أحفلْ متى قامَ عُوّدي
فمنهنّ: سبقي العاذلاتِ بشَربةٍ   كُمَيْتٍ متى ما تُعلَ بالماءِ تُزْبِدِ
وكرّي، إذا نادى المضافُ محنّبًا   كسيدِ الغضا، نبّهْتَهُ، المتورِّدِ
وتقصيرُ يومِ الدَّجنِ والدجنُ معجِبٌ   ببهكنةٍ تحت الطِّرافِ المعمّدِ
كَأَنَّ البُرِينَ وَالدَّمَالِيجَ عُلِّقَتْ   عَلَى عُشَرٍ، أَوْ خِرْوَعٍ لَمْ يُخَضَّدِ[117]

But for three things, that are the joy of a young fellow,
I assure you I wouldn't care when my deathbed visitors arrive-
First, to forestall my charming critics with a good swig
of crimson wine that foams when the water is mingled in;
Second, to wheel at the call of the beleaguered a curved-shanked steed
streaking like the wolf of the thicket you've startled lapping the water
And third, to curtail the day of showers, such an admirable season,
dallying with a ripe wench under the pole-propped tent,
Her anklets and her bracelets seemingly hung on the boughs
of a pliant, unriven gum-tree or a castor-shrub.[118]

The "three pleasures" invoked here are: wine, symbolizing liberation from the weight of anxiety and the burden of time; valor and generosity, representing the affirmation of personal worth in a society that equated honor with dignity and giving; and dalliance with women, a celebration of corporeal beauty before it withers under the passage of years.

These three delights are elements of a philosophy of intensified living in the shadow of inevitable extinction. They resonate with Epicurus' dictum that "pleasure is the beginning and end of living in bliss",[119] not as reckless indulgence but as a rational response to human fragility. For Epicurus, the pleasant life is secured through sober reflection, careful examination of choices, and the liberation from beliefs that agitate the soul, with reason standing at its head. In this framework, pleasure is inseparable from rationality, dignity, and justice; there can be no life of

115 Shaḥāda 1995, 127; and see also: Shaḥāda 1995, 127–136.
116 Shaḥāda 1995, 127, 133.
117 Ṭarafa ibn al-ʿAbd, *Dīwān*, 25–26.
118 Arberry 1957, 86.
119 White 2021, 454.

pleasure without reason, and no virtuous life without delight.[120] In Ṭarafa's vision, too, joy, valor, and generosity emerge as existential strategies against the finitude of time, transforming ephemeral experience into a stance of defiance and affirmation.

3.3 Isolation as the Price of Choice

Ṭarafa ibn al-ʿAbd's rebellion against tribal norms does not appear as a passing caprice or a matter of unruly behavior; rather, it unfolds as a profound existential stance, grounded in his individual vision that transcends the logic of the collective. It articulates an acute awareness of the self's freedom and its right to meaning and pleasure. This rebellion acquires an inward philosophical dimension: it not only rejects the external authority of the tribe but demands the establishment of individual values outside its moral and social framework. The stance reaches its culmination in his verses:

وما زال تشْرابي الخمورَ، ولذّتي   وبيعي وإنفاقي طريفي ومُتلدي
إلى أن تحامَتْني العشيرةُ كلُّها   وأُفردتُ إفرادَ البعيرِ المعَبَّدِ[121]

> Unceasingly I tippled the wine and took my joy,
> unceasingly I sold and squandered my hoard and my patrimony
> Till all my family deserted me, every one of them,
> and I sat alone like a lonely camel scabby with mange.[122]

The poet acknowledges that his immersion in pleasure and departure from the tribe's conventions led to his total isolation. His clan rejected him like a *maʿbbad* camel[123]— afflicted with mange and therefore shunned by the herd. Yet, this iso-

---

120 "When we say that pleasure is the end, we do not mean the pleasures of the dissolute or those of indulgence, as some mistakenly maintain, whether out of disagreement or malicious distortion. Rather we mean not feeling either any bodily pain or any mental turmoil. For it is not a continuous string of drinking parties and revels that produces a pleasant life, nor the delights of boys and women, or of fish and everything else a lavish table offers: no, it is sober reasoning that both uncovers the rationale for all choice and avoidance, and also drives out the beliefs that deliver souls into the grip of great uproar." White 2021, 454–455.

121 Ṭarafa ibn al-ʿAbd, *Dīwān*, 25.

122 Arberry 1957, 86.

123 The expression *al-baʿīr al-muʿabbad* literally denotes a camel subdued by mange, whose hair has fallen off and which is therefore separated from the herd for treatment. Ibn Manẓūr, *Lisān al-ʿArab*, 6:51. While Arberry rendered it as 'lonely camel', a more precise translation would be 'mangy camel', or, to preserve the nuance of isolation, 'a mangy camel ostracized from the herd'. The latter better conveys both the physical condition and the social exclusion implied in the Arabic expression.

lation is not presented in a context of remorse or repentance; to the contrary, it is framed as an inevitable consequence of a free stance, an existential price paid by the self for the preservation of its autonomy. It is an isolation born of a divergent vision, not of moral fault —the self is cast out because it chose to be the master of its own time, clinging to its delight and rebelling against the tribal ethic that located supreme value in discipline and collective interest.

In this sense, social exclusion becomes a poetic declaration of individual independence, whereby the poet redefines pride not through communal approval but through the authenticity of subjective experience and the courage to live beyond the established order. The simile of the "mangy camel" embodies the harshness of rejection and the completeness of rupture, but within the poem, it is transfigured into a symbolic condensation of an existentially conscious choice, redefining the self outside the tribal hierarchy and granting it a defiant autonomy.

3.4 The Philosophy of the Moment: Presence beneath the Shadow of Time

Ṭarafa ibn al-ʿAbd's stance toward death does not proceed from denial or defiance of fate, but from an acute recognition of mortality's authority, countered by a precise clinging to life as the only available sphere for action and meaning. He declares:

كريمٌ يُروي نفسَه في حياته   ستعلَمُ، إن مُتْنا غدًا، أيُّنا الصَّدي[124]

> I'm a generous fellow, one that soaks himself in his lifetime;
> you'll know tomorrow, when we're dead, which of us is the thirsty one.[125]

The verse contrasts the fulfilled and the deprived: the man, who "soaks" or "irrigates" himself with life's fullness while alive, stands opposed to those who withhold themselves and remain *ṣadī* (thirsty). This imagery corresponds to Ṭarafa's earlier expression *arwī hāmatī* (I irrigate my soul),[126] so that the motif of irrigation intertwines across the poem as a metaphor for seizing life before its depletion.

In the verse above, generosity extends beyond the external, material giving to the ability to irrigate the self within its finite span. The noble man is he who exercises his right to existence in full awareness before dryness overtakes him. Pleasure

124 Ṭarafa ibn al-ʿAbd, *Dīwān*, 26.
125 Arberry 1957, 86.
126 Ṭarafa ibn al-ʿAbd, *Dīwān, sharḥ al-Aʿlam al-Shantamarī*, 48; Arberry 1957, 86.

thus becomes a cognitive act rather than an instinctual indulgence; life becomes fullness, not waiting—choice, not submission.

From this existential perspective on time, death, and life, the value system collapses altogether. The individual sensibility erupts, dismantling collective consciousness and annulling the legitimacy of values rooted in a superficial grasp of daily and social life. As in the earlier image of the equalizing grave,[127] death cancels distinctions, leaving the *ṣadī*—the one who fails to drink of life—defeated in the struggle with time.[128]

This conception is bound to the sense of mortality i.e., the acute awareness of the fragility of all that matters. Life, or the moment, derives its meaning from its precariousness and its likelihood of vanishing. What endows existence with significance in Ṭarafa's vision is precisely its susceptibility to loss: value arises not from permanence but from fragility itself.[129] Meaning is thus not drawn from duration but from the risk latent in every instant, from the dread of its possible extinction at any time. In this way, Ṭarafa's poetic consciousness turns toward the moment as the locus of dignity and significance. As previously noted, this awareness that the days are not permanent possessions but borrowed time destined to be reclaimed is crystallized in a verse already cited.[130]

4 Conclusion

Time in Ṭarafa ibn al-ʿAbd's *Muʿallaqa* does not function as a neutral or passive background but as an active existential force that shapes human destiny. It appears as a coercive power that erodes vitality, brings mortality, and compels all beings toward inevitable annihilation. At the same time, it is conceived as a temporary loan—a symbolic economy in which life consists of what may be drawn before it vanishes. Time is thus a multifaceted phenomenon: it embodies memory, fate, decay, transformation, presence, and absence simultaneously, and is experienced psychologically through anxiety, grief, and joy, in close dialogue with the harsh conditions of the desert.

This temporal awareness is rendered through a dense symbolic vocabulary. The ruins (*aṭlāl*) embody the persistence of the past within decay, a visible presence haunted by absence. The caravan and the ship articulate movement, fluctuation,

---

127 Ṭarafa ibn al-ʿAbd, *Dīwān*, 26; Arberry 1957, 87.

128 Abū Deeb 2000, 184.

129 Hägglund 2019, 10–11.

130 al-Shaybānī, *Sharḥ al-Muʿallaqāt*, 81; al-Tabrīzī, *Sharḥ al-Qaṣāʾid*, 200.

and the uncertainty of fate, dramatizing life's exposure to risk and flux. The she-camel, finally, becomes the vehicle of endurance and transformation, symbolizing active participation in time and the capacity to move from grief toward renewal. Through these images, time emerges both as an annihilating force and as a stimulus for awareness, a paradoxical agent that demands awareness of mortality while inspiring celebration of life.

Vision in Ṭarafa's *Muʿallaqa* is both sensory and metaphorical, mediating the awareness of time's passage and its existential effects. The poet's gaze upon ruins, fading tattoos, fleeting traces, and the steady camel enacts a dynamic interplay of seeing and temporal consciousness: perception does not merely register what is visible but transforms absence into presence, memory into vision, and loss into an act of consciousness. In this way, vision links the sensory to the contemplative, binding external images to inner recognition of temporality. Ṭarafa's repeated use of expressions such as *arā* ("I see") anchors the poem in the act of perception itself, where observation becomes not only the means but also the metaphor of reflection. Vision here is thus an active engagement with the interplay of presence and absence woven by time, a process that triggers memory, emotion, and existential reckoning.

The *Muʿallaqa* articulates a complex philosophical meditation on time as an existential field where human life is defined by the tension between mortality and presence, loss and celebration. It proposes a philosophy of living that embraces the fleeting present moment with dignity and joy despite the inevitability of death. Time is acknowledged as an agent of destruction but as a space of meaning, choice, and resistance. The poet's stance is one of conscious defiance, transforming sorrow into action and isolation into autonomy. In this way, Ṭarafa's *Muʿallaqa* transcends lament to affirm a sensuous and thoughtful engagement with life, reorienting the self within its fragile moment and asserting awareness, presence, and freedom in the face of annihilation.

Bibliography

ʿAbd al-Salām, Ḥasan (1991), *Al-Mawt fī al-Shiʿr al-Jāhilī*. Cairo: Maṭbaʿat al-Ḥusayn al-Islāmiyya.

Abū Deeb, Kamāl (2000), "Ṭarafa wa-Azmat al-ʾIntimāʾ (al-Qism al-Awwal)." In *Ṭarafa b. al-ʿAbd: Dirāsāt wa-Abḥāth Multaqā al-Baḥrayn*. Beirut: al-Muʾassasa al-ʿArabiyya li-l-Dirāsāt wa-l-Nashr, 169–195.

Abū Deeb, Kamāl (1977), *al-Ruʾā al-Muqannaʿa: Naḥw Manhaj Binyawī fī Dirāsat al-Shiʿr al-Jāhilī*. Cairo: Maṭābiʿ al-Hayʾa al-Miṣriyya al-ʿĀmma li-l-Kitāb.

Abū Suwaylim, Anwar ʿAlyān (1983), *al-ʾIbil fī al-Shiʿr al-Jāhilī*. Riyad: Dār al-ʿUlūm.

al-ʿArīḍ, ʿAbd al-Jalīl (2000), "Ṭarafa b. al-ʿAbd wa-ṣūrat al-nāqa fī shiʿrihi." In *Ṭarafa b. al-ʿAbd: Dirāsāt wa-Abḥāth Multaqā al-Baḥrayn*. Beirut: al-Muʾassasa al-ʿArabiyya li-l-Dirāsāt wa-l-Nashr, 55–91.

al-Bahbītī, Najīb (1970), *Tārīkh al-Shiʿr al-ʿArabī ḥattā al-Qarn al-Thālith al-Hijrī*. 4th ed. Cairo: Dār al-Fikr/ Maktabat al-Khānjī.
al-Dukhaylī, Ḥasan (2011), *Al-Faḍāʾ al-Shiʿrī ʿinda al-Shuʿarāʾ al-Luṣūṣ fī al-ʿAṣrayn al-Jāhilī wa-l-Islāmī*. Amman: Dār Ḥāmid li-l-Nashr wa-l-Tawzīʿ.
al-Ghalāyīnī, Muṣṭafā (1998), *Rijāl al-Muʿallaqāt al-ʿAshr: Kitāb Adab wa-Tārīkh wa-Lugha*. Beirut: al-Maktaba al-ʿAṣriyya.
al-Ghayḍāwī, ʿAlī (2001), *Al-Iḥsās bi-l-Zamān fī al-Shiʿr al-ʿArabī: min al-Uṣūl ḥattā Nihāyat al-Qarn al-Thānī li-l-Hijra*. Manūba: University of Manouba, Publications of the Faculty of Arts.
al-Jihād, Hilāl (2007), *Jamāliyyāt al-Shiʿr al-ʿArabī: Dirāsa fī Falsafat al-Jamāl fī al-Waʿy al-Shiʿrī al-Jāhilī*. Beirut: Markaz Dirāsāt al-Waḥda al-ʿArabiyya.
al-Jubūrī, Yaḥyā (1986), *al-Shiʿr al-Jāhilī: Khaṣāʾiṣuhu wa-Funūnuhu*. 5th ed. Beirut: Muʾassasat al-Risāla.
al-Qaysī, Nūrī (1980), *al-Shiʿr wa-l-Tārīkh*. Baghdad: Dār al-Ḥurriyya li-l-Ṭibāʿa.
al-Ṣāʾigh, ʿAbd al-ʾIlāh (n.d.), *al-Zaman ʿinda al-Shuʿarāʾ al-ʿArab qabl al-Islām*. Cairo: ʿAṣmī lil-Nashr wa-l-Tawzīʿ.
al-Shaybānī, Abū ʿAmr, *Sharḥ al-Muʿallaqāt al-Tisʿ, wa yalīhi Muʿallaqat al-Ḥārith al-Yashkurī*, edited and explained by ʿAbd al-Majīd Hammū. Beirut: Muʾassasat al-Aʿlamī li-l-Maṭbūʿāt, 2001.
al-Tabrīzī, Yaḥyā ibn ʿAlī, *Sharḥ al-Qaṣāʾid al-ʿAshr*, edited and annotated by Muḥammad ʿAbd al-Ḥamīd. Cairo: Maktabat Muḥammad ʿAlī Ṣubḥ wa-Awlādih, n.d.
al-Ṭālib, ʿUmar (1989), *al-Qalaq wa-l-Ightirāb fī al-shiʿr al-Jāhilī*. al-Maghrib: Dār ʿUkāẓ.
al-Yūsuf, Yūsuf (2001), *Maqālāt fī al-Shiʿr al-Jāhilī*. 3rd ed. Ramallah: Wizārat al-Thaqāfa al-Filasṭīniyya.
Arberry, Arthur John (1957), *The Seven Odes: The First Chapter in Arabic Literature*. London: G. Allen & Unwin.
ʿAṣfūr, Jābir (1992), *al-Ṣūra al-Fanniyya fī al-Turāth al-Naqdī wa-l-Balāghī ʿinda al-ʿArab*. Beirut: al-Markaz al-Thaqāfī al-ʿArabī.
ʿAṭwān, Ḥusayn (1982), *Waṣf al-Baḥr wa-l-Nahr fī al-Shiʿr al-ʿArabī*. Beirut: Dār al-Jīl.
Badawī, ʿAbd al-Raḥmān (1947), *al-Insāniyya wa-l-Wujūdiyya fī al-Fikr al-ʿArabī*. Cairo: Maktabat al-Nahḍa al-Miṣriyya.
Badawī, ʿAbd al-Raḥmān (1945), *Shūbinhawir*. 2nd ed. Cairo: Maktabat al-Nahḍa al-Miṣriyya.
El Masri, Ghassan (2020), *The Semantics of Qurʾanic Language: al-Āḫira*. Leiden: Brill.
Fūghālī, Bādīs (2008), *al-Zamān wa-l-Makān fī al-Shiʿr al-Jāhilī*. Amman: Jādārā lil-Kitāb al-ʿĀlamī, ʿĀlam al-Kutub al-Ḥadīth.
Hägglund, Martin (2019), *This Life: Secular Faith and Spiritual Freedom*. New York: Pantheon Books.
Hammad, Ahmad Zaki (2009), *The Gracious Quran: A Modern phrased Interpretation in English. Arabic-English*, 6th ed. Lisle: Lucent Interpretations LLC.
Ḥannūn, Nāʾil (1986), *ʿAqāʾid mā baʿd al-Mawt fī Ḥaḍārat Bilād Wādī al-Rāfidayn al-qadīma*. 2nd ed. Iraq: Dār al-Shuʾūn al-Thaqāfiyya al-ʿĀmma.
Heidegger, Martin (2001), *Being and Time*, translated by John Macquarrie and Edward Robinson. Oxford/Cambridge: Blackwell.
Ibn Manẓūr, *Lisān al-ʿArab*. Cairo: Dār al-Ḥadīth, 2003.
Imhof, Agnes (2018), "Labīd b. Rabīʿa." *Encyclopaedia of Islam Three Online*. https://doi.org/10.1163/1573-3912_ei3_COM_35759.
Imruʾ al-Qays, *Dīwān Imruʾ al-Qays*, edited by Muḥammad Abū al-Faḍl Ibrāhīm. Cairo: Dār al-Maʿārif, 1990.
Jihād, Hilāl (2001), *Falsafat al-Shiʿr al-Jāhilī: Dirāsa Taḥlīliyya fī Ḥarakat al-Waʿy al-Shiʿrī al-ʿArabī*. Damascus: Dār al-Madā li-l-thaqāfa wa-l-nashr.
Jumʿa, Ḥusayn (2002), "al-Zamān fī Madākhil Naqd al-Shiʿr al-Qadīm." *Majallat al-Maʿrifa* 470, 30–49.
Khulayf, Yūsuf (1981), *Dirāsāt fī al-Shiʿr al-Jāhilī*. Cairo: Maktabat Gharīb.

Labīd ibn Rabīʿa al-ʿĀmirī, *Dīwān Labīd ibn Rabīʿa al-ʿĀmirī.* Beirut: Dār Ṣādir, n.d.
Macquarrie, John (1972), *Existentialism.* Philadelphia/London: Westminster/Hutchinson.
Meyerhoff, Hans (1960), *Time in Literature.* Berkeley: University of California Press.
Montgomery, James E. (2012), "Ṭarafa." *Encyclopaedia of Islam New Edition Online*. https://doi.org/10.1163/1573-3912_islam_SIM_7405.
Montgomery, James E. (ed.) (2022), *Fate the Hunter: Early Arabic Hunting Poems*. New York: New York University Press.
Muṣliḥī, Ṣalāḥ (2000), "Muʿallaqat Ṭarafa b. al-ʿAbd: al-Mawqif wa-l-bunya." In *Ṭarafa b. al-ʿAbd: Dirāsāt wa-Abḥāth Multaqā al-Baḥrayn.* Beirut: al-Muʾassasa al-ʿArabiyya li-l-Dirāsāt wa-l-Nashr, 217–260.
Nāṣif, Muṣṭafā (2000), "Mushkilat al-Maṣīr fī Muṭawwalat Ṭarafa." In *Ṭarafa b. al-ʿAbd: Dirāsāt wa-Abḥāth Multaqā al-Baḥrayn*. Beirut: al-Muʾassasa al-ʿArabiyya li-l-Dirāsāt wa-l-Nashr, 29–43.
Nāṣif, Muṣṭafā (1981), *Qirāʾa Thāniya li-Shiʿrinā al-Qadīm.* Beirut: Dār al-Andalus.
Nūr al-Dīn, Ḥasan (ed.) (1990), *Ṭarafa b. al-ʿAbd: Sīratuhu wa-Shiʿruhu.* Beirut: Dār al-Kutub al-ʿIlmiyya.
Plekhanov, George (1977), *al-Fann wa-l-Taṣawwur al-Māddī li-l-Tārīkh*, translated by George Ṭarābīshī. Beirut: Dār al-Ṭalīʿa.
Ricoeur, Paul (1984), *Time and Narrative*, translated by Kathleen McLaughlin and David Pellauer. Chicago/London: The University of Chicago Press.
Ṣafwat, Aḥmad (n.d.), *Jamharat Rasāʾil al-ʿArab fī ʿUṣūr al-ʿArabiyya al-Zāhira*. Beirut: al-Maktaba al-ʿIlmiyya.
Shaḥāda, ʿAbd al-ʿAzīz Muḥammad, *al-Zaman fī al-Shiʿr al-Jāhilī.* Irbid: Muʾassasat Ḥammāda lil-khadamāt wa-Dirāsāt al-Jāmiʿiyya, 1995.
Stetkevych, Suzanne (1985), "Al-Qaṣīdah al-ʿArabiyyah wa Ṭuqūs al-ʿUbūr." *Majallat Majmaʿ al-Lughah al-ʿArabiyyah bi-Dimashq* 60.1, 55–85.
Stetkevych, Suzanne (1993), *The Mute Immortals Speak: Pre-Islamic Poetry and the Poetics of Ritual.* Ithaca: Cornell University Press.
Ṭarafa ibn al-ʿAbd, *Dīwān Ṭarafa ibn al-ʿAbd, sharḥ al-Aʿlam al-Shantamarī, wa-talīhi ṭāʾifa min al-shiʿr al-mansūb ilā Ṭarafa*, edited by Durriyya Khaṭīb wa-Luṭfī al-Ṣaqqāl. 2nd ed. Beirut: al-Muʾassasa al-ʿArabiyya li-l-Dirāsāt wa-l-Nashr; Jordan: Dār al-Fāris li-l-Nashr wa-l-Tawzīʿ, 2000.
Ṭarafa ibn al-ʿAbd, *Dīwān Ṭarafa ibn al-ʿAbd*, edited by Mahdī Nāṣir al-Dīn. Beirut: Dār al-Kutub al-ʿIlmiyya, 2002.
ʿUbayd b. al-Abraṣ, *Dīwān ʿUbayd b. al-Abraṣ*, edited and annotated by Ashraf ʿAdra. Beirut: Dār al-Kitāb al-ʿArabī, 1994.
Weipert, Reinhard (2007), "ʿAbīd b. al-Abraṣ." *Encyclopaedia of Islam Three Online*. Accessed 30 October 2025. https://doi.org/10.1163/1573-3912_ei3_SIM_0019.
White, Stephen (ed. and trans.) (2021), *Diogenes Laertius: Lives of Eminent Philosophers: An Edited Translation*. Cambridge: Cambridge University Press, 411–462.
Zuhayr b. Abī Sulmā, *Dīwān Zuhayr b. Abī Sulmā*, annotated by Alī Fāʿūr. Beirut: Dār al-Kutub al-ʿIlmiyya, 1988.

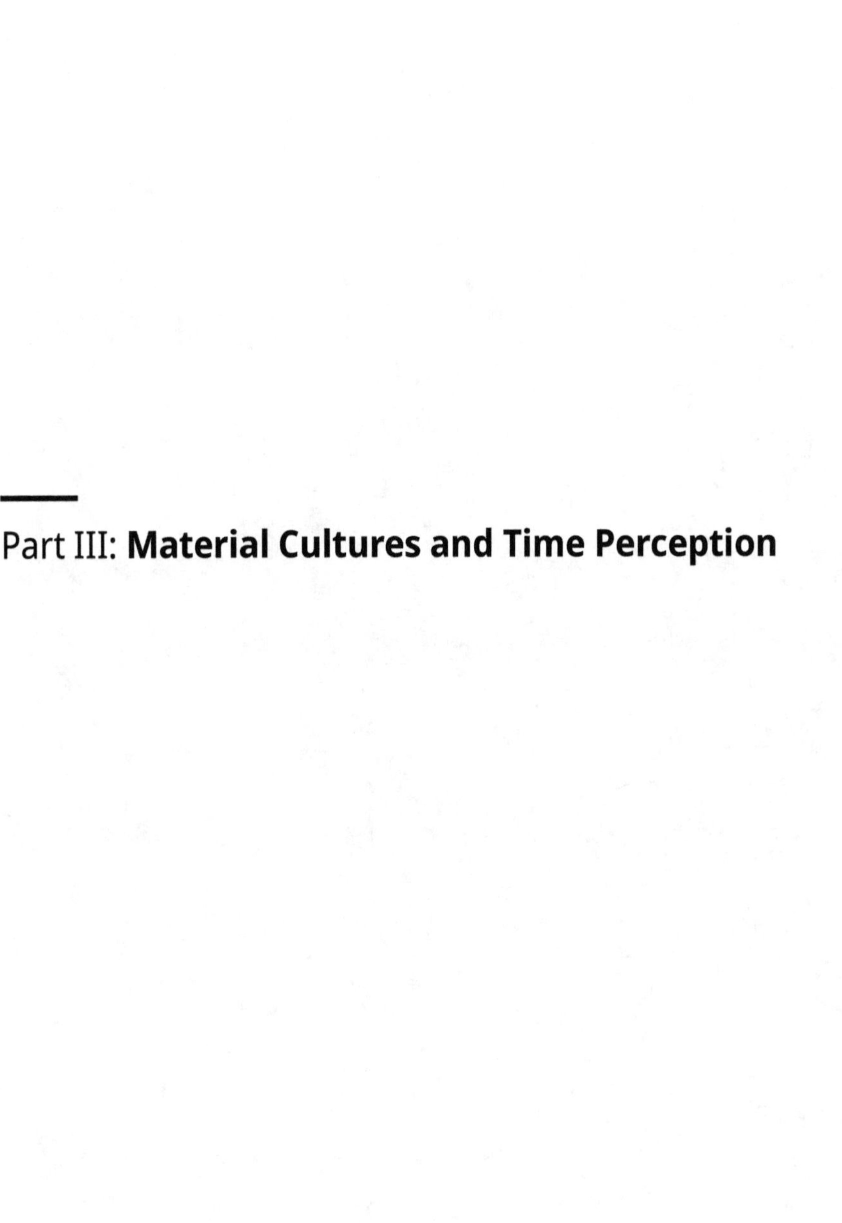

Part III: **Material Cultures and Time Perception**

Inbal Kol

Illuminating Time

Sensory Experience of Light in Early Islamic Art and Architecture

> What can 'art' mean in a culture where the primary organ of perception is not the eye or the ears, but the heart? It requires a shift from the visible to the sensible, in which attention is directed not outwardly toward the object, but inwardly, within the heart.
> — Wendy M. K. Shaw, *What Is "Islamic" Art?*

1 Introduction

Focusing on the formative centuries of Islam (7th–10th centuries), this article examines how mosque architecture was designed to emphasize the symbolic and perceptual importance of light, shaping worshippers' experience of both temporal progression and divine eternity. Architects utilized natural light not only for illumination but also as a medium through which the passage of time and the concept of timelessness could be perceived. By shaping the entry of light through domes, courtyards, and lattices, architects crafted spatial rhythms that draw worshippers into a sensory experience where time feels both immediate and infinite.

Wendy Shaw's concept of "seeing with the heart" offers a valuable framework for understanding this phenomenon. Shaw suggests that, in Islamic visual culture, perception extends beyond the eye to include the heart, facilitating an inward, sensory experience of the divine.[1] Building on this idea, this study examines how light in early mosques serves as a perceptual tool, guiding worshippers' awareness of temporal cycles while evoking a sense of the eternal. Drawing on Shaw's ideas, I argue that architecture in these sacred spaces functions as a sensory environment where light, shadow, and spatial layout mediate between human temporality and divine eternity. This approach enables an analysis of how natural and artificial light interact. Sunlight entering through well-placed openings creates a dynamic flow of illumination that follows prayer times and daily routines. Artificial light, such as oil and glass lamps, extends this sense of time into the night, strengthening the connection to divine cycles. By examining the sources of light, the mosque can be seen as a space that transforms temporal theology into a lived, perceptual experience.

1 Shaw 2019, 115.

Finally, this study places these observations within a broader theoretical framework. Drawing on Henry Corbin's notion that the visible acts as a medium through which the invisible can be understood, I propose that light in mosque architecture serves as a physical manifestation of abstract concepts related to time and the divine. Through precise manipulation of lighting and shadows, sacred spaces prompt worshippers to sense a flow of time that appears both limited and infinite, anchoring philosophical and theological ideas in a concrete, sensory experience.

2 Light as a Medium of Perception and Presence

The role of light in early Islamic architecture is not merely a physical phenomenon but also a medium that engages with temporal and divine perception. Building on Shaw's insights into inward perception, the following discussion examines how these principles manifest concretely in mosque architecture, particularly through the manipulation of light and spatial design. Shaw argues that, in Islamic culture, the primary organ of perception is not the eye but the heart; hence, the notion of "seeing with the heart" provides a crucial framework for understanding these architectural strategies. Shaw emphasizes that Islamic art and architecture cultivate inward, sensory engagement, encouraging the worshipper to feel and experience the divine presence. According to Shaw, this shift from external, visual perception to inward, sensory experience is essential for understanding Islamic art and architecture.[2] The goal is not merely to observe or listen, but to feel and experience the divine presence in a personal and profound way.

This approach is particularly pertinent in the context of mosque design, where the environment is meticulously crafted to inspire spiritual contemplation and foster a sense of connection with the divine. The interplay of light and shadow is intended to evoke a sense of divine presence, guiding the worshipper toward inner reflection and spiritual harmony. According to Shaw, the atmosphere created by light in the mosque is intended to resonate with the worshipper's heart, encouraging a deeper and more personal encounter with the sacred.[3] In other words, sacred Islamic architecture can be seen as a space for contemplation, a place where abstract philosophical and theological ideas about time are made sensory, spatial, and experiential.[4]

This transition from prioritizing visuals to engaging all the senses fosters a more profound connection with the environment, going beyond simple visual perception

2 Shaw 2019, 115–117.
3 Shaw 2019, 116.
4 Akkach 2012, 33–36.

to include a sensory experience that is both tangible and emotional. As a result, the space assumes a sacred quality, enabling the worshipper's heart to align with the divine.[5] This notion resonates with the Qur'ānic metaphors in which the heart is described as the seat of understanding and spiritual sight (e.g., Q 22:46: "Have these people [of Mecca] not travelled through the land with hearts to understand and ears to hear? It is not people's eyes that are blind, but their hearts within their breasts.").

Building on this approach, light is used not only to illuminate but also to embody the divine and eternal, prompting reflection on the passage of time while simultaneously reminding the worshipper of God's perpetual presence. The experiential encounter with the divine and the temporal is achieved through various architectural and design elements, including the filtering of sunlight through geometric windows, the interplay of shadows within the prayer hall, and the focused illumination of the *mihrab*.[6] The mosque, with its deliberate design and careful utilization of light, becomes a space where human temporality intersects with divine eternity. In Islamic sacred spaces, the intentional use of light reflects a theological understanding of time as fluid and dynamic, encompassing both personal and cosmic dimensions. Each moment thus becomes more than a fleeting point in time; it serves as an opportunity to connect with the ever-constant divine order, much like the sight-based temporal awareness described in this volume by Hentschel in *Mālik's Muwaṭṭa'*, where observing the movement of light and shadow marks the right moment for prayer and situates human action within divine rhythm.[7]

As art historian and archaeologist Oleg Grabar claimed, Islamic architecture cannot be reduced to just form or its historical background; its importance lies in the experience it creates. The built environment acts as a bridge between the physical and spiritual worlds, forming a transcendent reality. Light, space, and design work together to create an immersive experience that appeals to worshippers both mentally and physically. Therefore, the way a mosque is perceived depends less on its historical or visual features and more on the strength and continuity of the experience it offers, linking the tangible with the spiritual.[8]

Building on this understanding of light's essential role, the *mihrab*—the niche indicating the direction of prayer—stands out as a particularly important architectural element that captures the interaction of light and time. The *mihrab* is often highlighted by natural light at specific times of day, thereby reinforcing the worshipper's temporal and spiritual direction. This relationship between light and religious practice not only emphasizes the practical function of illumination but also

5 Shaw 2019, 116.

6 Hentschel in this volume; Akkach 2012, 49–51.

7 Akkach 2012, 49–51.

8 Grabar 1992, 18–20, 172–174.

reflects the Islamic theological view of time as flexible and influenced by divine will.[9] Another architectural feature that participates in the interplay of light and shadow is the *muqarnas*. The *muqarnas*, a structural element in early Islamic art, consists of tiered, niche-like cells (stalactite structures) that project and recede in complex geometries. The dynamic interplay of light and shadow created by these surfaces produces a pattern that feels both spatial and temporal, contributing to a sense of depth and continuity for viewers. The *muqarnas* serves a dual purpose: acting as a transition between structural changes and controlling the flow of daylight within space. As the sun moves across the tiers, creating variations in shadow length, the resulting pulsations of light emphasize these transitions, improving the visual experience. Beyond its structural and spatial roles, the *muqarnas* also carries symbolic meaning: in Islamic architecture, light is seen as a divine element, symbolizing the descent of spiritual illumination into the material world. The *muqarnas* has been described by Nasrollahi as "an architectural manifestation of a precise Islamic concept symbolizing the descent of light into the world of material forms," emphasizing its role in linking the physical and spiritual realms.[10]

Yasser Tabbaa, though focusing on later examples, approaches it differently: he interprets the *muqarnas* not merely as a symbol of divine light but as a spatial expression of theological ideas such as atomism and occasionalism, reflecting the world's continual re-creation by God.[11] In this way, the *muqarnas* serves not just as decoration but as a temporal and spiritual enhancer. The variation of light and the gradation of forms create a feeling of a heavenly garden, emphasizing the coexistence of material and spiritual experiences within the sacred space.[12]

Building on this cosmological-theological framework, Majdi Faleh shifts attention from meaning to perception. He argues that light in Islamic architecture transcends simple illumination, interacting with geometric forms, patterns, and surfaces to create a continuous, transformative experience of space.[13] The projection of light through *muqarnas* generates constantly shifting patterns and gradations of brightness and shadow, engaging the viewer both visually and spiritually. According to Faleh, "each pattern, geometry, and form is a living element inside the building,"[14] emphasizing the close connection between architectural form, light, and spiritual contemplation. While Faleh, like Tabbaa, primarily focuses on later examples, his theoretical insights are similarly relevant to early Islamic architecture, providing a

9 Akkach 2012, 49–51.
10 Nasrollahi 2015, 99.
11 Tabbaa 1991, 71–72.
12 Tabbaa 1991, 71–72.
13 Faleh 2016, 172–174.
14 Faleh 2016, 178.

framework for understanding how *muqarnas* can serve as both a spatial and temporal enhancer, as well as a mediator of the experience of light, shadow, and the divine.[15]

The *muqarnas* is not only a theological or phenomenological device but also a profoundly geometric one, embodying the mathematical order that underlies Islamic architecture. The interaction of light with architectural features such as domes, windows, and minarets highlights the importance of geometry and order in Islamic architecture. Geometric patterns and *arabesques* are not merely decorative elements; rather, they play a vital role in the dynamic relationship between light and space. As the sun's position changes throughout the day, light interacts with these patterns, thereby creating a dynamic environment that reflects the fleeting nature of human life. At the same time, this movement of light through sacred spaces symbolizes the constancy of God's presence, suggesting that while human existence is temporary, the divine remains eternal and unchanging. As a result, the mosque goes beyond its practical function as a place of worship and becomes an architectural symbol of the theological concept of time. Through the skillful arrangement of light and space, believers are prompted to contemplate the dualistic nature of existence, which encompasses both temporal and divine aspects.[16]

The lighting inside the mosque, whether from the soft glow of lanterns, direct sunlight, or the grand chandeliers that hang in the prayer hall, is carefully arranged to create an atmosphere of reflection and reverence. The intentional play of light and shadow not only indicates the passage of time but also serves as a spiritual guide, encouraging worshippers to reflect on their place within the divine order. As Hentschel emphasizes, these temporal markers enable individual worshippers to perceive the "right moment" within sacred time, effectively integrating themselves into the rhythm of the mosque's spiritual and temporal framework. By guiding attention through light and shadow, the architecture actively shapes the experience of sacred time.[17] In Islamic architectural theory, the mosque is seen as more than just a physical building; it is designed to shape space in a way that places the worshipper in the presence of the divine, turning movement through and interaction with the space into a spiritual experience.[18] Light in these sacred spaces becomes both a physical and symbolic element, representing divine guidance and inviting worshippers to connect with the eternal. By working with light and time this way, Islamic architecture creates

15 Faleh 2016, 180.

16 One might also consider whether the repetition of geometric patterns, through which form and meaning are transmitted across surfaces, reflects in visual terms the structure of *isnād* chains and the collective continuity of knowledge transmission through time as discussed by Amir and Yahav in this volume.

17 Hentschel in this volume.

18 Nasrollahi 2015, 99.

a spiritual environment that prompts followers to consider their existence and their connection to the eternal by bridging the earthly world with the divine.[19]

From the orchestration of time, space, and geometry, the meaning of light in Islamic architecture extends into the realm of theology. The Qur'ān describes God as "the Light of the heavens and the earth" (Q 24:35), emphasizing light as a sign of divine presence and guidance. Hence, in mosques, light serves a purpose beyond its practical role, becoming a theological symbol. This is especially evident in the *mihrab*, where the fall of natural light at specific times of day or the use of lamps aligns with the rhythm of prayer, linking daily worship to the metaphor of divinely guiding light. These design choices shape space not only physically but also spiritually, guiding worshippers toward an awareness of the divine presence and encouraging a contemplative experience.[20]

This intrinsic relationship between light and Islamic architecture demonstrates that illumination is not merely a functional or decorative element, but a medium through which spiritual presence is made visible. Classical masterpieces of Islamic architecture act as crystallized forms of light, clear and transparent, simultaneously illuminating and being illuminated.[21] In these spaces, light defines both the physical and spiritual dimensions, shaping the perception of the sacred and marking temporal progression through its movement. While architects traditionally aimed to shield interior spaces from external heat, and shade was seen as a divine blessing, the Muslim soul longs for light as a symbol of Divine Presence.[22] In this context, the reverberation of the word (the prayer and the call to prayer) combined with the play of light sanctifies the architecture, guiding the worshipper toward the One and creating a constant sense of the divine everywhere, as the Qur'ān states: "wherever you turn, there is His Face" (Q 2:115).[23] The dance of illumination and spatial design thus turns the mosque into a perceptual and temporal space where the worshipper directly connects with the divine order, experiencing the unity of creation through both light and sacred architecture.

Light reflects divine order by following the day-night cycle and signaling God's presence. Inside the mosque, sunlight moving throughout the day marks the passage of time, while also emphasizing human temporality. Moreover, the role of light in the mosque goes beyond simply indicating time; it also promotes a sense of community. In this way, light acts as a symbolic connection between individual worship and collective devotion, echoing Qur'anic principles of unity (*tawḥīd*) and

---

19 Lange 2021,150; Shaw 2019, 117.
20 Nasrollahi 2015, 98–99.
21 Nasr 1987, 51.
22 Nasr 1987, 51.
23 Nasr 1987, 54.

social harmony.[24] Light also plays a vital role in shaping the spiritual atmosphere of the mosque. It helps create a sense of purity and tranquility, allowing worshippers to focus on prayer and connect with the divine. When filtered through intricate windows or stained glass, it transforms the space into a medium of spiritual engagement. This demonstrates that light is not merely an aesthetic feature, but a crucial component of the spiritual experience within the mosque, thereby deepening the worshipper's engagement with the sacred space.[25] In this way, the mosque transcends its physical form, becoming a metaphysical tool that helps worshippers understand the relationship between time, light, and the divine.[26]

3 Light in Early Islamic Architecture

Having examined perception and sensory experience, the focus now turns to time as the driving force for form and structure in Islamic architecture. Light in early Islamic sacred spaces not only mediates inward perception and shapes temporal experience; it also articulates how time is governed by God and governs all life. A well-known ḥadīth reported by Abū Huraira in Ṣaḥīḥ al-Bukhārī and Ṣaḥīḥ Muslim provides further insight into this concept. The Prophet Muhammad warns: "Do not curse Time (*ad-dahr*), for indeed God is Time."[27] In this ḥadīth, *ad-dahr*—understood in pre-Islamic poetry as an impersonal and often hostile force of fate—is redefined as an expression of divine agency. What was once blind destiny becomes the unfolding of God's will in temporal form. Architecture, in this context, reflects this theological shift: by controlling light and shadow, by marking the visible passage of day and night, the mosque transforms time into a site of divine presence. Through this interplay, light not only illuminates material forms but articulates the rhythms and transitions of sacred time, marking moments of prayer and reflection while connecting the earthly to the divine. In this way, architectural materialization renders the meaning of the ḥadīth perceptible; it makes the flow of *ad-dahr* appear ordered, sacred, and ultimately governed by God.

Having traced how light and time in early Islamic thought intertwine as expressions of divine rule and guidance and how architecture invites perception of this relation through sensory experience, the next step is to examine how these ideas mate-

24 Shaw 2019, 119.

25 Nasrollahi 2015, 98–99.

26 Shaw 2019, 119.

27 Böwering 1997, 60–61.

rialize in specific architectural forms, as seen in elements such as domes, windows, and geometric patterns that channel and diffuse light throughout the space.

The Great Mosque of Damascus, which was completed circa 715 CE, offers an early architectural embodiment of these theological and temporal concepts (Fig. 1).[28] Its extensive use of clerestory windows and mosaics creates a carefully modulated illumination, producing dynamic interplay between sunlight, shadow,

Fig. 1: Great Mosque of Damascus interior in daylight, Damascus, Syria. Digital photograph, 1986. © Aga Khan Trust for Culture / Stefano Bianca (photographer), https://www.archnet.org/sites/31?media_content_id=681732 (last accessed on January 8, 2026).

28 Hillenbrand 1994, 54–60.

and reflective surfaces (Fig. 2).[29] As the sun moves across the sky, light animates the mosaics and architectural forms, reinforcing Qur'ānic imagery of "gardens graced with flowing streams" (Q 9:72) and evoking the temporal and spiritual rhythm of sacred space. According to Finbarr Flood, the shifting play of light in Damascus engages the viewer in a continuously transforming experience of space, one that emphasizes the temporal progression of both material and divine realities.[30] Robert Hillenbrand further notes that these architectural arrangements facilitate a perception of continuity and eternity, as the movement of light produces temporal markers that punctuate daily ritual practice while connecting the worshipper to the divine.[31]

Fig. 2: Great Mosque of Damascus, Golden Mosaics and clerestory windows, Damascus, Syria. Digital photograph, 1986. © Aga Khan Trust for Culture / Stefano Bianca (photographer), https://www.archnet.org/sites/31?media_content_id=681730 (last accessed on January 8, 2026).

In the more specific architectural details of the Damascus Mosque, *muqarnas*, which are often placed over or around the *mihrab*, or in semi-domes, serve to focus attention on key moments of prayer. The upper tiers are illuminated during specific periods of the day, directing the viewer's attention toward the focal point, while the

29 Flood 2001, 47–57.
30 Flood 2001, 47–57.
31 Hillenbrand 1994, 59.

lower tiers remain relatively obscured, delineating the sacred space and enhancing the spiritual resonance of light and shadow. This exemplifies the potential of *muqarnas* to serve as a medium for embodying temporal, symbolic, and contemplative dimensions within the context of Islamic architecture, extending beyond its structural and decorative functions.

Building on this architectural and symbolic heritage, the Great Mosque of Córdoba (784–988 CE) exhibits impressive scale and sophistication in its use of light. In this hypostyle mosque, light filters through grilled windows and is diffused by a forest of columns and double arches, creating a dynamic play of light and shadow across the prayer hall (Fig. 3). This intentional arrangement of natural light symbolizes the transmission of divine presence and guidance into the world.[32] The movement of light throughout the day marks the rhythm of prayer and reflects both human temporality and the possibility of glimpsing the eternal. This shifting illumination is not merely aesthetic but a deliberate design gesture that embodies the passage of time as a divine act. As sunlight shifts, it marks the rhythm of daily prayers and underscores both the human experience of temporality and the chance to catch a glimpse of the eternal.

Besides its symbolic role, light in both places also serves a practical purpose. It illuminates the space for prayer and reorientation, providing the necessary physical illumination for worship while also representing the spiritual light that guides believers. Using light in architectural design reflects the connection between the material and spiritual aspects of time. Each moment in the mosque, marked by the entry of light, becomes a point of convergence between the transient and the eternal.[33]

As Grabar observes in his detailed analyses of both the Great Mosque of Damascus and the Great Mosque of Córdoba, each structure (through its distinct architectural evolution) reveals key stages in the development of sacred spaces in early Islamic architecture. Regarding the mosque in Damascus, Grabar notes that its *mihrab* is one of three that already existed in the medieval period. He further explains that the columns of the hypostyle hall are largely spolia, repurposed from earlier architectural contexts, while the arches themselves recall pre-Islamic building traditions of the region. These elements not only demonstrate continuity with the architectural past but also reinterpret it within a new sacred order, one that merges earlier visual languages into an Islamic theological framework.[34]

---

32 Arel and Öner 2017, 425.
33 Akkach 2012, 41–44.
34 Grabar 1973, 105.

Fig. 3: The Great Mosque of Cordoba, prayer hall. Digital photograph by Yunus Hentschel, 2024. Courtesy of the photographer.

In his discussion of the Great Mosque of Córdoba, Grabar highlights that its *mihrab* functions as a whole chamber, appearing as though it opens from within the mosque toward another, unseen realm (Fig. 4).[35] This effect is achieved through the intentional use of empty space designed to receive and contain light. The luminous aura surrounding the *mihrab* transforms it into a focal point of divine presence. Similarly, the alternating pattern of red and white voussoirs in the *ablaq* arches creates a rhythmic contrast of light and shadow, further intensified by natural illumination. Together, these visual strategies enhance the sacred atmosphere of the interior. As Grabar emphasizes, ornamentation in these mosques works in harmony with architectural design, serving not merely decorative purposes but guiding the believer's perception, both physical and spiritual, toward the most significant parts of the sacred space.[36] The *mihrab*, highlighted by light, thus becomes a visual and sensory mediator of divine presence, demonstrating how early Islamic architecture

35 Grabar 1973, 115.
36 Grabar 1973, 126.

unites structure, decoration, and illumination to shape the worshipper's contemplative experience.

Fig. 4: The Great Mosque of Córdoba, the *mihrab* chamber is visible through the archway. Digital photograph by Yunus Hentschel, 2024. Courtesy of the photographer.

4 Time in Islamic Thought and Architecture

Beyond the sensory and visual dimensions of worship experienced within early Islamic mosques lies a deeper theological and philosophical conception of time and light. This conception forms the foundation of Islamic cosmology, theology, and philosophy, and is manifested in religious practices and social structures. A central principle in Islamic thought is that time is not an autonomous or eternal entity but a divine creation. The Qur'ān states this clearly: "when He wills something to be, His way is to say, 'Be'—and it is!" (Q 36:82), and "every day He is at work" (Q

55:29). These verses emphasize that all events and the flow of time are continuously created and controlled by God's will. From this perspective, time does not exist independently; rather, each moment is a renewed act of divine creation. This understanding causes Islamic cosmology to reject the idea that time exists independently. Instead, each moment is continuously renewed by the divine, highlighting both the world's fleeting nature and God's ongoing creative power.

Böwering explains, "in every instant, God is creating the world anew; there are no intermediate causes. God can be thought of as continually creating the universe from nothing... each moment within time is the direct creation of the eternally active God."[37] Thus, the world's existence is not self-sustaining but is constantly maintained by God's creative act, highlighting the fragility and transient nature of all creation.

The interplay of sunlight and shadow within sacred architecture mirrors this theological conception of temporality. It is not merely decorative but symbolizes the temporal rhythm of sacred space, guiding worshippers' movement and focus during prayer. In this context, Henry Corbin's notion of the *Imago Templi* provides a complementary, although non-architectural, perspective. According to Corbin, the *Imago Templi* is conceptualized as an imaginal archetype that materializes within the "man-temple," thereby transforming the human being into a living temple.[38] Corbin proposes that the inner temple serves as a medium for reflecting unseen realities.[39] By analogy, the dynamic play of light and shadow in Islamic sacred architecture can be seen as rendering the invisible perceptible, translating temporal change into an experience of spiritual presence.

This philosophical reflection on the nature of history and temporality in Islamic thought is further emphasized by the duality between divine time and human time. Otfried Weintritt notes that Islamic historiography emphasizes a succession of distinct moments rather than a continuous chain of cause and effect.[40] In this context, time is viewed as atomistic, with events occurring in separate, isolated moments rather than as a continuous flow. This atomistic perception of time not only shapes theology but also profoundly influences Islamic historical consciousness, which tends to highlight significant, exemplary moments—particularly those associated with the early Islamic period. As a result, this formative era is viewed as one of spiritual and moral purity, from which later generations have deviated, awaiting ultimate judgment and restoration.[41]

37 Böwering 1997, 59.
38 Corbin 1986, 386–387.
39 Corbin 1986, 386–387.
40 Weintritt 2008, 86.
41 Weintritt 2008, 86–88.

The integration of these dimensions—divine, human, and practical—reflects the dynamic and complex nature of time in Islamic thought. This unity is reflected architecturally in sacred spaces designed to embody both divine eternity and human temporality. The play of light and shadow, the use of detailed geometric patterns, and the focus on areas meant for reflection and meditation all express these theological and philosophical ideas. Among these, the mosque stands out as a paradigmatic example: here, the call to prayer, which demarcates specific times throughout the day, serves as a central link between the temporary and the divine order. This spatial arrangement encourages worshippers to connect with both the human and divine aspects of time, creating a layered experience that reflects the close relationship between these principles. In this way, the architecture itself becomes a medium of contemplation, translating metaphysical ideas about time into lived, sensory, and spatial experience.[42]

Ultimately, the concept of time in Islam extends beyond merely measuring events. As Böwering explains, Islamic thought distinguishes between a vertical, theoretical dimension where the individual is forever connected to God and marked by moments of existence, and a horizontal, practical dimension, in which the community of believers creates its own temporal framework through the calendar, marking the start of a new era in human history. This duality demonstrates that time in Islam operates simultaneously as a divine creation and as a framework for collective life, linking cosmic order with human devotion.[43]

Taken together, these various philosophical, theological, and social perspectives on time provide a rich conceptual foundation that is not confined to abstract thought but finds material expression in the very spaces, images, and rituals of Islamic civilization. Thus, when light animates sacred space, marking prayer times, shaping perception, and structuring movement, it does more than illuminate; it enacts the very principles of divine temporality that define Islamic cosmology. The integration of time and light in Islamic art and architecture reflects the broader theological and philosophical foundations of time in Islamic thought. As articulated by Böwering and Weintritt, time in Islam is not merely a chronological progression but a dynamic, divinely guided force that profoundly intersects with human experience.[44] Light, within this framework, becomes a material expression of the divine order—both marking temporal rhythm and signifying God's eternal presence. The deliberate interplay of light and architecture in Islamic spaces encourages contemplation, guiding worshippers to reflect on the nature of time and its divine connec-

42 Akkach 2012, 33–36.
43 Böwering 1997, 65.
44 Böwering 1997, 65; Weintritt 2008, 90.

tion. In these spaces, the temporal and the eternal converge, transforming architectural experience into an act of spiritual reflection.

5 The Symbolism of Shadow and the Limits of Light in Islamic Architecture

Having established the theological and philosophical foundations of time and light in Islamic thought, it is essential to consider their counterpart: shadow. In Islamic architecture, the relationship between light and shadow extends these metaphysical ideas into visual and spatial form. Just as time is understood as a series of divinely renewed moments, shadow represents the transient dimension of existence, the fleeting, material aspect of creation that reveals its dependence on divine illumination. Within this context, shadow becomes more than a visual absence; it emerges as a symbolic and theological presence that defines the sacred experience of space.

Building on the discussion of light and time, the interplay of shadow in early Islamic sacred spaces complements and enhances the sensory and spiritual experience of the worshipper. In Islamic thought, the relationship between light and shadow is not merely a physical phenomenon, but also a profound metaphorical and theological concept. Light, as discussed above, symbolizes divine illumination, knowledge, and God's presence. However, every light has an unavoidable shadow, and in Islamic symbolism, shadows strongly represent the temporal and material world, as well as the limits of human existence. Shadows, unlike light, suggest impermanence, obscurity, and the finite nature of human life.

Shadows, often seen as symbols of obscurity or absence, paradoxically enhance the experience of light. Just as the human perception of divine light relies on the inward engagement described by Shaw, the perception of shadow similarly requires reflection, emphasizing the contrast between the temporal and the eternal. In the Islamic spiritual and philosophical framework, the material world cannot exist without the transcendent divine. The Qur'ān frequently contrasts the clarity of divine truth (represented by light) with the ambiguity and darkness of human ignorance or sin (represented by darkness). In this sense, the shadow is not merely a negation of light but a vital part of the cosmic order that highlights God's presence.

As Oleg Grabar observes, Islamic architectural representations employ visual oppositions—between structure and ornament, or between the real and the imagined—that function not as literal depictions but as mediators, guiding the viewer beyond the physical into a realm of spiritual meaning.[45] Here, shadow operates as a temporal and contemplative dimension within sacred space, giving perceptible form to the invisible processes of divine and human temporality discussed above. In this context, the play of light and shadow across ornamental surfaces becomes directly relevant to how these contrasts are perceived and how they shape the spatial and spiritual experience of the mosque.

In architecture, the duality between light and shadow is evident in the design of sacred spaces. The play of natural light filtering through windows, domes, and arches creates intricate shadow patterns that change throughout the day, emphasizing the cyclical nature of time. This dynamic interaction can serve as a visual metaphor for the passage of time and the eternal truths of divine order. Keith Critchlow's exploration of geometric design in Islamic architecture highlights the importance of both light and shadow in shaping the worshipper's experience. The detailed arabesques and patterns on mosque walls, often designed with light and shadow in mind, reflect the transcendent nature of divine beauty while reminding viewers of the limited nature of their earthly existence.[46]

The manipulation of light and shadow in mosques is a deliberate architectural strategy that shapes not just physical space, but also spiritual experience. The mihrab, as the focal point of prayer, is often illuminated by natural light at specific times of the day, symbolizing God's guidance, while shadowed areas create a sense of mystery and sacredness. This interplay does more than create visual effects; it guides how worshippers move, focus, and engage within the space. Grabar explains, "architecture is, in these architecturally fashioned objects, a visual access to an action, to a way of behaving, and is not restricted to representing something or evoking it."[47] In this sense, the contrast between light and shadow in the mosque can be understood as a means through which architecture provides access to spiritual action and experience, rather than merely representing the physical environment. This architectural design mirrors the Islamic concept of time, where each moment of prayer is an opportunity to bridge the gap between the finite human experience and the eternal divine presence.

In mosques, this duality is not only a physical phenomenon but also a visual symbol of the spiritual journey of the believer. The play of light and shadow in mosque architecture encourages worshippers to reflect on their place within the

---

45 Grabar 1992, 172–174.
46 Critchlow 1976, 45–47.
47 Grabar 1992, 193.

divine order, reminding them of God's hiddenness while guiding them toward eternal truth.[48]

6 Conclusion

Building on the framework outlined in this article and following Wendy Shaw's insight into "seeing with the heart," this study has shown how early Islamic architecture transforms light, shadow, and spatial design into a perceptual and spiritual experience that mediates between temporal progression and divine eternity. By orchestrating natural illumination through domes, windows, and intricate geometric patterns, architects created sacred spaces that invite worshippers to engage inwardly, sensing the flow of time while connecting with the eternal presence of God. This approach highlights the centrality of sensory perception in experiencing the divine, situating the human encounter within a broader cosmological and theological order.

At the same time, the analysis recognizes the limits of visibility and the invisible aspects of divine temporality. While light renders God's temporal action perceptible, shadow reminds us that the essence of time and divine agency remains elusive, only glimpsed through fleeting sensory moments. This duality highlights the interplay between the material and the spiritual, underscoring that sacred architecture reveals not the totality of the divine but rather traces of its presence in space and time. The research also invites reflection on its historical scope: it remains uncertain to what extent early Muslim worshippers would have consciously perceived the theological orchestration of light and time, or whether the symbolic program we reconstruct reflects the interpretive lens of later scholars. These questions highlight the provisional nature of interpretation and the complex relationship between lived experience and historical reconstruction.

Finally, early Islamic architecture demonstrates the transformation and reinterpretation of sacred forms inherited from Late Antiquity. Through innovative spatial arrangements, the manipulation of light, and the integration of symbolic geometry, architects of the 7th–10th centuries created a distinctive mode of sacred expression that both honors its precedents and establishes a novel theological and aesthetic language. In this way, the mosques studied here stand as heirs to previous sacred architectural traditions while simultaneously asserting their own perceptual, spiritual, and temporal visions.

---

48 Shaw 2019, 117–121.

Bibliography

Akkach, Samer (2012), *Cosmology and Architecture in Premodern Islam: An Architectural Reading of Mystical Ideas*. Albany, NY: State University of New York Press.

Arel, Hasan Ş., and Merve Öner (2017), "Use of Daylight in Mosques: Meaning and Practice in Three Different Cases." *International Journal of Heritage Architecture* 1.3, 421–429.

Böwering, Gerhard (1997), "The Concept of Time in Islam." *Proceedings of the American Philosophical Society* 141.1, 55–66.

Corbin, Henry (1986), *Temple and Contemplation*, translated by Philip Sherrard and Liadain Sherrard. London: KPI.

Critchlow, Keith (1976), *Islamic Patterns: An Analytical and Cosmological Approach*. Rochester, VT: Inner Traditions International.

Faleh, Majdi (2016), "Islamic Light in the Architecture of the Sublime." *WIT Transactions on The Built Environment* 159, 171–181.

Flood, Finbarr Barry (2001), *The Great Mosque of Damascus: Studies on the Makings of an Umayyad Visual Culture*. Leiden: Brill.

Grabar, Oleg (1973), *The Formation of Islamic Art*. New Haven: Yale University Press.

Grabar, Oleg (1992), *The Mediation of Ornament*. Princeton, NJ: Princeton University Press.

Hillenbrand, Robert (1994), *Islamic Architecture: Form, Function, and Meaning*. Edinburgh: Edinburgh University Press.

Lange, Christian (2021), "Eternal Sunshine of the Spotless Mind: Light and Luminous Being in Islamic Theology." *Critical Research on Religion* 9.2, 142–156.

Nasr, Seyyed Hossein (1987), *Islamic Art and Spirituality*. Albany: State University of New York Press.

Nasrollahi, Fatemeh (2015), "The Transcendent Soul of the Muslim Architect and Spiritual Impact of the Islamic Architecture." *Journal of Islamic Studies and Culture* 3.2, 86–99. https://jisc.thebrpi.org/journals/jisc/Vol_3_No_2_December_2015/10.pdf (last accessed on November 25, 2025).

Shaw, Wendy M. K. (2019), *What is "Islamic" Art? Between Religion and Perception*. Cambridge: Cambridge University Press.

Tabbaa, Yasser (1991), "The Muqarnas Dome: Its Origin and Meaning." *Muqarnas* 8, 61–72.

Weintritt, Otfried (2008), "Interpretations of Time in Islam." In *Time and History: The Variety of Cultures*, edited by Jörn Rüsen. New York/Oxford: Berghahn Books, 85–92.

Filiz Tütüncü Çağlar

Curating the Past: The Ottoman Imperial Museum and Historical Consciousness

Ne içindeyim zamanın, ne de büsbütün dışında
Neither am I within time, nor entirely outside of it.
—Ahmet Hamdi Tanpınar

1 Introduction

In the second half of the nineteenth century, the Ottoman Empire established its first state museum, the Imperial Museum (*Müze-i Hümâyûn*), as part of a wider set of reforms that sought to regulate the past with the same administrative discipline applied to the present. Initially functioning for its early decades largely as a storehouse for antiquities, the museum gradually became a site where fragments of the empire's history were gathered, sorted, and displayed in ways that reflected the shifting priorities of a rapidly modernizing state. This chapter examines how the Imperial Museum, particularly in the period from its institutionalization in 1869 to the early twentieth century, engaged with the past through its practices of collecting, classifying, and exhibiting.[1] While much has been written about its legal framework and archaeological fieldwork, much less is known about how the museum actually operated: how objects were chosen and arranged, what principles guided these decisions, and how these choices shaped Ottoman encounters with antiquity.

Drawing on the museum's catalogues, guidebooks, archival material, and contemporary commentaries, this study reconstructs the museum's evolving spatial organization and the curatorial logic behind it. The picture that emerges is one of persistent reconfiguration rather than stability. Galleries were continually expanded and reorganized as new objects arrived, and as practical conditions dictated. Within its halls, antiquities were arranged to impose order from a diverse

1 This chapter began as an empirical inquiry inspired by the thematic focus of the Einstein Center Chronoi on time and temporality, evolving into a broader investigation of the temporal practices of the Ottoman Imperial Museum and its implications for global museum historiography. I gratefully acknowledge the generous support of the Einstein Center Chronoi, whose 2024 fellowship (January–December) enabled the development of this research. My warm thanks go to the Chronoi team for their consistent support, as well as my co-fellows for many stimulating conversations. I am also grateful to Prof. Dr. Burak Onaran for sharing his valuable insights during the early stages of my research.

and fragmented past, even though that order remained provisional and often improvised. I argue that the museum's approach to antiquity was neither coherent nor fixed. Instead, it developed through pragmatic responses to the demands of a modernizing state caught between redefining its temporal horizons and asserting cultural authority and international legitimacy. The collections, exhibited in spacious galleries, made antiquity visible and meaningful primarily for the benefit of an international audience and the Ottoman educated urban elite. These practices unfolded at a time when multiple temporal frameworks—Islamic, bureaucratic, and Western—coexisted. As a result, the museum functioned simultaneously as a repository and as a site where objects acquired layered temporal meanings, after having been indexed by their production, period of use, style, and symbolic resonance within late Ottoman society.

To frame this inquiry, I draw loosely on François Hartog's concept of the museum as a *temporal agent*—an institution that shapes historical consciousness through acts of selection, ordering, and display.[2] Rather than applying this model directly to the Ottoman case, I use it heuristically to explore a set of guiding questions: how did the museum engage with time in its collecting, research, display, and mediation practices? Which pasts were prioritized, and how were they made visible? And finally, how were newly discovered antiquities connected to the present and to visions of the future? The limited accessibility of the museum archives and the fragmentary nature of the evidence necessitate a deliberately exploratory approach.[3] The aim is not to produce definitive conclusions, but to open new lines of inquiry to reconstruct the museum's curatorial logic.

In doing so, the chapter contributes to broader debates on the visual and temporal dimensions of museological practice—issues central to this volume. As a modern imperial institution that was secular in character, yet deeply embedded in Ottoman politics and scholarship, the Imperial Museum embodied historically specific ways of perceiving and organizing time. Its displays and classifications provide a point of departure for understanding how non-European actors engaged with their own pasts in an era of global museumification. As the empire's first museum and its most prominent cultural institution, the Imperial Museum had a relationship to the past that was central to late Ottoman cultural life and remains crucial for interpreting the global history of museum-making beyond Europe. More specifically, this chapter contributes by reconstructing the museum's internal spatial and classificatory approaches, through a close reading of Gustave Mendel's catalogues, and by interpreting these practices through a historically grounded discussion of

2 Hartog 2021.

3 A short history and critique of the museum's archives can be found in Bobou et al. 2025, 151–155.

time, improvisation, and institutional instability. These perspectives shift attention from legal framework and fieldwork practices alone to the museum's curatorial operations as sites where historical consciousness was actively formed.

2 Rethinking Historiographies

For much of the twentieth century, the history of the Imperial Museum was narrated as a sequence of administrative reforms based largely on official archives and with an overwhelming emphasis on Osman Hamdi Bey (1842–1910), the director who shaped its institutional character after 1881. This reliance on bureaucratic documentation produced a historiography that is descriptive in method and fragmented in scope. It also fostered a recurrent narrative in which the museum's story became closely tied to debates over the fate of antiquities, often casting Osman Hamdi as a key figure—whether protector or facilitator—in the transfer of objects to European collections. This institutional focus yielded an account that seldom questioned how the museum itself actually functioned: how objects were collected, classified, and displayed; how these practices shaped historical knowledge; or how the institution operated beyond Osman Hamdi's directorship. The museum's trajectory after his death in 1910 and the implications of the Young Turk Revolution of 1908 for cultural policy likewise remain insufficiently explored.

In recent decades, several analytical studies have expanded our understanding of the museum's formation, legal reforms, and archaeological practices within a global context. Among these, three authors have been especially influential in defining the field's contours, each offering a distinct interpretation of the museum's purpose and development.[4] Wendy M. K. Shaw situates the museum primarily within wider narratives of Ottoman modernization and cultural diplomacy, presenting it as a counter-hegemonic institution that visually asserted Ottoman sovereignty in the face of European archaeological dominance. She emphasizes the museum's displays as instruments for staging imperial continuity within the context of the Tanzimat reforms.[5] Zeynep Çelik shares Shaw's attention to politics and representation but shifts the emphasis outward, analyzing how debates over antiquities unfolded in the press, diplomacy, and international public opinion.[6] These two studies position the museum within a contested global arena, highlighting its role in mediating Ottoman identity at the turn of the twentieth century.

4 Shaw 2003; Çelik 2016; Eldem 2018.

5 Shaw 2003, 218–224.

6 Çelik 2016.

A more skeptical perspective comes from Edhem Eldem, who shifts attention to the museum's formative years, from the early collections of 1846 to Osman Hamdi's appointment in 1881. He argues that the museum did not emerge from a coherent ideological program but was instead a top-down bureaucratic and pragmatic attempt at Westernization. He presents it as part of a cultural 'checklist' intended to demonstrate the empire's modernity.[7] Eldem critiques Shaw's interpretation as "wishful thinking," cautioning against retroactively attributing coherence or nationalist ambition to a fragmented record. His intervention is valuable for exposing the limits of institutional modernity in the museum's early formation. While the present discussion takes Eldem's critique seriously, it also builds on his acknowledgment that the institution's more stable scientific foundations were laid only later, under Osman Hamdi, and asks how such classificatory and scholarly practices took shape despite enduring structural constraints.

Other scholars have also sought to rethink the museum through alternative theoretical frameworks. Drawing on Pierre Bourdieu, Lorenzo Posocco interprets Osman Hamdi as a cultural intermediary, embedded in elite networks of symbolic capital, framing curatorial practice as socially and institutionally embedded rather than as the expression of a purely autonomous ideological project.[8] Sezen Ünlüönen extends this line of inquiry through a comparative approach, aligning the Imperial Museum with contemporary institutions in colonized or semi-colonized settings. She interprets it as a "testament to imperial powerlessness": an institution that, despite its imperial symbolism, struggled with chronic shortages of funds, expertise, and space—conditions shared by many museums outside Europe.[9] Rather than framing these features simply as failures, she sees them as constitutive of a distinctly Ottoman museological practice that was adaptive, uneven, and fundamentally contingent.

Elucidating the museum's connections to Ottoman modernity, its role in cultural diplomacy, and its place within broader discourses of archaeology and identity, these studies have considerably refined our understanding of the Imperial Museum. Their interventions moved the discussion well beyond mainstream narratives that either celebrate institutional modernization or simply lament the displacement of antiquities. Yet, certain enduring tendencies persist, particularly the expectation that late Ottoman institutions must be understood either as coherent modernizing projects or as imperfect imitations of European models. Such inherited frameworks continue to inform how the museum's history is approached. Vir-

7 Eldem 2018, 272.

8 Posocco 2021, 37.

9 Ünlüönen 2024, 3.

ginia Aksan's call for a conceptual historiography attentive to silences, gaps, and interpretive assumptions remains relevant here, urging analyses that move beyond descriptive accumulation of archival facts toward a more critical examination of the epistemological foundations of institutional narratives.[10]

Building on these insights, this chapter seeks a middle ground beyond the binary of triumphalist modernization and failed imitation. Following Aksan's call for a historiography freed from inherited teleologies, this approach views the Imperial Museum as a site where historical consciousness was unevenly constructed through improvisation, negotiation, and practical constraints. Rather than viewing the museum as the product of a stable institutional program, this study considers it as a peculiar landscape shaped by pressure, uncertainty, and evolving strategies for defining the empire's relationship to the past. I examine curatorial acts, such as classification, display, and sequencing, as temporal interventions and empirical practices, employing temporality as an analytical focus to connect Ottoman museology with broader cultural and political contexts. By combining historiographical critique with close reading of museum practices, I treat curatorial choices not as ideological manifestations of a predetermined agenda but as pragmatic responses to the demands and limitations of a rapidly changing political and intellectual environment. Through this approach, the museum emerges as a temporal agent that contributed to shaping experiences of time and history in the late Ottoman world, even though contingent decision-making processes marked its operations.

3 Museums and Temporality

This study draws on insights from the growing scholarship on museum temporality to sharpen its empirical focus, particularly regarding how time was materially and institutionally handled at the Imperial Museum. Recent scholarship has demonstrated that museums are not neutral repositories of objects; they are active agents in shaping temporal experience. Through processes of selection, ordering, and display, they organize the past in ways that generate meaning in the present. As Jen Walklate has argued, time is "a key ethical and political feature of the museum," affecting how collections are framed, histories are constructed, and audiences are addressed.[11] In this chapter, I approach the Imperial Museum as a space where multiple temporalities were negotiated through curatorial practice.

---

10 Aksan 2008, 114–115.
11 Walklate 2023, 5.

The concepts deployed here are kept deliberately modest in scope rather than serving as a prescriptive theoretical model. They serve as prompts to explore how the museum's routine operations in collecting, classifying, arranging, and publishing turned the material remains of the past into a structured historical experience and, ultimately, into a vocabulary through which the late Ottoman society made sense of its relationship to antiquity. This perspective helps illuminate how the museum's curatorial acts contributed to the production of historical consciousness at a moment when notions of time, progress, and historical depth were being actively redefined within the empire.

François Hartog's work offers a useful point of reference in thinking about how museums intervene in perceptions of time.[12] Rather than simply mirroring existing temporal norms, museums actively configure them by stabilizing certain narratives, arranging the past into sequences, and rendering history legible. From this perspective, one may ask how the Imperial Museum's excavations, displays, and publications participated in this process: which pasts were elevated, which temporal regimes they invoked, and how their visual and textual presentation shaped meaning for different audiences. Susan A. Crane's notion of "fixed ephemerality" further highlights the paradox that lies at the heart of museums: they freeze the past while simultaneously mobilizing it as evidence of change and progress.[13] Over time, the Imperial Museum came to embody this tension, as its rapidly expanding collections required curators to balance permanence with transformation, and continuity with rupture.

This perspective matters because the Ottoman case diverges significantly from the coherent institutional models often assumed in studies of European museums. The Imperial Museum's curatorial strategies were not shaped by such a unified vision but reflected the practicalities of acquisition, limited space, and shifting bureaucracies. Temporality was, therefore, not a fixed backdrop but an active field of curatorial decision-making. Cataloguing, prioritizing certain sites or periods, reorganizing galleries, and revising typologies took shape as provisional solutions to collection urgencies. These practices produced hierarchies, as well as absences and gaps. In doing so, the museum's evolving arrangements not only made the past visible and relevant for its audiences but also contributed to articulating new forms of imperial identity grounded in claims to historical depth and civilizational belonging.

12 See Hartog 2021.

13 Crane 2006, 98–99.

At the same time, this temporally inflected approach raises methodological concerns. Applying concepts such as “temporal regimes” or “museum chronology” risks anachronism, especially given the fragmentary evidence and the particularities of the Ottoman institutional context. Administrators and curators of the Imperial Museum did not articulate their work in temporal terms, nor did they operate within a self-conscious theoretical framework. For this reason, it is important to emphasize that the heuristic use of temporality adopted here serves strictly to illuminate processes that are otherwise difficult to discern: how objects acquired historical meaning through their arrangement, and how curatorial practices contributed to shifting forms of imperial identity. Temporality, in this analytical sense, becomes one essential tool for understanding how history was curated and how the Ottoman museum articulated new forms of imperial self-understanding.

4 Historical Background: Time and History in the Late Ottoman Empire

4.1 Ottoman Temporal Culture

The late Ottoman period witnessed profound shifts in how time was organized, perceived, and politicized. From the mid-nineteenth century into the early twentieth century, the empire experienced an intensified engagement with both traditional and newly introduced temporal frameworks.[14] Recent studies have shown how new infrastructures, such as railways, steamships, telegraph networks, printing technologies, and the proliferation of public clocks, reshaped temporal awareness, producing what François Georgeon and Frédéric Hitzel have described as a distinct temporal culture.[15] These innovations accelerated communication, compressed distances, and placed unprecedented value on punctuality and regulation, framing time as a scarce and governable resource.

Among the most visible changes was the introduction of European-style timekeeping systems, most notably the widespread use of mechanical clocks and the construction of clock towers across the empire. These towers functioned both as tools of public discipline and as symbolic assertions of imperial sovereignty: instruments through which the state sought to regulate not only space but also

14 İhsanoğlu and Günergun 1996.

15 Georgeon and Hitzel 2012, 1–10.

time itself.[16] Reformist discourse increasingly linked punctuality, scheduling, and the efficient use of time to the ideals of order, civilization, and progress. Time thus became a moral as well as a practical category.[17]

Yet these modernizing impulses did not replace older temporalities. The Islamic lunar calendar (*hicrî*), the fiscal solar calendar (*rûmî*), and the Gregorian calendar coexisted, creating a complex and sometimes contradictory temporal order in legal, bureaucratic, and commercial life. This plurality generated a layered temporal consciousness, in which newly imported, linear and quantitative conceptions of time were grafted onto longstanding cyclical and religious rhythms. The result was a palimpsest of overlapping temporalities, which created both new possibilities and frictions.[18]

The Imperial Museum was very much a product of this temporal environment. Its development paralleled wider efforts to accelerate communication, standardize administration, and order the empire's past as a means of shaping its future. Like the telegraph or the railway, the museum was conceived as a tool to impose order on antiquities and histories. Standing at the heart of this new temporal culture, it embodied the same ambition: to discipline time, to make the empire's long past visible and available to the present, and to align its historical patrimony with an emerging modern order.

4.2 Birth of Modern History

From the Tanzimat era onwards, history in the Ottoman world became both an intellectual pursuit and a key instrument of reform and identity formation.[19] A defining feature of this period was the adoption of new historiographical frameworks that, while developed in conversation with European scholarship, assumed distinctly Ottoman forms. The tripartite division of history into "ancient, medieval, and modern," the growing interest in pre-Ottoman and non-dynastic pasts, and the elevation of material remains as historical sources all marked a departure from the *vakanüvis* (court chronicler) tradition toward more secular and scholarly approaches to the past.[20]

16 Wishnitzer 2015, 148.

17 Wishnitzer 2015, 134–138.

18 İhsanoğlu and Günergun 1996; Georgeon and Hitzel 2012, 1–10.

19 Arıkan 1985, 1584–1594.

20 Karateke 2013, cited in Papatheodorou 2017, 77.

Several figures stand out as pioneers of this transformation. For instance, Ahmet Cevdet Pasha, a leading statesman and scholar, produced his monumental *Tarih-i Cevdet* in twelve volumes (completed in 1884 and revised in 1891), a work that broke with earlier courtly historiography and established new critical methods. Ahmet Vefik Pasha represents another facet of this intellectual climate: steeped in both Ottoman and French scholarly traditions, he translated classical texts, built an impressive personal library, and pioneered a new universalist historical consciousness.[21] Namık Kemal, Hayrullah Efendi, and Ahmet Lütfi Efendi introduced further innovations, often situating Ottoman history within a wider world-historical narrative; in the case of Namık Kemal, this project was infused with civic and nationalist ideals. By the early twentieth century, these developments converged with an increasingly Turkist discourse, exemplified by the *Türk Derneği* (Turkish Society) (founded in 1908) and later the *Türk Ocağı*, in which history became a central tool for mobilizing nation-building projects.

These shift in historical horizons also brought renewed interest in the Middle Ages. As Johann Strauss has demonstrated, late Ottoman intellectuals and readers developed a nascent interest in medieval history, both Islamic and European, which was mediated through translations, textbooks, and periodicals.[22] This fascination with the medieval past formed part of a wider effort to situate the Ottoman experience within a universal chronology of civilizations, broadening the temporal scope of Ottoman historical imagination beyond dynastic boundaries.

This intellectual ferment culminated in the establishment of the *Tarih-i Osmani Encümeni* in 1909, a historical commission whose founding statement explicitly linked knowledge of "the ancient life and traditions of nations" with the cultivation of patriotism.[23] Although the commission was officially framed as an inclusive Ottomanist initiative, its early publications often displayed a more Turkist emphasis. This institutionalization of historical scholarship marked the transition from the Enlightenment-inspired universalism of the Tanzimat to the increasingly nationalized historiography of the Second Constitutional Era (1908–1918).

Within this vibrant environment, ideas of order, progress, and discipline became central themes. As Avner Wishnitzer has argued, late nineteenth- and early twentieth-century Ottoman military and political elites—shaped by the new tempos of the telegraph, railway, and modern schooling—interpreted reform as a process of disciplining both time and society.[24] Influenced by positivism and, to some extent, by social Darwinism, these elites envisioned institutions such as the

21 Arıkan 1985.
22 Strauss 2012, 213–216.
23 İnalcık 2006.
24 Wishnitzer 2012, 281–315.

army as the "school of the nation," with the regulation of time and conduct as essential tools for collective renewal. Order—rooted in Auguste Comte's positivist conviction that social order was the necessary precondition for progress—gave these temporal strategies a significance that reached far beyond the barracks.

Scientific debates of the period reinforced this outlook and political debates. For late Ottoman reformers, evolutionary thinking was compelling not for its biological claims but for its broader implications. It offered new conceptual tools for organizing knowledge, restructuring institutions, and accelerating social and political change. Concepts such as evolution, adaptation, and classification were adopted into cultural debates, informing questions such as how to align Ottoman institutions with global standards, how to "catch up" with Europe, and how to create a modern, historically conscious state.[25] In the museum context, such evolutionary and classificatory idioms made typology, comparison, and ordered display appear as natural techniques for representing the past. It was in this intellectual climate, where speed, order, and historical awareness converged, that disciplines such as archaeology, epigraphy, art history, and numismatics took root. These fields, closely connected to the mission of the Imperial Museum, anchored the study of the past not only in texts but also in the systematic study of material remains. Historical publications, translations, architectural studies, and a proliferation of visual culture (photographs, engravings) all contributed to a wider diffusion of historical knowledge.[26]

This period also saw a surge of interest in the material traces of the past. Archaeological surveys, architectural documentation, and restoration of monuments came to signify the outlook of a state seeking to present itself as historically grounded and culturally authoritative.[27] A particularly telling example is the long-running effort to stabilize and restore the Column of Constantine (*Çemberlitaş*) in Istanbul. Falling masonry from the column threatened nearby residents, prompting petitions that led to the formation of a commission chaired by Osman Hamdi Bey in 1888. Despite financial and technical hurdles, the restoration revealed a growing awareness of ancient monuments as imperial markers. Later interventions to prevent the construction of modern multi-story buildings around the column further highlighted an emerging concern for the historical character of urban space.[28]

Yet, this transformation was neither seamless nor uniform. Across historical and art-historical accounts of the period, terminology and periodization remained

25 Wishnitzer 2012, 310–311.

26 Ersoy 2016, 331–335; Çelik 2016, 110–119.

27 For a close analysis of the study of the material past of Byzantine Istanbul, see Sümertaş 2021.

28 Sönmez 2014.

fluid, experimental, and at times inconsistent.[29] Rather than signaling disciplinary immaturity, this linguistic and conceptual instability reflects a moment of intellectual experimentation similar to the tensions that also appeared in the museum's evolving classification systems and display strategies.

Among the prominent figures shaped by this new intellectual climate was Halil Edhem Bey (1861–1938), Osman Hamdi's younger brother.[30] Educated in Germany and Switzerland, he engaged in archaeology, epigraphy, numismatics, Islamic art and architecture and urban history. As founder of the journal *Tarih-i Osmani Mecmuası*, a leading, member of the *Tarih-i Osmani Encümeni (Ottoman Historical Commission)*, and later of the *Türk Tarih Kurumu* (Turkish Historical Society), he embodied the synthesis of European scholarly methods with emerging Ottoman historical consciousness.[31] His scholarly formation would later shape his approach to museum work, as discussed below.

4.3 Formation of the Imperial Museum

The foundation of the Imperial Museum in 1869 was part of this wider culture of reform and historical awareness. Following the first Antiquities Law (*Asâr-ı Atîka Nizamnâmesi*) of 1869, which aimed to protect antiquities and centralize their management, the museum became the institutional expression of these concerns. Its origins, however, date back to 1846, when early collections of antiquities and old armaments were assembled in Hagia Eirene within the Topkapı Palace complex. As these holdings grew, they were moved in 1880 to the nearby Tiled Pavilion (*Çinili Köşk*) (Figs. 1 and 2).[32]

Foreign expertise played an important role in this early phase. The first two directors, Edward Goold and Philipp Anton Dethier, and later Albert Dumont prepared the first inventories, advised on the conversion of spaces, and offered archaeological expertise, setting the stage for a more formal institution.[33] The real turning point came in 1881 with the appointment of Osman Hamdi Bey. Under his leadership, the museum evolved from a modest assemblage into a more structured and internationally engaged institution that sought to protect antiquities and assert the cultural prestige of the Ottoman state.

29 Sürün 2013, 18–19.
30 Eldem 2010, 255–259.
31 İnalcık 2006, 3–6.
32 Eldem 2010; Koçak 2011; Shaw 2003; Çelik 2016.
33 Goold 1871; Cezar 1995, 231–243; Dumont 1868, 1883.

Fig. 1: The Çinili Köşk (Tiled Pavilion), garden of Topkapı Palace, later housing the first archaeological displays of the Imperial Museum. Photograph by Abdullah Frères, ca. 1880s. İstanbul Üniversitesi Merkez Kütüphanesi, Abdülhamid II Albums, 90819–0017.

The rapid growth of the collections soon exceeded the capacities of the Hagia Eirene and the Tiled Pavilion, making a purpose-built museum essential. Designed in stages by Alexandre Vallaury, a Levantine architect trained at the *École des Beaux-Arts* in Paris, the new neoclassical building opened in 1891. Its symmetrical façade, porticoes and pediments, long, linear wings, and U-shaped courtyard reflected the Beaux-Arts ideals of clarity and monumentality (Fig. 3). The façade, modelled on the celebrated *Sarcophagus of the Mourning Women* excavated by Osman Hamdi in Sidon in 1887, turned the building itself into a monumental homage to the antiquities it housed.[34] This architectural symbolism, combined with its location adjacent to the Topkapı Palace, emphasized imperial prestige rather than public accessibility.

34 Kula (Say) 2014, 118–140; Üstoğlu Coşkun 2025, 227.

Fig. 2: Antiquities displayed inside the Çinili Köşk. Photograph by Pascal Sébah, late 19th century. İstanbul Üniversitesi Merkez Kütüphanesi, Abdülhamid II Albums (Grande salle, 91529–0008).

As the museum expanded in 1903 and 1907, spatial constraints required a constant reconfiguration of displays. By the 1890s, the main building housed Greek and Roman antiquities, while Islamic art remained in the Tiled Pavilion, and a separate Museum of the Ancient Orient, opened in 1917, was reserved for Near Eastern collections.[35] In principle, this separation introduced a chronological and civilizational order; in practice, it was undermined by limited space, rapid pace of acquisitions, and shortages of staff and resources. By 1911, Adolphe Reinach observed that the museum lacked basic infrastructure—labels, up-to-date visitor guides, and sufficient personnel—and noted that thousands of objects remained uncatalogued in storage.[36]

In 1892, Osman Hamdi appointed Halil Edhem as deputy, who succeeded him as director from 1910 to 1931. Combining historical scholarship with administrative skill, Halil Edhem consolidated and modernized the institution at a time of profound political change and tension, effectively bridging late Ottoman and early Republi-

35 Shaw 2000.

36 Reinach 1911.

Fig. 3: The Imperial Museum complex viewed from the central courtyard. Photograph by Sébah & Joaillier, after 1907. İstanbul Üniversitesi Merkez Kütüphanesi, Abdülhamid II Albums, 90518-0001.

can approaches to antiquities and museum practices. Although his vision of transforming the museum into a national institution remained constrained by resources, he established a new museological discourse through his books and articles on the responsibilities of museums, preservation, and the scholarly value of collections.[37] He envisioned the museum as a space where multiple histories could meet: ancient and modern, Ottoman and Western, archaeological artifacts and fine arts.

This vision extended into the creation in 1915 of the *Elvah-ı Nakşiye*, a fine arts collection housed in the *Sanayi-i Nefise Mektebi* (Academy of Fine Arts), founded by Osman Hamdi in 1883 as the empire's first modern art school to train artists in European techniques while cultivating a national school of painting and sculpture.[38] Located across from the museum, the academy formed part of a larger project to make art and archaeology mutually reinforcing fields. By placing the *Elvah-ı Nakşiye* in this space, Halil Edhem sought to integrate Ottoman and European art

---

37 The breadth of Halil Edhem's scholarly and curatorial output is reflected in publications such as Halil Edhem 1904, 1915a, 1915b, 1924, and 1932. Also see Bahrani, Çelik, and Eldem 2011a and 2011b.
38 Cezar 1995, 455–475; Artun 2010; Eldem 2010, 259.

histories into a universal, chronological narrative—from ancient sarcophagi to nineteenth-century painting—and to align the Imperial Museum with institutions such as the Louvre and Berlin's Altes Museum.[39] Through articles, catalogues, administrative work, and public advocacy, Halil Edhem argued for the systematic preservation of monuments and collections at risk from neglect, vandalism, or urban development.[40]

Despite these initiatives, the museum remained caught between ambition and constraint. Reliant almost entirely on state funding, it struggled to keep pace with the volume of finds generated by excavations, and the constant reshuffling of galleries became unavoidable. Nonetheless, it continued to serve as the central authority for the management of antiquities and monuments, and continually strove to extend this authority to the distant corners of the empire. As part of these efforts, provincial museums were founded in Konya, Bursa, Jerusalem, and later in Çanakkale, and Antalya, functioning mainly as regional depots that kept finds near their sites and reduced the risks of transport to the capital. Modest in scale and housed in schools or municipal courtyards, these institutions represented the first attempts to decentralize the administration of antiquities while keeping provincial collections firmly under the supervision of the Imperial Museum. As Shaw notes, this expansion unfolded within a broader and often contested field in which foreign missions, local authorities, and the Imperial Museum negotiated control over the movement and preservation of antiquities.[41] These broader ambitions became tangible in the museum's daily work with objects. The next section turns to its practices of collecting, classifying, and displaying to consider how the museum actively shaped late Ottoman understanding of the past.

5 Engaging with the Past: The Imperial Museum in Practice

The Imperial Museum emerged as a central node in the empire's expanding infrastructure for managing, studying, and interpreting antiquities. Through its routine practices of collecting, preserving, investigating, classifying, and displaying antiquities, the museum became a key arena where the Ottoman elite articulated their relationship to history. These activities were not purely technical or administrative procedures, but served as a means for asserting sovereignty over the past. By

---

39 Artun 2010; Halil Edhem 1924. An examination of the Universal Survey Museum can be found in Duncan and Wallach (1980).

40 Eldem 2010, 255–259.

41 Shaw 2003, 169–171.

determining which objects were protected and how they should be understood, the museum generated new forms of knowledge and rendered antiquity intelligible to both Ottoman and foreign audiences.

The analysis that follows articulates the museum's work across four domains of practice: the legal authority through which antiquities were claimed and protected; the museum's involvement in archaeological fieldwork and the production of knowledge; the curatorial strategies through which objects were ordered and interpreted; and the institutional and public settings in which these practices were communicated. These domains show how the Imperial Museum became a place where historical consciousness was constructed in the late Ottoman Empire.

5.1 Possessing and Preserving the Past: The Legislation and Appropriation of Antiquity

The museum's earliest and most decisive form of engagement with the past was through acts of possession and preservation. By the late nineteenth century, intensifying Western demand for antiquities, driven by collectors, museums, and archaeological missions, combined with widespread looting and an unregulated antiquities market, pushed the Ottoman government to centralize control over ancient sites and their remains. The Imperial Museum became the state's principal instrument through which this authority was exercised.

Earlier attempts to regulate antiquities had already been made in 1869 and again in 1874, both under the name *Asâr-ı Atîka Nizamnâmesi.*[42] These regulations introduced the first formal definitions of antiquities and sought to place archaeological activity under state supervision. By specifying which classes of objects counted as "ancient" and subject to protection, they also drew new temporal boundaries across the landscape, separating everyday material culture from a category of remains identified as belonging to a distant past. Yet they proved largely ineffective. The 1869 law lacked clear enforcement mechanisms and relied heavily on local discretion, while the 1874 revision neither restricted the export of objects nor curtailed the influence of foreign excavators. Neither succeeded in centralizing authority or establishing the museum as the primary custodian of the material past. Their limitations created the conditions that made a more comprehensive and enforceable framework necessary by the early 1880s.

A more robust framework was introduced with the Antiquities Law of 1884, which broadened the definition of objects deemed worthy of protection, placed

42 Çal 1997; Koçak 2011, 61–65, 83–85; Cezar 1995, 327–333.

archaeological fieldwork under state control, and explicitly prohibited the export of antiquities beyond imperial borders.[43] These restrictions applied equally to foreign archaeologists and Ottoman subjects, creating a new regime of exclusive state custodianship. In seeking to prevent the transfer of objects to Europe, the law also mirrored the centralizing and monopolizing tendencies of European imperial museums.

The revised law of 1906 expanded the definition of "antiquities" to include Islamic material culture, reflecting a growing recognition of later historical layers as part of the empire's patrimony.[44] Enforcement, however, remained uneven as the Sultan's personal authority still permitted exceptions, particularly in the form of diplomatic gifts to Austria and Germany. Osman Hamdi also appears to have made occasional compromises in negotiations with foreign missions, often to ensure that the museum secured its legally mandated share of finds. This was likely a pragmatic strategy, shaped by chronic funding shortages and the logistical challenges of transporting objects to Istanbul.[45] Even with these inconsistencies, the Antiquities Law established a durable legal foundation that reinforced the museum's institutional position and defined the administration of antiquities as a matter of state interest.[46]

These measures had wide-ranging consequences. They slowed the removal of artifacts from Ottoman territory, consolidated the museum's role as the central authority over antiquities, and contributed to the emergence of archaeology as a scientific discipline within the empire. They also enabled a steady expansion of the museum's collections. Contemporary accounts noted how excavations and state confiscations significantly increased the flow of objects to Istanbul, enriching the museum's holdings under the strengthened legal regime.[47]

After 1908, the deposition of Abdülhamid II brought an additional wave of objects into the museum, as the extensive collections of Yıldız Palace—including weapons, glassware, ceramics, and luxury objects—were transferred to the museum. Similar transfers also affected natural history collections and other palace holdings, transforming what had previously been royal property into state collections. At the same time, however, these additions caused considerable disruption in the galleries, as these materials did not fit within the thematic and chronological

43 Çal 1997; Eldem 2010, 53–63; Koçak 2011, 100–102.

44 Koçak 2011, 160–162.

45 Popular historians such as Yaşar Yılmaz (2023) have interpreted these compromises as evidence of Osman Hamdi's complicity in the transfer of antiquities to European museums. Such readings, however, often overlook the structural constraints, limited resources, and political pressures that shaped museum governance at the time.

46 With only minor modifications, this framework remained in force into the Republican period and was not replaced until 1973 (Shaw 2000, 68, fn. 23).

47 Reinach 1911.

framework the museum sought to maintain.[48] The influx of palace material thus intensified the tension between the legal accumulation of objects and the museum's fragile attempts to stage a coherent historical narrative. Field reports and correspondence from this period also indicate a notable tightening of enforcement following the Young Turk Revolution: foreign archaeologists now found it much harder to remove objects from the country, suggesting that the museum's legal authority over antiquities was beginning to be more assertively applied.

5.2 Investigating and Collecting the Past: Archaeological Practice and Knowledge Production

Once legal authority over antiquities had been established, the Imperial Museum increasingly moved from being merely a custodian of artifacts to becoming an active participant in the discovery and production of knowledge about the past. By the late nineteenth century, archaeological investigation had become a central part of its work, not only as a means of securing objects for the museum but also as a way of asserting intellectual and administrative control over antiquity.

Large-scale excavations across the empire were entirely dominated by foreign missions, particularly German, Austrian, French, and British.[49] Yet the museum asserted a supervisory role and positioned itself as a formal partner institution alongside these expeditions. By issuing permits and dispatching its own representatives (commissars) to monitor the work, it enforced the rule that finds were to be documented and registered before being transferred to Istanbul. Although foreign

---

48 Alongside the Imperial Museum, late nineteenth-century Istanbul saw the creation of other significant collections that remain understudied in the historiography of Ottoman museology. Among these was the Yıldız Palace complex, which contained an observatory, workshops, a library of forty thousand volumes, an armory, zoological and botanical collections, and a fine arts museum, organized—albeit for the Sultan's private world—according to modern principles of classification. The period also witnessed the growth of natural history collections, such as the Natural History Museum established by Abdullah Bey at the Medical School (which housed 10,000 fossils from the Istanbul region) as well as the collections at Saint-Joseph College. These developments reflected contemporary European models and helped shape an environment that encouraged the musealization of art and science. They were further supported by the exhibition culture flourishing in Pera, the predominantly European quarter of Istanbul where diplomatic missions, cultural institutions, and commercial galleries were concentrated. All of these initiatives contributed to the emergence of a broader museum culture in the late Ottoman capital. (Artun 2010; also see the special issue of *Toplumsal Tarih* (2019) on the Natural History Collection in the Ottoman Empire. I am grateful to Dr. Nurçin İleri for bringing this volume to my attention.)

49 For foreign excavations in the Ottoman Empire, see Cezar 1995, 281–311.

teams often sought to circumvent these restrictions through diplomatic pressure, the very presence of museum representatives on-site marked a notable shift from passive oversight to active participation.[50]

In parallel, the museum began to develop its own excavation initiatives. The earliest Ottoman-directed digs were small-scale salvage operations, carried out by provincial officials or by the museum itself when antiquities were exposed by accidental discoveries, construction, or illicit digging. These interventions were often intended to prevent the immediate loss of portable objects rather than to conduct systematic research. Under Osman Hamdi Bey's directorship, however, a more ambitious phase began. Excavations were used deliberately to enrich the museum's collections and to demonstrate the empire's capacity to conduct archaeological research.[51] His expedition at the Royal Necropolis of Sidon, which brought to the museum a series of celebrated sarcophagi, including the Alexander Sarcophagus, exemplified this strategy.[52] For Osman Hamdi, fieldwork was a prerequisite to curatorial work, a means of gathering the empire's ancient remains into a central institution, and a way of situating Istanbul among major cultural centers of Europe.[53]

Gradually, a more explicitly scientific agenda took shape. Excavations directed by museum officials, including Theodore Macridy, Halil Edhem, and Osman Hamdi's son Edhem Bey, began to place greater emphasis on surveying sites, establishing chronological frameworks, and documentation.[54] These projects were much smaller in scale than the foreign-led missions but marked a clear shift toward archaeology as a discipline in its own right rather than as an instrument of curatorial acquisition. For example, Macridy's work at Notion, Sidon, and Boğazköy, among others, was characterized by an increasing interest in the careful study of finds not merely for enriching the museum collections but also for their scholarly potential.[55] Even salvage work reflected this new orientation. Haydar Bey's shipment of crates filled with seemingly insignificant sherds and fragments from Raqqa reveals a change in priorities—from collecting display-worthy objects to assembling data, even though the research and publication stages were not always realized, whether because of limited expertise, time, or funding.[56]

---

50 This is well exemplified by Theodore Macridy's work as a commissar at sites such as Ephesus, Baalbek and Boğazköy as I have discussed elsewhere (Tütüncü Çağlar *forthcoming*).

51 Cezar (1995, 311–325) offers a list of excavations carried out on behalf of the Imperial Museum.

52 Osman Hamdi, Reinach, and Chantre 1892.

53 Osman Hamdi, letter to Carl Humann, 1884 (Eldem 2014b, 106–107).

54 I have discussed Ottoman archaeological initiatives in Tütüncü Çağlar 2023.

55 For a fuller investigation of Macridy's work and role as an Ottoman archaeologist, see Tütüncü Çağlar forthcoming.

56 Tütüncü Çağlar 2017.

This shift reflected broader trends in the professionalization of archaeology and the museum's aspiration to align with international scholarly standards. Post-excavation work was equally significant. Objects were classified, restored, and studied, sometimes in collaboration with European specialists and sometimes independently by the museum officials.[57] Earlier reports were published mainly in French and through European presses to reach an international scholarly audience. These publications, which included field reports, catalogues, and journal articles, helped circulate Ottoman archaeological knowledge in international circles and situated the museum as a contributor to global debates on antiquity. In later decades, publications also began to appear in Ottoman Turkish and in the local press.

In this way, the museum's engagement with archaeology went beyond the acquisition of objects. Excavations provided information as well as artifacts; classification and analysis transformed these fragments into historical evidence; and publication disseminated this evidence as part of a shared, universal past. Archaeology thus allowed the Imperial Museum to project authority beyond its physical walls, asserting a scientific as well as custodial claim over antiquity. Nevertheless, the museum's ambitions to produce authoritative knowledge were continually challenged by limited funding, understaffing, and the overwhelming volume of incoming material. Despite such constraints, these decades laid the foundations of a professional Ottoman archaeology and positioned the museum as a key actor in shaping the empire's archaeological map.

5.3 Curating and Classifying the Past: Spatial Organization, Object Hierarchies and the Archaeological Turn

As the Imperial Museum's collections expanded rapidly through excavations, confiscations, and acquisitions, curators faced the dual challenge of managing an ever-growing volume of material while imposing a system that could turn disorder into meaning. Decisions about placement, grouping, and description shaped how time, value, and history were articulated within the galleries. Yet this transformation from a storehouse into a scientific museum remained uneven, constantly disrupted by the arrival of new objects, space and personnel shortages, and the absence of an established and coherent curatorial vision.

This trajectory paralleled broader developments in late nineteenth- and early twentieth-century museology. European museums were moving away from the

57 See, for instance, published field reports of Demosthene Baltazzi Bey (1881 and 1888), one of the first archaeologists who carried out excavations on behalf of the Imperial Museum.

earlier "art gallery" model to what Carol Duncan has called the "civilizing rituals" of classification, where objects were not just conserved but arranged to produce knowledge.[58] Typological and evolutionary display systems created authoritative visions of the past that framed history as a story of progress and ranked cultures within civilizational hierarchies, a pattern widely discussed for universal survey museums in Europe.[59] Ottoman practices drew from these models, but their implementation was conditioned by practical constraints and the museum's unprecedented pace of growth over a relatively short period.

Descriptions of the Hagia Eirene and later in the Tiled Pavilion present them as storage spaces rather than curated galleries, with antiquities and weapons piled in confusion and Byzantine objects pushed to the corners. Even as late as 1893, André Joubin found the Tiled Pavilion "resembling a bazaar," its halls crowded with objects "piled up or thrown in complete disorder against the walls" (Fig. 2).[60] The first systematic attempt to impose order came in 1882, when Osman Hamdi invited the French archaeologist Salomon Reinach to catalogue the collections. Reinach's *Catalogue du Musée Impérial d'Antiquités* established a taxonomy, but also fixed a hierarchy that privileged classical antiquities, while describing Byzantine objects as "lacking artistic value."[61]

The Sidon discoveries of 1887 and the construction of the new museum building in 1891 magnified these imbalances. The new "Sarcophagus Museum" devoted its central galleries almost exclusively to the Sidon sarcophagi, while the other antiquities remained crowded in the Tiled Pavilion. To address these issues, Osman Hamdi appointed André Joubin to classify and catalogue the holdings.[62] Joubin grouped objects by type and style, distinguishing Greek, Roman, and Byzantine material. His *Catalogue sommaire des monuments funéraires* (1893) and subsequent catalogues introduced a spatial typology: the central hall of the Tiled Pavilion was devoted to Greek and Roman sculpture, with adjacent rooms housing bronzes, terracottas, Cypriot material, Himyarite and Hittite objects, and finally a small room for Byzantine sculpture.[63]

Joubin's efforts marked an important turning point in the museum's self-conception. Earlier displays had echoed the aesthetic priorities of an "art gallery," whereas his new arrangement aligned the museum more closely with research-oriented archaeological institutes. This object-centered, taxonomic approach mir-

58 Duncan 1995; Moser 2006.
59 Duncan and Wallach 1980, 451.
60 Joubin 1893a; Du Crest 2002.
61 Reinach 1882.
62 Eldem 2010, 312.
63 Joubin 1893b; Du Crest 2002.

rored contemporary European practices, where museums increasingly treated archaeology as a scientific and historical discipline rather than a purely artistic one. In Istanbul, however, this transition remained partial. Although displays became gradually more systematic, the shortage of resources and space prevented them from achieving the clarity and narrative coherence seen in Berlin or Paris.

A more substantial shift occurred with the 1903 expansion of the museum. A surviving photograph of the new gallery dedicated to Byzantine antiquities shows lions from the Boukoleon Palace and a Medusa medallion flanking the staircase, and the Sidamara sarcophagus standing among an array of capitals, reliefs, and architectural fragments (Fig. 4). For the first time, the Byzantine past received its own room, yet the mode of presentation remained accumulative rather than explanatory.[64]

Fig. 4: The Imperial Museum, the new Byzantine Gallery, Ground Floor, Hall V [original caption: "Müze-i Hümâyûn, Yeni dairede Bizantin salonu"]. Photograph by Sébah and Joaillier, c. 1903–1907. İstanbul Üniversitesi Merkez Kütüphanesi, Abdülhamid II Albums, 90518–0006.

64 Eldem 2021.

The most significant effort to impose order came with Gustave Mendel's work between 1908 and 1914.[65] Unlike Joubin, Mendel organized the museum through a dual logic: first, objects were listed according to the halls in which they stood; second, within each hall, they were grouped by archaeological site and type.[66] This hybrid system produced a three-dimensional index of historical time, linking the stories of fieldwork to the experience of the galleries. Each catalogue entry followed a rigorous scholarly format (dimensions, material, findspot, bibliography, and parallels), demonstrating an intellectual discipline that the galleries themselves often could not sustain. The catalogue was a surrogate of the museum's interior—a way of creating order on paper when it could not be fully imposed in space, which reflected the messy reality of a museum overwhelmed by acquisitions.[67]

Indeed, using Mendel's floor plan, it is possible to reconstruct the museum's internal layout (Fig. 5). The central galleries (Halls I–III) were dominated by Sidon: the Alexander Sarcophagus and other funerary monuments stood at the heart of the building. Surrounding halls displayed sculptures and fragments from Asia Minor (Assos, Pergamon, Miletus, Magnesia, Didyma, and Tralles), while the latest wing grouped material from Aphrodisias, Priene, Cyme, Gordion, and other later excavations. This provenance-based logic was clearest in these spaces, which traced the flow of objects from excavations supervised by the museum.

Yet provenance was not the only organizing principle. By the early twentieth century, thematic and typological arrangements began to emerge alongside it. Hall XX was dedicated to busts and stelae from various sites, creating a cross-regional typological comparison. Hall VII focused on theatre-related reliefs from Assos, Aeolia, Milas, Pergamon, and Tralles. These arrangements indicate a gradual shift from a strictly site-based model to an analytical one that allowed comparison. A loose chronology also appeared in some halls: busts and sculptures were arranged from Archaic to Classical and Roman forms. This was not a building-wide chronological sequence but a room-level one, reflecting the increasing influence of archaeological periodization (Fig. 6).

65 Mendel 1908, 1910, 1912–1914; Eldem 2014a.

66 Lechat 1922.

67 Mendel 1912–1914; among many reviews, see, for instance, Lechat 1922.

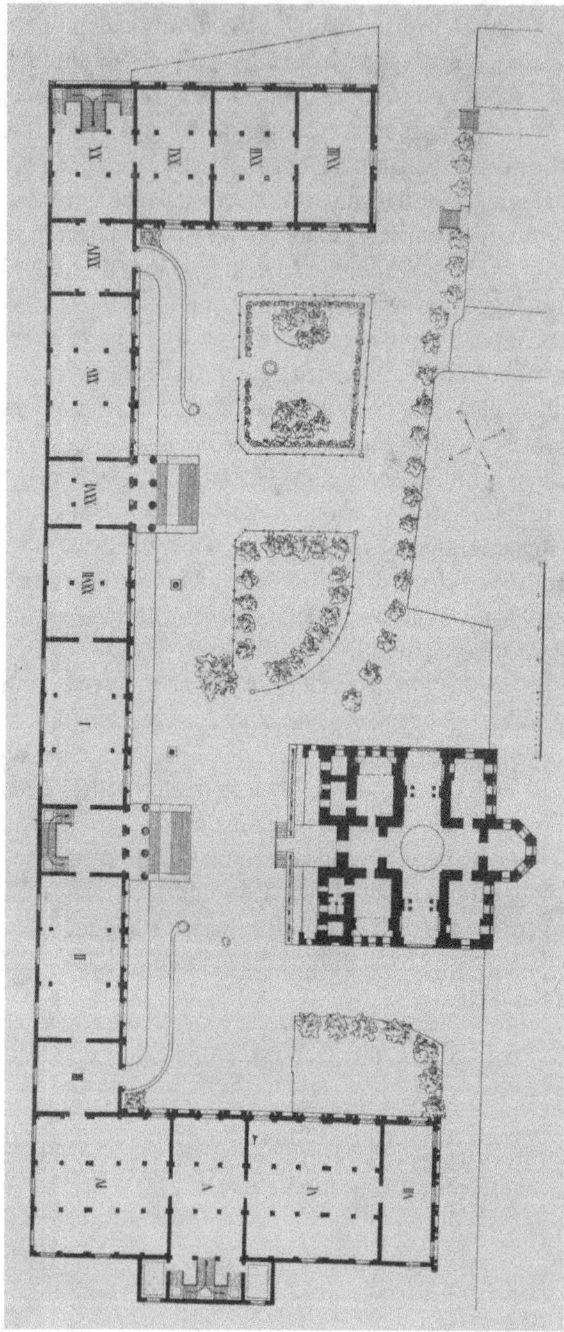

Fig. 5: Plan of the Imperial Museum, the Çinili Köşk (Tiled Pavilion) and the courtyard, drawn by Gustave Mendel in Catalogue des sculptures grecques, romaines et byzantines, Vol. I (1912).

Fig. 6: Interior view of the museum galleries, showing vitrines and sculptural displays. Sébah & Joaillier, c. 1900s. [original caption: "Üst katta büyük galeri"]. Photograph by Sébah & Joaillier, c. 1903–1907. İstanbul Üniversitesi Merkez Kütüphanesi, Abdülhamid II Albums, 90518–0016.

Despite these attempts at structure, Halls VIII–XIX revealed the constraints of the museum. These galleries contained an eclectic mix of Yıldız Palace porcelains, Palestinian antiquities, terracottas, Greek vases, Egyptian and Mesopotamian objects, bronzes, and Himyarite and Palmyrene material.[68] Even Mendel's meticulous catalogues could not conceal the fact that physical arrangements were shaped as much by spatial limitations as by curatorial logic.

This hybrid system of provenance, thematic grouping, and a loose internal chronology reveals how the museum curated time as a mosaic rather than a linear sequence. Instead of a unified narrative, the displays materialized a vision of the past constructed through accumulation, juxtaposition, and constant reorganization. Geography remained the main framework, but Mendel's catalogues show that it was increasingly supplemented by typological and thematic experiments. The result was a form of classification that sought to reflect diverse temporalities and object types within the available space. The museum presented antiquity as something assembled, layered, and provisional, as an archive of the empire's long past.

Hierarchies nevertheless persisted. Greek and Roman antiquities received the greatest curatorial investment and were presented as the apex of civilization. The Byzantine collection, though increasingly visible, remained secondary.[69] Islamic art was marginal and, although incorporated by Osman Hamdi into the collection, was shaped largely by Western demand.[70] Halil Edhem formalized this marginalization by establishing the Islamic collection as a separate museum in the Tiled Pavilion in 1908. Ancient Near Eastern and Egyptian antiquities were similarly scattered throughout the galleries, without systematic classification.

The 1889 internal regulations (*Müze-i Hümayun Nizamname-i Dahilisi*) codified the museum's structure into six departments:[71]

1. Greek, Roman, and Byzantine
2. Assyrian, Chaldean, Egyptian, Phoenician, Hittite, African, and Asian
3. Islamic arts
4. Numismatics
5. Manuscripts
6. Natural history and the museum library

In practice, these departments reflected the aspiration of the museum rather than actual display, as resources, the volume of new acquisitions, and available staff and space dictated constant rearrangement. Even at its most organized stage, the

---

68 Mordtmann 1895.

69 Eldem 2021.

70 Shaw 2000.

71 Papatheodorou 2017, 151–153.

museum struggled with basic conditions. Thousands of objects—including Hittite ceramics from Boğazköy, figurines from Samsun, and friezes from the Miletus Bouleuterion—remained unexhibited.[72] As Reinach conveyed, guides and labels were scarce and outdated, and the galleries never fully reflected the order established in the catalogues. The gap between institutional ambition and practical capacity remained a defining feature of the museum's curatorial landscape.

5.4 Mediating the Past: Reception and Knowledge

Unlike many European museums of the period, the Imperial Museum never became a fully public institution. Its mediation of the past grew primarily out of scholarly ambitions rather than a clear vision of outreach. The museum's very location, enclosed within the Topkapı Palace grounds, reinforced its semi-public character. Before the opening of Gülhane Park in 1912, entry required special permission; even afterward, the museum remained a destination for a narrow urban elite, visiting intellectuals, and foreign scholars rather than a general Ottoman public.[73] There is little evidence of a steady flow of casual visitors, which suggests that the museum's limited accessibility remained a structural feature of its late Ottoman existence.[74]

From the 1890s onward, publications became the museum's primary medium for communicating its work and presenting antiquities. Excavation reports, catalogues, and handbooks functioned as substitutes for systematic displays. They were almost exclusively produced in French, targeting an international scholarly readership, while their high prices drew criticism in Ottoman circles.[75] The years between 1890 and 1915 saw a remarkable increase in such publications, ranging from

72 Reinach 1911.

73 Çelik 2016, 37.

74 According to contemporary guidebooks compiled by Zeynep Çelik, the museum hours were 8:30 a.m.–4:30 p.m. in 1895, 11:00 a.m.–4:00 p.m. in 1900, 10:00 a.m.–5:00 p.m. in 1905 (except Fridays), 9:30 a.m.–3:30 p.m. in summer and 10:00 a.m.–4:00 p.m. in winter in 1909 (except Fridays), and by 1912, 9:30 a.m.–4:30 p.m. in summer and 10:00 a.m.–4:00 p.m. in winter, with Fridays (and later Sundays in summer) reserved for closure. These schedules were broadly comparable to those of major European museums, such as the British Museum, which was open weekdays from 10:00 a.m. to 4:00, 5:00, or 6:00 p.m., depending on the season. Admission to the Imperial Museum was free during this period (Çelik 2016: 232, fn. 53).

75 Koç 2011.

reports on Sidon, Mt. Nemrud, and Palmyra to catalogues of coins, seals, ceramics, and bronzes, culminating in Mendel's extensive volumes.[76]

These publications, with their detailed typological descriptions and provenance data, transformed objects into standardized, portable knowledge, allowing the museum to join global academic networks. Yet they also reinforced the fact that, for most Ottomans, the experience of antiquity was mediated through books rather than through direct contact with objects. Printed guides intended for general audiences were rare. The most significant initiative was the *Rehnuma*, a visitor's guide, commissioned by Osman Hamdi, and written by his son-in-law, Mehmed Vahid Bey, who was one of the empire's first art historians. Published in 1903/1904 and updated several times in later years, it offered the first structured introduction for non-specialists, but quickly fell out of date due to the constant influx of new objects.[77] As mentioned earlier, labels, interpretive signage, and visitor aids remained rudimentary.

Despite these limitations, the museum was not entirely indifferent to the idea of cultivating a local audience. Brief Ottoman-Turkish summaries of new discoveries appearing occasionally in the periodical press indicate modest efforts to broaden access to the collections.[78] Such initiatives, however, remained marginal in comparison to the museum's overwhelmingly scholarly orientation. For much of this period, visitors were few and consisted primarily of foreign scholars and local elites. Only under Halil Edhem's directorship did the museum begin to attract school groups. Even then, the institution's educational engagement was oriented mainly toward the Academy of Fine Arts rather than the broader public.

The Young Turk Revolution briefly raised hopes for a more open, public museum, but again structural obstacles prevented this ambition from being realized. As Eldem has argued, the museum thus remained caught between two identities: an institution aspiring to scholarly authority and an archive for the Ottoman state, yet one without the resources and infrastructure to function as a modern public museum.[79]

---

76 Çelik 2016, 79–84; Koç 2011. For a small selection of a much larger publishing output, see Osman Hamdi and Osgan Effendi 1883; Mordtmann 1895; İsmail Galib, Mehmed Mübarek Galib, Ahmed Tevhid, and Halil Edhem 1894; Halil Edhem 1904 and 1915a.

77 Mehmed Vahid Bey 1903–1904; Sürün 2013, 231–233, fn. 341.

78 Ersoy 2016, 331–335.

79 Eldem 2018.

6 Conclusion

The trajectory of the Imperial Museum illustrates how the late Ottoman state sought to manage, interpret, and ultimately exhibit the material traces of its past. Far from being a mere repository, the museum emerged as an institutional response to several demands: the need to safeguard antiquities, to assert scholarly authority, and to organize an expanding body of material remains into meaningful historical narratives. Within this framework, the museum gradually defined its role through a series of pragmatic and often improvised decisions shaped by scientific ambition, limited resources, and the steady influx of objects. At its core, the museum served as a site where the state negotiated its claims to the past, using antiquities to articulate new forms of historical authority.

What emerges from this study is a portrait of an institution characterized by flux. Its galleries and catalogues reveal a hybrid classificatory logic that combined provenance, typology, and a loose sense of chronology. Instead of producing a coherent, linear narrative, the museum assembled a series of fragmented pasts, arranged them side by side in a way that reflected the uncertainties of its own time. This pattern was as much a product of constraint as of deliberate design, yet it enabled the museum to operate as a space where different ways of thinking about history could coexist and, at times, intersect. From a comparative perspective, these hybrid practices challenge narratives that assume museums in the non-Western world merely replicate European norms. The Ottoman case shows how global museological forms were appropriated, reworked, and adapted to local institutional conditions, producing neither imitation nor rejection but a distinct synthesis. In this sense, the museum confirms recent analyses that stress constraint and fragility, yet it also shows how curatorial experimentation and scientific routines persisted within those limits.

The museum's curatorial and publishing practices acted as forms of mediation. By transferring the authority of objects into catalogues and reports—mostly in French—it created a corpus of standardized knowledge that reached an international scholarly audience, while remaining largely inaccessible to a broader Ottoman public. This tension between scholarly ambition and limited accessibility defined the museum's character throughout the late Ottoman period. The catalogues are therefore indispensable sources: beyond compensating for the limits of exhibition practice, they reveal the internal rhythms of the institution—its labor, priorities, and emerging curatorial vocabulary—and preserve forms of order that the galleries could not consistently sustain.

This study has highlighted only one dimension of a much larger institutional history. Future research could profitably shift attention to the individuals who made the museum function, particularly its curators, assistants, and archaeologists, as well as networks of foreign scholars and collectors who shaped the flow of objects into its stores.[80] Likewise, further work might explore the circulation of antiquities between provincial sites and the capital, and examine the reciprocal influences between the museum and its European counterparts. These directions point to a more connected history of knowledge production, one that sees the Imperial Museum not as an isolated institution but as a node in a much broader and entangled landscape.

Seen in this light, the Imperial Museum was never a fully accomplished project nor a stabilized institution. It remained an ongoing experiment in managing, classifying, and displaying antiquities amid the shifting conditions of the late empire and the changing expectations of scholarship. Many of these dynamics persisted into the Republican period and still resonate in the Istanbul Archaeological Museums today, where extraordinary collections remain housed within an institution periodically disrupted by renovations, relocations, and varying levels of accessibility for visitors and scholars.

Bibliography

Ağca Diker, Sevgi (2024), "Müze-i Hümâyûn ve Teşkilatı [The Imperial Museum and its Organization]." *Türk Kültürü İncelemeleri Dergisi* 51 (Bahar), 113–154.

Aksan, Virginia (2008), "Theoretical Ottomans." *History and Theory* 47 (1), 109–122.

Arıkan, Zeki (1985), "Tanzimat'tan Cumhuriyete Tarihçilik." *Tanzimat'tan Cumhuriyet'e Türkiye Ansiklopedisi*, vol. 6, Istanbul: İletişim Yayınları, 1583–1594.

Artun, Ali (2010), "Halil Edhem'in Modern İstanbul Müzesi." In *Osman Hamdi Bey'in Ölümünün Yüzüncü Yılı Sempozyumu*. Istanbul: MSGSÜ. Accessed 10 July 2025. https://aliartun.com/yazilar/halil-edhemin-modern-istanbul-muzesi.

Bahrani, Zainab, Zeynep Çelik, and Edhem Eldem (2011a), "Interlude: Halil Edhem on the Museum of Pious Foundations." In *Scramble for the Past: A Story of Archaeology in the Ottoman Empire, 1753–1914*, edited by Zainab Bahrani, Zeynep Çelik, and Edhem Eldem. Istanbul: SALT, 418–421.

Bahrani, Zainab, Zeynep Çelik, and Edhem Eldem (2011b), "Interlude: The Museum as a Civic Tool." In *Scramble for the Past: A Story of Archaeology in the Ottoman Empire, 1753–1914*, edited by Zainab Bahrani, Zeynep Çelik, and Edhem Eldem. Istanbul: SALT, 480–481.

Baltazzi, Demosthene (1881), "Borne des Pergaméniens." *Bulletin de Correspondance Hellénique* V, 283–284.

Baltazzi, Demosthene (1888), "Inscriptions de l'Éolide." *Bulletin de Correspondance Hellénique* XII, 358–376.

Bobou, Olympia, Filiz Tütüncü Çağlar, Miriam Kühn, Eleanor Q. Neil, and Rubina Raja (2025), "Shelving Urban Excavations: Revisiting Ottoman and Mandate-Period Archives in Western Asia." *Journal of Urban Archaeology* 12: 149–176.

80 For an examination of the organization of the museum personnel, see Ağca Diker 2024.

Cezar, Mustafa (1995), *Sanatta Batı'ya Açılış ve Osman Hamdi Bey* [The Westernization of Art and Osman Hamdi Bey]. Istanbul: Erol Kerim Aksoy Kültür, Eğitim, Spor ve Sağlık Vakfı.

Crane, Susan A. (2006), "The Conundrum of Ephemerality: Time, Memory, and Museums." In A Companion to Museum Studies, edited by Sharon Macdonald. Malden, MA: Blackwell, 98–110.

Çal, Halit (1997), "Osmanlı Devletinde Âsâr-ı Atîka Nizamnameleri [Antiquity Laws in the Ottoman State]." *Vakıflar Dergisi* 26, 391–400.

Çelik, Zeynep (2016), *About Antiquities: Politics of Archaeology in the Ottoman Empire*. Austin: University of Texas Press.

Du Crest, Xavier (2002), "André Joubin à Constantinople: un chargé de mission au Musée impérial ottoman (1893–1894)." *Histoire de l'art* 51, 127–134.

Dumont, Albert (1868), "Le Musée Sainte-Irène à Constantinople." *Revue archéologique*, Nouvelle Série 18, 237–263.

Dumont, Albert (1883), *Catalogue du Musée Impérial d'Antiquités: Antiquités grecques et latines*. Constantinople: Typographie et Lithographie Centrales.

Duncan, Carol (1995), *Civilizing Rituals: Inside Public Art Museums*. London: Routledge.

Duncan, Carol, and Alan Wallach (1980), "The Universal Survey Museum." *Art History* 3 (4), 448–469.

Edhem, Halil (1904), *Müze-i Hümayun Kurşun Mühür Kataloğu: Arab ve Arab-Bizantin ve Osmanlı Kurşun Mühürlerine Mahsusdur* [The Catalogue of Lead Seals in the Imperial Museum: Arab, Arab-Byzantine and Ottoman Seals]. Istanbul: Mahmud Bey Matbaası.

Edhem, Halil (1915a), *Meskûkât-ı Kadîme-i İslâmiyye Katalogu: Meskûkât-ı Osmânî* [The Catalogue of Ancient Islamic Coins: Ottoman Coins]. Istanbul: Mahmud Bey Matbaası.

Edhem, Halil (1915b), *Kayseriyye Şehri: Mebâni-i İslâmiyye ve Kitâbeleri*. Istanbul: Matbaa-i Orhaniye.

Edhem, Halil (1924), *Elvah-ı Nakşiye Koleksiyonu*. Istanbul: Matbaa-i Amire.

Edhem, Halil (1932), "Müzeler." In *1. Türk Tarih Kongresi, Konferanslar, Müzakere Zabıtları*. Ankara: T.C. Maarif Vekaleti, 532–566.

Eldem, Edhem (2010), *Osman Hamdi Bey Sözlüğü*. Ankara: Kültür ve Turizm Bakanlığı.

Eldem, Edhem (2014a), *Mendel -Sebah: Müze-i Hümayun'u Belgelemek / Documenting the Imperial Museum*. Istanbul: Istanbul Arkeoloji Müzeleri Yayınları.

Eldem, Edhem (2014b), *Nazlı'nın Defteri. Osman Hamdi Bey'in Çevresi. Nazlı's Guestbook, Osman Hamdi Bey's Circle*. Istanbul: Homer.

Eldem, Edhem (2018), "The (Still)Birth of the Ottoman 'Museum': A Critical Reassessment." In *Collecting and Empires: An Historical and Global Perspective*, edited by Maia W. Gahtan and Eva-Maria Troelenberg. London: Harvey Miller Publishers.

Eldem, Edhem (2021), "Byzantium in Istanbul: The Byzantine Collections of the Istanbul Archaeological Museum." In *From Istanbul to Byzantium. Paths to Rediscovery 1800–1955*, edited by Brigitte Pitarakis. Istanbul: Pera Museum.

Ersoy, Ahmet E. (2016), "Ottomans and the Kodak Galaxy: Archiving Everyday Life and Historical Space in Ottoman Illustrated Journals." *History of Photography* 40 (3), 330–357.

Eyice, Semavi (1985), "Arkeoloji Müzesi ve Kuruluşu." In *Tanzimat'tan Cumhuriyet'e Türkiye Ansiklopedisi* 6. Istanbul: İletişim Yayınları. 1596–1603.

Galib, İsmail, Mehmed Mübarek Galib, Ahmed Tevhid, and Halil Edhem (1894), *Müze-yi Hümayun Meskukat-i Kadime-yi Islamiye Katalogu*. Constantinople: Mihran Matbaasi.

Gerçek, Ferruh (1999), *Türk Müzeciliği* [Turkish Museology]. Ankara: T.C. Kültür Bakanlığı.

Goold, Edward (1871), *Catalogue explicative, historique et scientifique d'un certain nombre d'objets contenus dans le Musée Impérial de Constantinople fondé en 1869 sous le grand vésirat de Son Altesse A'ali Pacha*. Constantinople: Zellich.

Georgeon, François, and Frédéric Hitzel, eds. (2012), *Les Ottomans et le temps*. Leiden: Brill.

Grosvenor, Edwin A. (1900), *Constantinople*. Boston: Little, Brown and Company.
Hamdi, Osman, and Osgan Effendi (1883), *Le Tumulus de Nemroud-Dagh: Voyage, Description, Inscriptions av. Plans et Photographies*. Constantinople: F. Loeffler.
Hamdi, Osman, Theodore Reinach, and Ernest Chantre (1892), *Une Nécropole Royale à Sidon. Fouilles de Hamdy Bey*. Paris: Ernest Le Roux.
Hartog, François (2017), *Regimes of Historicity: Presentism and Experiences of Time*, translated by Saskia Brown. New York: Columbia University Press.
Hartog, François (2021), "The Museum and Temporalization." *Time & Society* 30 (4), 462–476.
İhsanoğlu, Ekmeleddin, and Feza Günergun (1996), "Osmanlı Türkiyesinde 'Alaturka Saat'ten 'Alafranga Saat'e Geçiş." In *X. Ulusal Astronomi Kongresi (2–6 Eylül 1996)*. Istanbul: İstanbul Üniversitesi Fen Fakültesi, Boğaziçi Üniversitesi Kandilli Rasathanesi ve Deprem Araştırma Enstitüsü, 434–441.
İnalcık, Halil (2006), "Türkiye'de Modern Tarihin Kurucuları." *Muhafazakâr Düşünce* 2.7, 3–44.
Joubin, André (1893a), *Müze-i Hümayun. Luhûd ve Makabir-i Atika Kataloğu*. Istanbul: Mihran.
Joubin, André (1893b), *Musée Impérial Ottoman. Monuments funéraires. Catalogue sommaire*. Constantinople: Imprimerie Mihran.
Karateke, Hakan T. (2013), "The Challenge of Periodization – New Patterns in Nineteenth-Century Ottoman Historiography." In *Writing History at the Ottoman Court: Editing the Past, Fashioning the Future*, edited by H. Erdem Cipa and Emine Fetvaci. Bloomington, IN: Indiana University Press, 129–131, 145–147.
Koç, Havva (2011), "Müze-i Hümâyûn'da Yayın Çalışmaları (Cumhuriyet Dönemine Kadar)." In *Gelenek, kimlik, bireşim: kültürel kesişmeler ve sanat. Prof. Dr. Günsel Renda'ya armağan*, edited by Zeynep Yasa Yaman and Serpil Bağcı. Ankara: Hacettepe Üniversitesi Edebiyat Fakültesi, Sanat Tarihi Bölümü, 151–164.
Koçak, Alev (2011), *The Ottoman Empire and Archaeological Excavations: Ottoman Policy from 1840–1906, Foreign Archaeologists, and the Formation of the Ottoman Museum*. Istanbul: Isis Press.
Koşay, Hâmit Zübeyr, E. Zarif Orgun, Sadi Bayram, and Erdoğan Tan (2013), *Osmanlı İmparatorluğu ve Türkiye Cumhuriyeti Çağlarında Türk Kazı Tarihi* [History of Turkish Excavations in the periods of Ottoman Empire and the Turkish Republic]. Ankara: Türk Tarih Kurumu.
Kula (Say), Seda (2014), *Beaux-Arts Kökenli Bir Mimar Olarak Alexandre Vallaury'nin Meslek Pratiği ve Eğitimciliği Açısından Kariyerinin İrdelenmesi*. PhD dissertation, İstanbul Teknik Üniversitesi.
Lechat, Henri G. (1922), "Mendel, Musées impériaux ottomans: Catalogue des sculptures grecques, romaines et byzantines, tome III, 1914." *Revue des Études Anciennes* 24.1, 70–71.
Mehmed Vahid Bey (1903), Müze-i Hümâyûn-ı Osmânî'ye Mahsus Muhtasar Rehnümâ [guidebook]. Istanbul.
Mendel, Gustave (1908), *Catalogue des Figurines Grecques de Terre Cuite*. Constantinople: Musée Impérial.
Mendel, Gustave (1910), *Catalogue des poteries byzantines*. Musées Impériaux Ottomans. Constantinople.
Mendel, Gustave (1912–1914), *Catalogue des sculptures grecques, romaines et byzantines*. Musées Impériaux Ottomans. 3 Vols. Constantinople.
Mordtmann, Johannes Heinrich (1895), *Antiquités Himyarites et Palmyréniennes. Catalogue Sommaire*. Constantinople: Mihran Imprimeur.
Moser, Stephanie (2006), "Introduction: Museum Display, Representation, and Ancient Egypt," *Wondrous Curiosities*. Chicago, IL: University of Chicago Press.
Papatheodorou, Artemis (2017), *Ottoman Policy-Making in an Age of Reforms: Unearthing Ottoman Archaeology in the 19th and Early 20th Centuries*. PhD dissertation, Oxford University.

Posocco, Lorenzo (2021), "Osman Hamdi Bey and the Dawn of the Ottoman Museum: a Bourdieusian Approach." *International Journal of Humanities Social Sciences and Education (IJHSSE)* 8.10, 29–41.

Reinach, Adolphe (1911), "Au Musée de Constantinople." *Revue des Études Anciennes* 13/3, 370–377.

Reinach, Salomon (1882), *Catalogue du Musée Impérial d'Antiquités*. Constantinople: Direction du Musée.

Shaw, Wendy M. K. (2000), "Arts in the Ottoman Imperial Museum, 1889–1923." *Ars Orientalis* 30, 55–68.

Shaw, Wendy M. K. (2003), *Possessors and Possessed: Museums, Archaeology, and the Visualization of History in the Late Ottoman Empire*. Berkeley: University of California Press.

Sümertaş, Firuze Melike (2021), *From Antiquarianism to Urban Archaeology: Transformation of Research on 'Old' Istanbul throughout the Nineteenth Century*. PhD dissertation, Boğaziçi University.

Strauss, Johann (2012), "La perception du Moyen Âge dans l'Empire ottoman (XIXe–début XXe siècle)." In *Les Ottomans et le temps*, edited by François Georgeon and Frédéric Hitzel. Leiden: Brill, 199–238.

Sönmez, Ali (2014), "Osmanlı'da Bürokratik Tartışmalar ve Mali Sorunların Gölgesinde Çemberlitaş'ın Tamiri Meselesi." *Tarihin Peşinde* 11, 1–28.

Sürün, Mustafa (2013), *Cumhuriyet Öncesi Sanat Tarihi Yaklaşımları (1850–1923 Sanat Tarihi Yayınları Üzerine bir İnceleme)*. PhD dissertation, Marmara Üniversitesi.

Toplumsal Tarih (2019), *Tasniften Teşhire: Osmanlı'dan Cumhuriyet'e Doğa Tarihi Müzeleri*, No. 311 (Kasım).

Tütüncü Çağlar, Filiz (2017), *From Raqqa with Love*. PhD dissertation, University of Victoria.

Tütüncü Çağlar, Filiz (2023), "Changing Perceptions of the Past: An Archaeological Perspective." In *Objektzeiten: Die Relationierung historischer Zeiten durch Relikte (6.–20. Jahrhundert)*, edited by Mirjam Hähnle and Julian Zimmermann. Freiburg: Rombach Verlag, 291–315.

Tütüncü Çağlar, Filiz (forthcoming), "Rethinking the History of Archaeology through Ottoman Archival Material: The Case of Theodore Macridy." In *Unleashing Knowledge and Structuring Notes Archaeological "Archives" and Their Historiographies*, edited by John Frey and Rubina Raja. Turnhout: Brepols.

Ünlüönen, Sezen (2024), "Rethinking the Nineteenth-Century Museum via the Ottoman Imperial Museum." *Literature Compass* 21/1–3, e12710, 1–9. Accessed 30 October 2025. https://doi.org/10.1111/lic3.12710

Üstoğlu Coşkun, Deniz (2025), *Reinstituting Knowledge on Construction Techniques and Materials of a Late Ottoman Imperial Building: Istanbul Archaeological Museum*. PhD dissertation, Middle East Technical University Ankara.

Yılmaz, Yaşar (2023), *Zincirli'den Eserlerimizin Götürülüşü – Osman Hamdi Bey'in Öteki Yüzü*. Istanbul: Korpus Kültür Sanat Yayıncılık.

Walklate, Jen (2023), *Time and the Museum: Literature, Phenomenology, and the Production of Radical Temporality*. London and New York: Routledge.

Wishnitzer, Avner (2012), "With the Precision of a Watch? Time Organization in the Ottoman Army, 1826–1918." In *Les Ottomans et le temps*, edited by François Georgeon and Frédéric Hitzel. The Ottoman Empire and Its Heritage 49. Leiden: Brill, 281–315.

Wishnitzer, Avner (2015), *Reading Clocks, Alla Turca: Time and Society in the Late Ottoman Empire*. Chicago: University of Chicago Press.

Part IV: **Philosophical and Comparative Perspectives**

Jack Shardlow

Reflecting Islamic Time Perception through Western Contemporary Philosophy

The vision of time is broad, but when you pass through it, time becomes a narrow door.
— Frank Herbert, Dune

1 Introductory Remarks

This volume explores issues that I have a longstanding interest in—concerning our human, subjective experience of temporal phenomena, and its relation to time itself—through a lens which is largely alien to me—regarding Islamic Thought and Qur'ānic studies. Mindful of my own limitations and competencies, I don't here propose to break any new ground on the latter; nor is this the place for novel argumentation towards substantive conclusions in the context of the former. Instead, my aims are a little more subtle and modest. In the context of the excellent research collected here, I propose to add a little by way of reflection, drawing out some philosophically interesting—and, perhaps, surprisingly contentious—claims; tracing some of the history of thought on these ideas in Islamic and Western contexts; and connecting these to contemporary debates in Western Philosophy, an area of research I call home. In doing so, I trust that the broad interest and appeal of the issues discussed in this volume may be heightened and emphasised.

The scholarship assembled here, fascinating in its own right, has many interesting points of connection with discussions of time and temporal experience in contemporary Western Philosophy; there is potential for fertile discussion of how insights from each area could intellectually cross-pollinate. In the scope of the current contribution, however, I can't hope to do justice to each and every interesting point raised—nor can I afford to be exhaustive in appeal to relevant ideas from contemporary Western Philosophy. Rather than review and reflect on each in turn, which would provide only superficial analysis and fail to do justice to the interests and complexities of each, to provide a balance of detail and brevity, I propose to identify a couple of key themes across the contributions. With these themes, I will introduce and explain ideas from the history of philosophy, Western and Islamic, before developing some ideas from recent work in Western Philosophy, which also picks up on and pursues such themes to a greater extent. I do not advocate for any particular directions future research ought to take, but I hope that, for those interested in these areas, relevant bidirectional insights can be brought to the fore, iden-

https://doi.org/10.1515/9783112240038-009

tifying avenues for where future work in Islamic studies and related disciplines, and in Contemporary Western Philosophy, can draw upon and develop ideas from one another in the context of time perception and the sense of sight.

It is worth noting (the perhaps obvious fact) that contemporary Western Philosophy is not a monolith. There is little interest in recounting the recent history of Western Philosophy here, but there have been substantive and stylistic divisions between traditions under this broad umbrella—for example, the prominent 'analytic' and 'continental' divide of the Twentieth Century—as well as there being thinkers and more narrow traditions that evade attempts at easy classification. This is said only to emphasise that there is another way in which the focus I will assume—a broadly analytical one—is partial and limited. With these qualifications made, we can turn to themes from the works assembled here and the structure of the discussion to follow.

Within the contributions to this volume, there are interesting issues concerning the representation of time in art, curation, architecture, poetry, and even law, and the different roles that the visual may play in each, due to the differing pictorial and linguistic forms of representation. There are issues concerning the distinctive forms of temporal awareness afforded by memory – both the memory of an individual, and something more akin to an actively maintained, cultural memory, via curatorial strategies employed in museums. The temporal content of dream experience is discussed, as is the epistemic value we are to attribute to the content of such experience. There is also, across several of the contributions, some allusion to questions about how our subjective perspective in and on time compares and contrasts with that of time itself, as conceptualised from a 'view from nowhere', or a divine perspective—these are related to questions that have proliferated a lot of papers and books in Western Philosophy over recent decades. For example, what is 'the now' of experience? How is this informed by thinking about distinctly visual experience? How does this factor fit into our experience of paradigmatically temporal phenomena, such as motion and change, and does memory play a fundamental role here? And how is (or isn't) this connected to the issue of whether there is an objective now, as a matter of scientific fact? Given the burgeoning literature on these issues in Twentieth and Twenty-First Century Philosophy, I will provide only a broad overview.

My contribution is structured as follows. In section 2, I briefly outline some historical interactions between Ancient Greek Philosophy and Islamic Thought on the topic of time. In section 3, I draw out, in more detail, some themes in papers within the present volume, which build upon ideas already present in those historical interactions discussed in section 2, and which continue to assume a place of prominence in some circles of contemporary Western Philosophy. In section 4, I present an overview of issues currently discussed in Western Philosophy concerning the idea that time passes; in section 5, I present an overview of discussions about 'the present' that we have a vantage point upon in conscious experience. My hope is that, in offering a philosophical elucidation of some of these ideas, and in outlining the complex philosophical debates about these ideas that continue to rumble on in Anglophone spheres, further avenues for interpretation may present themselves for, e.g., those engaged in Qur'ānic studies while focused on issues of time perception and vision.

2 A brief, selective History of Time and Temporality: Aristotle, al-Kindī, Ibn Sīnā

The exploration of the overlap and interaction between Ancient Greek Philosophy, Western Philosophy, and Islamic Thought, particularly on the topic of time, has a long intellectual history, touching upon major figures from each tradition.[1] Many discussions of time up to this day, still refer back to positions held by the likes of Aristotle and Plato, if not their predecessors Parmenides and Heraclitus. Of these philosophers, it was Aristotle who played a prominent role in discussions of time in early Islamic Philosophy.

Aristotle is taken to hold that there is no absolute time; there is no time independent of the events that occur in time. For Aristotle, all talk that is supposed to be about time can ultimately be reduced to talk about temporal relations among things/events.[2] Hence, while time is not independent of that which occurs in time, for Aristotle, there is 'relative time', insofar as there are temporal relations between events. Aristotle also argued that the world is eternal—that there is no beginning (or end) to time. His reasoning here, roughly, is that such a beginning would constitute a first moment of time, and in order for something to be a 'moment of time' it must fall between earlier and later periods of time, and falling between earlier and later periods would disqualify any such moment of time from being *the first* moment.[3] Whatever the merits of such a line of argument may be, Aristotle's claims proved influential.

Al-Kindī (d. c. 870 CE), often regarded as the first self-identified philosopher (*faylasūf*) in the Arabic-Islamic tradition, drew deeply on Aristotelian and Neoplatonic thought. In addition to his writings on Qur'ānic interpretation and polemics

1 E.g. Sorabji 1983.

2 The alternative, Platonic view, takes time to exist independently of whatever occurs within it, like a container within which things/events may be organised.

3 For the more precise, first-hand discussion, see Aristotle, *Physics*, Bk. VIII.

against the Christian doctrine of the Trinity, al-Kindī produced treatises on metaphysics, mathematics, optics, medicine, and music. He also stood at the center of the so-called 'Kindi circle', one of the two main groups of translators in the ninth century, who translated numerous works of philosophy from Greek into Arabic, including Aristotle's *Physics* and *Metaphysics*.[4] In his *On First Philosophy*, al-Kindī is directly responding to Aristotle's claims about time, drawing on Aristotelian critics to argue against the eternity of the world.[5] A century and a half later, Ibn Sīnā (Avicenna, d. 1037 CE) transformed that legacy, siding with Aristotle and against al-Kindī. Blending Aristotelian physics with Neoplatonic metaphysics, he constructed a systematic philosophy arguing that time, and motion/moving bodies, must have existed infinitely into the past.

In addition to his arguments about the eternity of the world, Ibn Sīnā's interests and works also engage with other aspects of time, which connect more centrally with themes from the current volume, about 'the now' and the 'passing of time'. For Ibn Sīnā, the now is the divide between past and future. But what is this 'now'? One natural assumption would be that, as a divide, the now must be strictly extensionless. Some interpreters, however, have read Ibn Sīnā as proposing a *nunc differens*—a temporally extended now, within which contrasts and movement can occur.[6] McGinnis shows this attribution is unlikely, pointing out that Aristotle gives several explicit arguments against an extended now, and Ibn Sīnā, quick to point out where he disagrees with Aristotle, offers no comment on any such radical divergence from Aristotle on the extended now.[7]

In addition to considering the now as a division between past and future—whether extended or extensionless—Ibn Sīnā also makes an appeal to the now as a *nunc fluens*: a flowing now. The notion of a "flowing now" appears to be particularly important. Fakhr al-dīn al-Rāzī (d. 1210 CE) notes in his *al-Mabāhith al-mashriqīyya* that, according to Ibn Sīnā, the flowing of the now is the producer and cause of time.[8] Whatever the precise interpretation of Ibn Sīnā's position, his work—and that of al-Kindī—illustrates a sustained engagement with questions of time that

4 See Endress 1997.

5 For more on al-Kindī's philosophy, and the influence of Aristotle, see Adamson 2024.

6 See Shayegan 1986. The 'nunc differens', as used by Kretzmann (1976) in his discussion of Aristotle, isn't obviously a notion of 'an extended present', as opposed to capturing the idea that, with the passing of time, the present instant is always different (nunc differens) or always the same (nunc fluens). However, the 'nunc differens' is used in this way—i.e., as an extended now—by McGinnis (1999, 96), in his own discussion of Ibn Sīnā on 'the now', so I here follow suit.

7 McGinnis 1999, 96.

8 Fakhr al-dīn al-Rāzī, *al-Mabāhith al-mashriqīyya*, vol. 1, 551. For recent discussion of Ibn Sīnā on time, see Lammer 2021.

stem from Ancient Greek philosophy and continue to develop within both the Islamic and later Western intellectual traditions.[9]

3 *Nunc fluens, nunc differens*, and Islamic Thought

There is a long history of ideas in Western Philosophy interacting with aspects of Islamic Thought on the topic of time, but what can be said of potential cross-overs and interaction in the present context? Well, as it happens, particular currents running through papers assembled within this very volume pick up on—and may shed light on—issues that are hotly contested in discussions of time and temporal experience in contemporary Western Philosophy. Specifically, we've seen how the *nunc fluens* and *nunc differens* are issues at the forefront when we consider the influence of Ancient Greek Philosophy on early Islamic philosophers; these two notions are also relevant to and discussed in the works collected within this volume—though not in these terms. Moreover, these two notions also retain significance in debates within contemporary Western Philosophy.

In sections 4 and 5, I outline some of the significance and some of what remains contentious when we turn our attention to the *nunc fluens* and *nunc differens* as discussed in recent philosophy. First, I'll sketch how these notions relate to some of the ideas expressed within the collected works in this volume, and I will return to this throughout.

The Nunc Fluens. The idea of time's passing is discussed in several contributions. Aweida discusses how the poetry of Ṭarafa picks up on 'the fleeting present', focusing on time as experienced in comparison and contrast to abstractly conceptualised. Kol also discusses such a contrast, but from a different angle, through reflection on how Islamic architecture from the 7th to the 10th Centuries presents a 'frozen' and 'infinite present', perhaps unlike our everyday experiences of time as passing. We find elements of both of these ideas in Çağlar's consideration of the dual temporal logic in museums, where curation can blend narratives of timelessness and progress, both 'freezing and mobilizing the time'. In each case, ideas in the aesthetics of poetry, architecture, and curatorial practices are tied to claims about how time is typically experienced and conceptualised, and how it might be otherwise experienced or conceptualised.

The passage of time is especially relevant in Koloska's discussion of the role of memory and our conception of time, and in her presentation of the Companions of the Cave. Koloska discusses how the narrative and visual imagery allow

9 For a recent concise and accessible discussion of Ibn Sīnā's account of time, see Lammer 2026.

us to 'witness' the passage of time, and, as presented, memory has a significant role to play here. This raises questions—often discussed in philosophy—concerning what it means to say that time passes; what it is to believe that time passes, and to experience time passing; and whether or not visual experience, or experiential memory, has a significant role to play in how we do (*if* we do) experience time as passing. The parenthetical qualification in the previous sentence is also an allusion to a direction taken in recent philosophical debates about the experience of time as passing, which is touched upon (indirectly) in Amir's contribution to this volume—concerning the epistemic value accredited to particular experiential reports (discussed in 4.3).

Nunc Differens. A related but importantly distinct idea; it doesn't necessarily concern the idea that time passes, but is centred on how we are to conceive of the present moment. In so far as this idea is touched upon in some of the contributing papers, it is typically conceptualised as the 'experienced present'—our vantage point in and upon time. For example, we again have the contrast between Ṭarafa's poetry celebrating the fleeting present, in Aweida's discussion, and Islamic architecture bringing to the forefront a notion of an infinite present, in Kol's. Çağlar offers a broader perspective on how, within the present, we can actively construct narratives of past and future, via consideration of museums as active producers of historical consciousness. Koloska directly refers to the present as a 'horizon,' which represents the vantage point from which we observe the past and future. Across these contexts, there is the very issue of what this horizon is — i.e., whether it is best thought of as a *nunc differens.*

How we are to best conceive of 'the present' and even 'the experienced present' is, again, an issue which has been at the centre of much debate for philosophers in the West who are concerned with how we think about and experience time. Rather than focusing upon how the Qur'ānic text may shape how we think about time, by creating a specific vantage point, I will shed light on what recent Western Philosophy has to say about our experiential 'horizon' in time, and how a tendency to focus on vision over other sensory modalities, and claims about the significance of the role attributed to memory, have led to some recent twists in this debate. The particular focus on vision has a tendency to exacerbate the spatialization of time – something which bleeds into how we ourselves present temporal narratives, as Çağlar, via Gielen, discusses in the context of 'museum chronotopics'. Here, perhaps, we would do well to reflect on the temporality of our experience across modalities, where we may be aided by Aweida's discussion of the multisensory content of Ṭarafa's writing.

4 *Nunc Fluens*: In the World? In Experience?

What are we appealing to when we make use of the *nunc fluens*? Typically, the idea is not merely that there are earlier and later times, but that there is a metaphysically robust sense of passage *from* one *to* another. This is thought to contrast with space. Space is typically conceived of as a domain in which objects can move, but space itself is thought to be static—i.e., objects in space may be attributed dynamic properties, but space itself is not attributed dynamic properties. By contrast, time is not simply said to be a domain in which objects can have dynamic properties; time itself is said to have dynamic properties, insofar as *time passes*.

If, in saying that time passes, we are not simply taking ourselves to be using metaphorical language and instead commit ourselves (even implicitly) to a metaphysical thesis about the nature of time, why do so? Why, that is, do we hold that time passes? The answer usually comes via an appeal to experience; that the reality of the *nunc fluens* is somehow manifest in our everyday experience of the world. To provide an overview of how this is debated in contemporary Western Philosophy, in this section I will outline how debates about the passage of time arise in metaphysics and physics (4.1.), how particular claims about our experiences and common-sense beliefs about time's passage are put to the test in empirical work (4.2.), and how the idea that we experience time as passing—divorced from the metaphysical issue of whether time in fact passes—has become disputed in recent philosophy of mind, connecting with points raised by Koloska and Amir (4.3.).

4.1 *Nunc fluens*: Metaphysics and Physics

A point of contention in recent Western Philosophy, when we turn to the question of the nature of time itself, has been the relevance, if any, of our experiences of time and temporal phenomena. What weight in our theorising, if any, ought we accredit to theorists' appeal to our subjective experience of time, and/or our common sense beliefs about time, i.e., beliefs that naturally arise in response to our experiences, as we navigate the world? In metaphysics, that branch of philosophy which is broadly concerned with what is necessary and what is possible, and therefore what is actual, theorists often begin with an articulation of initial appearances and common sense beliefs about a subject matter, since this provides us with the materials we are trying to pick apart, understand, and explain.[10] And, according to some theorists, the extent to which our theories cohere with this anthropocentric starting point

10 On this conception of metaphysics, see, e.g., Conee and Sider 2014, 236.

provides one way of assessing these very theories. The reasoning here seems to be something like the following: if a particular claim is believed by a significant proportion of all human subjects, then it seems reasonable to take this as (defeasible) evidence that the claim is true.[11] Even for dissenting theorists, initial appearances and common sense beliefs can be of interest, not because they are taken to provide any defeasible evidence for some theory or other, but because whatever view we take on the nature of things, we are due some explanation of how and why phenomena *appear* as they do, and of why certain beliefs are accepted as commonsensical by subjects across the world, even if such appearances and beliefs are thought to be misleading/erroneous.

How does this broad methodology work when we start talking about time? Well, while remaining interested in the *nunc fluens*, broadly construed, contemporary theorists have disputed the relevance of appeals to experience and common sense beliefs as an evidence base. Since Einstein, in physics and metaphysics, time is often said to be a single dimension of extension alongside the three spatial dimensions. In Parmenidean fashion, there is said to simply be a four-dimensional manifold of events, time being one of the four dimensions. It has often been reasoned that, as a consequence, time does not pass. Briefly, the idea here is that the relativity of simultaneity refutes the notion of an objectively present time, and the passage of time is supposed to be nothing more than a flowing objectively present time—a *nunc fluens*; hence, without the former, there can be no latter.[12]

Yet, a charge often raised against any conception of time that jettisons its apparent passage is that such a conception cannot do justice to our temporal experience. In Heraclitean fashion, some theorists have argued that our experience presents a world in temporal flux; from reflection on experience, time is often said to seem dynamic. Hence, our experience (and naïve beliefs and talk about time) has been supposed to support the claim that time passes.[13] Yet, for theorists making use of such appeals to experience, there are two claims that it is important to distinguish between. The first is that people do take themselves to experience, and intuitively have beliefs about, some aspect of time (e.g., that time passes); the second is the claim that such experience and intuitive beliefs provide support for a metaphysical thesis about time (e.g., that time passes). Beyond the contentious methodology which is assumed when one makes the second claim, briefly outlined above, it is also important for such theorists to find support for the first claim—i.e., to show

11 See, e.g., Loux and Zimmerman 2005, 5, and Zimmerman 2008, 222.
12 For one expression of this idea, see, e.g., Gödel 1990[/1949], 202–203.
13 See, e.g., Schlesinger 1980, 30.

that people's experience, naïve beliefs, and talk about time is as they claim—and this is an issue which has become hotly contested.

4.2 *Nunc fluens*: Experimental Philosophy

We've seen that the view of the nature of time emerging from much of modern physics does not uphold the passage of time (at least not as popularly conceived). But do people nevertheless naively believe that time passes, where 'time passing' is conceived of in a metaphysically robust sense? And do people take themselves to experience time as passing? If so, in what sense? I'll outline some research addressing these questions in the current subsection.

Addressing the issue of whether people perceive time as passing may seem relatively straightforward. You might think it only takes a moment's reflection to answer in the affirmative. Yet, the issue isn't whether people say things such as 'time seems to pass', rather, the issue is whether, with a metaphysically robust understanding of the notion of the passage of time in mind, people believe that they experience time passing *so understood*. Regardless of such a qualification, some theorists have maintained that it is introspectively *obvious* that we experience time as passing and naively believe that time passes.[14] However, such claims have recently been viewed with skepticism, at least in some circles, as the legitimacy of such theorists themselves, characterizing their appearances and beliefs as intuitive or obvious, has been called into question. The reason for such skepticism is, quite generally, that theorists' own beliefs and theories may unduly influence their claims. This worry has been a strong impetus behind the recent growth in experimental philosophy,[15] which tests whether philosophers' claims and intuitions are shared by the public at large.

Recent empirical work in experimental philosophy has focused on the relation between people's experience of time and their beliefs about those experiences. For example, Shardlow et al. investigated how people understand what it means for time to pass, and how this relates to their beliefs about their experience of time.[16] A majority of participants conceptualized time passing in a way which broadly conflicts with the time of modern physics. A majority also claimed to feel and see time passing—though a substantial minority did not. This might be interpreted as broadly supporting the claim that there is a *nunc fluens* in experience, that is not

---

14 See, e.g., Maudlin 2002.

15 See, e.g., Knobe and Nichols 2008.

16 Shardlow et al. 2021.

captured by the modern picture of time emerging from science—though, in and of itself, this does very little to elucidate the supposed experience or to draw out any decisive implications.

An even more comprehensive and exploratory study, by Lee *et al.*, directly asked participants about the extent to which they agreed with sets of brief statements about time—about whether time passes, about the reality of the present time, its relation to the past and future, and whether time has a direction.[17] The authors aimed not only to order which statements find more/less agreement within the public at large, but to analyze whether or not some subset of these statements cohere in the manner of a theory, aiming to probe whether or not we share a common-sense, folk theory of time. Perhaps surprisingly, across two experiments and several analyses, the authors found evidence of multiple and seemingly mutually incompatible intuitive theories of time, held by three distinct subpopulations. Two of these subpopulations, roughly 70% of participants overall, aligned closely with philosophers' characterizations of common-sense time insofar as the large majority agreed that the future is open, that the past is not mutable, and that time has a direction.[18] The third subpopulation differed in significant ways: while the majority agreed that the future was open, they did not do so as strongly as participants in the other two profiles; the majority also agreed that the past was not mutable, but again notably more weakly than those in the other two profiles; and there was a notable minority within the subpopulation who did not agree that time has a direction. These findings may be of interest for numerous reasons, but in the current context, it is interesting to note that, among these subpopulations, the authors were not able to uncover any clear patterns of (dis)agreement on statements about time passing. People's views on the *nunc fluens* remain somewhat elusive and difficult to probe clearly.

To summarise, people appeal colloquially to the experience of time passing on a day-to-day basis, and the question of whether time does in fact pass is a contentious one within philosophy. Shardlow et al. found that people do, by and large, think that they experience time passing, but in studies such as those of Lee et al. it has been difficult to find statements that convincingly capture whether people *believe* that time is passing and how such beliefs about time passing cohere with other beliefs about time.[19]

---

17 Lee et al. 2022.

18 The two subpopulations differed to the degree that people in each take the present moment to be objectively privileged.

19 Shardlow et al 2021; Lee et al. 2022.

4.3 *Nunc fluens*: Philosophy of Mind

To the extent that we do think that time passes, why do we do so? One idea expressed within this very volume (e.g., Koloska) and also by several philosophers, is that there is a significant role for memory in this story. For example, Mellor says that we come to believe that time passes because of how our memories accumulate over time.[20] We remember the past, but not the future, and at a later time we can remember more than we could remember at an earlier time—because there are now more experiences to remember, including previous episodes of recollecting—and, taken together, this may contribute to a sense in which we seem to be moving from the past and towards the future. In a similar vein, Velleman suggests that our sense of time as passing is connected to the way we think of ourselves as occupying distinct experiential perspectives over time, especially within the context of experiential memory (and imagination).[21]

While many people have been broadly sympathetic to the idea that memory plays *a* role in how we think of time as directional, and the past as fixed, for some, Mellor's suggestion is unable to provide the whole story regarding time passing. For those theorists who believe that we *experience* time as passing, and that we do so in almost every waking moment,[22] an appeal to memory can seem out of place and overly complex—insofar as it is thought that our experience of time as passing is present even when we are not actively recollecting, and seemingly requires no reflection on the contents of memories. For these theorists, even feeling a cool breeze on one's face may be sufficient for experiencing time as passing.[23]

To appreciate the contrast being drawn here, between inferring that some period of time has elapsed based on memory, and some other experience of time as passing, consider Koloska's presentation of the Companions of the Cave, and what is thought to be lacking for these companions. In this case, upon their awakening, the youths are said to be unaware of how much time has elapsed. Absent of any experience and memory for the period that they have been kept in stasis, that which we typically use to judge the duration of elapsed periods of time is lacking. As the Companions of the Cave have not been wakefully conscious, they do not have the availability of memory to help them to judge how much time has elapsed since they entered the cave. The case is different for those who may simply dwell in a cave for some period of time. For example, the French geologist Michel Siffre spent two months in a cave in 1962, without his watch or any other indicators of

20 Mellor 1998, 122.

21 Velleman 2006.

22 See, e.g., O'Shaughnessy 2000, 61.

23 See, e.g., Paul 2010.

time. Siffre later described losing track of the minutes and hours to such an extent that he believed he had only been in the cave for around one month, when it had in fact been two. The inaccurate estimate plausibly results from the fact that we typically depend on a wide variety of external indicators when judging the durations of elapsed periods of time—even in those cases where we have relevant memories to draw upon. Hence, there was, in Siffre's case, a sense in which he had a reduced awareness of how much time had elapsed, and his resulting estimate was inaccurate, though he was still able to make a somewhat reasonable estimate, in no small part because his memory for the periods of time spent in the cave was relatively intact. This is *a* difference between the case of Siffre and that of the Companions, but it is not the only difference between the two. Plausibly, over and above being able to make retrospective estimates of how much time had elapsed, while Siffre was wakefully conscious in the cave, he still enjoyed an ongoing experience of time as passing. The Companions of the Cave, by contrast, lacked such ongoing experience. Their lack, with regard to time consciousness, was therefore twofold: they did not have wakefully conscious experience, and hence the experience of time passing, while in stasis, and they did not have any memories to appeal to in order to estimate how long they had been in the cave.

Among theorists who are interested in articulating and accounting for our incessant experience of time as passing, it is common not to appeal to memory but to instead identify something in perceptual experience that corresponds to the apparent flow of time. This is something we find in the work of Prosser, who suggests that it is how we perceive objects persisting over time and persisting through change, which is responsible for time seeming to pass.[24] Broadly, the idea is that reflection on our experience of objects as persisting over time highlights a distinctive aspect of our phenomenology: a kind of dynamic and flowy character to the experience of objects undergoing motion and change. Prosser suggests that this flowy/dynamic character of change/motion experience is represented in experience, which we associate with time seeming to pass. Yet this has proved controversial, not least with those philosophers who maintain that, in a strict sense, there is no experience of time passing. For one example, Hoerl claims that, strictly speaking, time doesn't *seem* to pass; when we say that it does, we're actually making an error.[25] With reference to proposals such as Prosser's, Hoerl grants that there is an experienced difference between perceiving something moving and inferring on the basis of perception that something has moved. That is, there's a difference between perceptible motion and change, and perceiving something's being one way whilst

24 Prosser 2016.
25 Hoerl 2014.

recalling it being another. Yet, for Hoerl, that which is present in the former case, and absent in the latter, is *merely* perceptible motion/change, and not an experience of time itself being some way—i.e., not an experience of time as passing. Hoerl reasons that, insofar as we think that we experience time passing, we are actually making a mistake and simply appealing to the perception of motion/change; this is erroneously taken to be some experience of time itself passing. The latter—the apparent experience of time passing—is, for Hoerl, not something that we actually enjoy.

Why recount this philosophical dispute here? There are two reasons. First, I hope that it is of interest to recognise the complexity of the issues we are faced with when we turn to what might have seemed to be a rather innocent and uncontroversial issue, regarding the *nunc fluens*. In contemporary Western Philosophy, there is disagreement over the import of developments in physics over the past century and whether these commit us to denying that time passes. There is disagreement over the import of our experience of time when it comes to discussions of the nature of time. There is disagreement over what aspect of our experience leads us to claim that time passes, and there is even disagreement concerning whether or not we do experience time as passing.

The second reason for recounting this dispute is to illustrate how the state of the debate in this isolated corner of contemporary Western Philosophy is facing the same issues Amir identifies in his discussion of the history of Islamic Thought. Amir's discussion presents us with a delicate dialectical manoeuvre, where one can grant that if one sees the Prophet in a dream, the content of the dream is true, while also maintaining that, if what seems to be the Prophet, in the dream, says anything which contradicts established principles, then the dream cannot be true. These two seemingly contradictory claims are made consistent by holding that, in the latter case, the dreamer either misunderstood or misremembered the Prophet's words, or else they did not see the Prophet at all, but *only thought so*. In this case, a deflationary explanation is provided, granting the dream-reporter some limited authority in how they recount their dream experience, while providing some explanation of how they are, in fact, mistaken about what they thought they had experienced. By weakening the authority of the dream-reporter, concerning the content of the dream, one can allow for dream-reports of what is (mistakenly) believed to be the Prophet, without granting that these are in fact dreams of the Prophet, and hence without granting that the content is true.

With regards to the *nunc fluens*, we can observe contemporary philosophers making similar dialectical moves to those Amir identifies. In this context, theorists wish to grant that people regularly express experiencing time passing,[26] while denying that they really enjoy any such experience. This is done by weakening the authority of the subject making the experiential report. It is granted that there is an aspect of experience being appealed to, when subjects report experiencing time as passing, just as there may be an aspect of one's dream experience being appealed to in supposed dream reports of the Prophet. And yet, the subject is also said to be making an error, because when the experience is accurately articulated, the subject is not said to be experiencing temporal passage, but something else which they mistake for the experience of time passing—just as it has been claimed for dreams. Hence, we can see how what might have appeared uncontroversial—that we experience time passing—has become disputed in recent philosophy, and some of the dialectical moves underwriting this dispute mirror those employed in the history of Islamic Thought.

5 *Nunc Differens*: The Experienced Present, the Visual, and the Temporal

So much for the idea of time passing. In contemporary philosophy, there is also much discussion of what Koloska refers to as the 'horizon;' the vantage point we occupy in and upon time in ongoing experience. Indeed, there has been significant debate over the very issue of what this horizon is—i.e., whether it is best thought of as extensionless, or a *nunc differens* (i.e., a temporally extended present)—mirroring issues we encountered in the discussion of Ibn Sīnā. In this philosophical debate, some theories are substantially influenced by the tendency to focus on visual experience, and, in explaining how we experience temporal phenomena over time, some theorists have also attributed a significant role to memory. Since vision and memory are prominent themes in the present volume, I trust that the structure of this debate, and the broad lessons that can be drawn from it, will be of interest.

An Augustinian line of reasoning is often taken to support rejecting the notion of a *nunc differens*—understood as a temporally extended present.[27] Augustine argues that in an interval of any duration, there must be earlier and later parts; hence, if we take the present to have duration, we will be forced to accept that within that duration, some earlier part will be past relative to some later part, and,

26 In line with the findings of Shardlow et al. 2021.

27 See Augustine's *Confessions*, Book XI.

therefore, the whole duration cannot be present. This issue will reoccur for any positive duration and, the suggestion goes, to avoid it, we must grant that the present is strictly durationless. Regardless of the merits of this reasoning, some have been sufficiently persuaded by it to suppose that it applies to time itself, and also to the experience of time: that the experienced present must be strictly instantaneous. Thus, our experience of time is taken, by such theorists, to be best modelled on the fleeting present of Ṭarafa's poetry, rather than the infinite present exemplified by the 7th to the 10th Century Islamic architecture Kol discusses.

That theorists have been willing to grant that the experienced present is strictly instantaneous might seem surprising. If this is so, how is it that we experience temporally extended phenomena such as motion/change? And how is it that we measure the duration of experienced events, such as the duration of a blinking light, or of a piercing sound? Augustine's answer appeals to memory. Given his commitment to an instantaneous present, he reasons that the measuring of the duration of an event is in memory; that the experience of any interval of time fundamentally depends upon memory.

The legacy of Augustine's reasoning lives on in some contemporary accounts of temporal experience, which look to account for our experience of temporal phenomena through an analogy with cinematic representation.[28] According to proponents of such an account, our stream of consciousness over time consists of a series of extensionless (or very brief) snapshots, each of which presents a momentary state of affairs—like static images. While no single snapshot is sufficient to present movement or change, the occurrence of successive snapshots in quick succession, together with the memory of immediately previous snapshots, is said to be sufficient to account for the rich experience we take ourselves to have of objects moving and changing, and events unfolding in the world around us. Thus, with a fundamental role credited to memory, an instantaneous experiential horizon in perceptual experience is maintained.

Such a use of an analogy with cinematic representation is controversial. Part of this controversy derives from how the cinematic analogy seems ill-placed when applied to non-visual sensory modalities; I'll return to this point below. Of more direct interest is what we may sacrifice when we take the experienced present to be instantaneous, conceiving of our experience over time in terms of a series of such instantaneous presentations. Granted, it is typically taken to be uncontroversial that *seeing* a rapid succession of static images *can* result in an experience of motion and change. Reels of film consist of static snapshots, and when presented in quick succession, the subjects depicted are experienced by an audience as dynamic, as

---

28 See, e.g., Chuard 2011, 2017.

objects moving and undergoing change. However, the idea that it is problematic to suppose that our own perceptions are similarly akin to a series of static snapshots has a long intellectual history, and can be traced at least as far back as Reid's discussion of Locke.

In Locke's *Essay Concerning Human Understanding*, he suggests that a single idea, presenting an object as occupying distinct locations, is not sufficient for an idea of succession; he claims that we only arrive at an idea of succession through having a succession of qualitatively different individual ideas that we are reflectively aware of.[29] Reid charges Locke with a problematic ambiguity when making his case for the role of reflection in deriving our ideas of duration and succession.[30] He draws attention to how, on one interpretation, which we can call the perceptual reading, Locke treats reflection as though it is structurally similar to sensory perception and is, as Locke says, "the perception of the operations of our own minds within us."[31] On another interpretation, which we can call the memory reading, Locke treats reflection as though it is structurally similar to memory, and is our capacity to remember things experienced previously.

On the perceptual reading, Reid charges Locke with providing no explanation of our awareness of succession. Because of the parallels between reflection and sensory perception, any problem with sensorially perceiving succession should present a structurally identical problem with becoming reflectively 'perceptually' aware of succession; any plausible solution at the level of reflection should also serve as a solution at the level of sensory perception. If sensory perception as of an object at more than one spatial position isn't sufficient for the idea of succession, reflection on ideas as of objects at more than one spatial position plausibly isn't sufficient either. Thus, taking our perceptual experiences to be a series of static presentations, by analogy with cinematic representation, provides no explanatory purchase and simply pushes the explanatory project one step further. On the memory reading, Reid says that it is misleading to claim that we experience succession; Reid says that "it is only by the aid of memory that we discern motion, or any succession whatsoever."[32] Hence, on the memory reading, there could be no awareness of succession without the twinned contributions of sensory perception and memory – thus, we do not *perceive* motion/change in any robust sense, though we may become inferentially aware of it. Reid also provides an independent route to this conclusion, based on the assumption that the operations of sensory percep-

29 Locke 1690.
30 Reid 1785.
31 Locke 1690, II.i.4.
32 Reid 1785, 271.

tion and reflection, "are confined to the present point of time, and [that] there can be no succession in a point of time."[33]

As a result of problems such as those identified by Reid, it has become more common in contemporary philosophy to appeal to an extended perceptual present in order to account for our experience of motion and change—this is typically referred to as the 'specious present', the terminology coming from Kelly via the more well-known William James.[34] This view, and the motivation in its favour, is well brought out through the contrast with Reid. Reid accepted that if we can perceive motion, then the contents of perception must span a temporal interval, but, since he rejected the latter, he accepted the denial of the former. On the contrary, Kelly, accepting the former—i.e., that we experience motion and change—was thereby willing to embrace the latter. In doing so, Kelly distinguishes between the 'present', which we have a conception of from reflection on experience, which has duration, and an abstract conception of 'present', a sense which is without duration.[35] Over the Twentieth Century, it has since become commonplace in Western Philosophy to take the specious present, a *nunc differens*, to be the present of experience, the locus of our vantage point in and on time.

In contemporary debates, as previously mentioned and by way of summary, some theorists continue to make use of the cinematic analogy, suggesting that a series of perceptions of static states of affairs, together with memories of previous such perceptions, is sufficient to account for how our experience strikes us—i.e., that there is no more to our experiences of motion/change than the perception of one static state of affairs and memories of others. Other theorists have made partial use of the cinematic analogy, granting that such an austere model is insufficient to account for the richness of our experiential lives (and especially our experiences of motion and change), while trying to maintain that we can explain our perception over time in terms of slightly more complicated snapshots, such as snapshots with 'motion-like vectors'.[36] Others again maintain that the cinematic analogy is entirely misguided, and that the present of experience is no snapshot, but must be temporally extended. Rather than weighing in on the nuances of this debate, before ending this discussion of the experienced present, it is worth simply reflecting on the use of the cinematic analogy.[37]

33 Reid 1785, 270.

34 Kelly 1882, James 1890.

35 If we assume that '*the* present' is, as a matter of metaphysical fact, durationless, then the experienced present is specious insofar as some duration is given as being present—hence its moniker.

36 See, e.g., Arstila 2018; Prosser 2016; Torrengo 2024.

37 See, e.g., McKenna 2021; Phillips 2010; Shardlow 2019.

The analogy with cinematic representation, when applied to our perceptual experience over time, is seemingly enabled by the tendency to focus on vision as the default case of perceptual experience, supposing that what can be said about vision can also be said about other sensory modalities. Theorists have modelled the structure of perceptual experience over time on a very familiar form of visual representation—a succession of static snapshots. Among the general things that may be said by way of a critique of such views, we might wonder whether we would have any temptation to support such a view if our starting point was, for example, auditory rather than visual experience. After all, in addition to change plausibly being *seen*—as we observe the pulsing of colour in a cuttlefish's mantle—we typically suppose that change can be heard in the rising of a melody, smelled in a growing stench, tasted in a subsiding flavour, and felt in bodily sensation as pressure is increased on one's skin. However familiar we may be with static visual images, thinking of them as instantaneous presentations of a visual scene, it isn't at all obvious that we can make sense of instantaneous presentations of sounds, smells, or flavours. If we consider Ṭarafa's ability to make poignant our multisensory, embodied experience of time, as presented by Aweida, we may become less satisfied with the tendency to focus on visual experience. All of this is just to say that we can be misled by focusing predominantly on the visual, and our theorising—in philosophy, and across various fields—may benefit if we give greater consideration to the likes of the auditory, tactual, and others.

6 Concluding Remarks

This paper has been a reflection on themes concerning time and vision—some implicit, and some explicit—running through the papers collected in this volume, through the lens of contemporary Western Philosophy. Some of the more explicit themes concern the passing of time and 'the now' of experience, these being themes that have been at the intersection of Ancient Greek Philosophy and Islamic Thought since al-Kindī and Ibn Sīnā, with each being influenced by Aristotle's discussion of such issues. The purpose of the brief overview provided herein, about how these themes are dissected and discussed in contemporary Western Philosophy, has been to shed light on some of the complexities in our conceptions of time—and of our experience of time—that may be disguised by some of the common but imprecise ways in which we typically talk about these topics. I have also, but only fleetingly, outlined how some of our claims about time, and our temporal experience, are informed by thinking about distinctly visual experience, rather than other sensory modalities. There is, of course, much more that could be said, both about the collected papers and the relevant philosophy, but my hope is that the brief overview of the varied contemporary debates on this topic will help to reveal possible avenues for interpretation and further discussion for those engaged in Islamic studies, art history, or museology while focused on issues of time and vision.

Bibliography

Adamson, Peter (2024), "al-Kindī." *The Stanford Encyclopedia of Philosophy*, edited by Edward Zalta and Uri Nodelman. https://plato.stanford.edu/archives/sum2024/entries/al-kindi (last accessed on October 30, 2025).

al-Rāzī, Fakhr al-dīn, *al-Mabāhith al-mashriqīyya*, vol. 1. Hydarabad: Majlis dā'irat al-ma'ārif, 1924/5.

Anonymous [E. Robert Kelly] (1882), *The Alternative: A Study in Psychology*. London: Macmillan and Co.

Aristotle, *Physics*. In *The Complete Works of Aristotle*, edited by Jonathan Barnes. Princeton, NJ: Princeton University Press, 1984.

Arstila, Valtteri (2018), "Temporal Experiences Without the Specious Present." *Australasian Journal of Philosophy* 96, 287–302.

Augustine of Hippo (1838), *Confessions of St. Augustine*, translated by Edward B. Pusey, London: J. H. Parker.

Callender, Craig (2017), *What makes time special?* Oxford: Oxford University Press.

Chuard, Philippe (2011), "Temporal Experiences and Their Parts." *Philosophers' Imprint* 11: article 11, 1–28.

Chuard, Philippe (2017), "The Snapshot Conception of Temporal Experience." In *The Routledge Handbook of Philosophy of Temporal Experience*, edited by Ian Phillips. London: Routledge, 121–132.

Conee, Earl, and Theodore Sider (2014), *Riddles of Existence: A Guided Tour of Metaphysics*, 2nd ed. Oxford: Oxford University Press.

Endress, Gerhard (1997), "The Circle of al-Kindi." In *The Ancient Tradition in Christian and Islamic Hellenism*, edited by Gerhard Endress and Remke Kruk. Leiden: Research School CNWS, 43–76.

Gödel, Kurt (1949/1990), "A remark about the relationship between relativity theory and idealistic philosophy." In *Kurt Gödel – Collected Works, vol. II*, edited by Solomon Feferman. Oxford: Oxford University Press, 202–207.

Hoerl, Christoph (2014), "Do We (Seem to) Perceive Passage?" *Philosophical Explorations* 17, 188–202.

James, William (1890/1983), *The Principles of Psychology*. Cambridge, MA: Harvard University Press.

Knobe, Joshua, and Shaun Nichols (2008), "An experimental Philosophy Manifesto." In *Experimental Philosophy*, edited by Joshua Knobe and Shaun Nichols. New York: Oxford University Press, 3–14.

Kretzmann, Norman (1976), "Time Exists – but Hardly, or Obscurely (Physics IV, 10, 217b29–218a33)." *The Aristotelian Society Supplementary* 50, 91–114.

Lammer, Andreas (2026), "Time and Modality? Avicenna's Account Vis-À-Vis the Eternity of the World." In *The Routledge Companion to Philosophy of Time*, edited by Nina Emery. New York: Routledge, 36–47.

Lammer, Andreas (2021), "Now Is Not the Time: Revisiting Avicenna's Account of the Now." In *Oxford Studies in Medieval Philosophy* Volume 9, edited by Robert Pasnau. Oxford: Oxford University Press, 77–146.

Le Poidevin, Robin (2007), *The Images of Time*. Oxford: Oxford University Press.

Lee, Ruth, Jack Shardlow, Christoph Hoerl, Patrick O'Connor, Alison Fernandes, and Teresa McCormack (2022), "Toward an Account of Intuitive Time." *Cognitive Science* 46: e13166. https://pubmed.ncbi.nlm.nih.gov/35731904 (last accessed on October 30, 2025).
Locke, John (1690/1975), *An Essay concerning Human Understanding*, edited by Peter Nidditch. Oxford: Oxford University Press.
Loux, Michael, and Dean Zimmerman (2005), "Introduction." In *Oxford Handbook of Metaphysics*, edited by Michael Loux and Dean Zimmerman. Oxford: Oxford University Press, 1–8.
Maudlin, Tim (2002), "Remarks on the passing of Time." *Proceedings of the Aristotelian Society* 102, 237–252.
McGinnis, Jon (1999), "Ibn Sīnā on the Now." *American Catholic Philosophical Quarterly* 73, 73–106.
McKenna, Camden (2021), "Don't Go Chasing Waterfalls: Motion Aftereffects and the Dynamic Snapshot Theory of Temporal Experience." *Review of Philosophy and Psychology* 12, 825–845.
Mellor, David Hugh (1998), *Real Time II*. London: Routledge.
O'Shaughnessy, Brian (2000), *Consciousness and the World*. Oxford: Oxford University Press.
Paul, Laurie (2010), "Temporal Experience." *Journal of Philosophy* CVII, 333 –359.
Phillips, Ian (2010), "Perceiving Temporal Properties." *European Journal of Philosophy* 18, 176–202.
Prosser, Simon (2016), *Experiencing Time*. Oxford: Oxford University Press.
Reid, Thomas (1785/2002), *Essays on the Intellectual Powers of Man*, edited by Derek Brookes and Knud Haakonssen. Edinburgh: Edinburgh University Press.
Schlesinger, George (1980), *Aspects of Time*. Indianapolis: Hackett.
Shardlow, Jack (2019), "Minima Sensibilia: Against the Dynamic Snapshot Model of Temporal Experience." *European Journal of Philosophy* 27, 741–757.
Shardlow, Jack, Ruth Lee, Teresa McCormack, Alison Fernandes, Patrick Burns, and Christoph Hoerl (2021), "Exploring people's beliefs about the experience of time." *Synthese* 198, 10709–10731.
Shayegan, Yegane (1986), *Avicenna on Time*. PhD dissertation, Harvard University.
Sorabji, Richard (1983), *Time, Creation and the Continuum. Theories in Antiquity and the Early Middle Ages*. London, Ithaca: Duckworth/Cornell University Press.
Torrengo, Giuliano (2024), *Temporal Experience: The Atomist Dynamic Model*. New York: Oxford University Press.
Velleman, J. David (2006), "So It Goes." *The Amherst Lecture in Philos*ophy 1, 1–23.
Zimmerman, Dean (2008), "The Privileged Present: Defending an 'A-theory' of Time." In *Contemporary Debates in Metaphysics*, edited by Theodore Sider, John Hawthorne, and Dean Zimmerman. Oxford: Blackwell Publishing, 211–225.

Contributors

Or Amir is a Senior Lecturer at the Department of Islamic and Middle Eastern Studies at the Hebrew University of Jerusalem.

Ula Aweida is a Postdoctoral Researcher in the ERC research group VISIONIS – Visuality in the Qur'an and Early Islam, Jerusalem.

Filiz Tütüncü Çağlar is a Postdoctoral Research Fellow at EUME – Forum Transregionale Studien, Berlin.

Yunus Hentschel is a Postdoctoral Researcher in the ERC research group VISIONIS – Visuality in the Qur'an and Early Islam, Jerusalem.

Inbal Kol is a Doctoral Fellow in the ERC research group VISIONIS – Visuality in the Qur'an and Early Islam, and a Ph.D. student in the Honors Program in the Humanities at the Hebrew University of Jerusalem.

Hannelies Koloska is a Senior Lecturer at the Department of Comparative Religion at the Hebrew University of Jerusalem and the Principal Investigator (PI) of the ERC research group VISIONIS – Visuality in the Qur'an and Early Islam.

Yehonatan Yahav is a Postdoctoral Researcher in the ERC research group VISIONIS – Visuality in the Qur'an and Early Islam, Jerusalem.

Jack Shardlow is a Postdoctoral Researcher at the Department of Philosophy at the University of Liverpool.

Contributors

Name Index

Subject Index

 | https://doi.org/10.1515/9783112240038-012

The following volumes have been published in this series:

Volume 2
Detel, Wolfgang. *Subjektive und objektive Zeit: Aristoteles und die moderne Zeit-Theorie*. Berlin/Boston: De Gruyter, 2021.

Volume 3
Singer, P. N. *Time for the Ancients: Measurement, Theory, Experience*. Berlin/Boston: De Gruyter, 2022.

Volume 4
Gertzen, Thomas L. *Aber die Zeit fürchtet die Pyramiden: Die Wissenschaften vom Alten Orient und die zeitliche Dimension von Kulturgeschichte*. Berlin/Boston: De Gruyter, 2022.

Volume 6
Zachhuber, Johannes. *Time and Soul: From Aristotle to St. Augustine*. Berlin/Boston: De Gruyter, 2022.

Volume 7
Golitsis, Pantelis. *Damascius' Philosophy of Time*. Berlin/Boston: De Gruyter, 2023.

Volume 8
Defaux, Olivier. *La Table des rois: Contribution à l'histoire textuelle des ›Tables faciles‹ de Ptolémée*. Berlin/Boston: De Gruyter, 2023.

Volume 9
Fischer, Julia (ed.). *Zwiegespräche über die Zeit: Dialoge in der Berlin-Brandenburgischen Akademie der Wissenschaften aus Anlass des sechzigsten Geburtstags von Christoph Markschies*. Berlin/Boston: De Gruyter, 2024.

Volume 10
Walter, Anke (ed.). *The Temporality of Festivals: Approaches to Festive Time in Ancient Babylon, Greece, Rome, and Medieval China*. Berlin/Boston: De Gruyter, 2024.

Volume 11
Ben Sasson, Menahem. *Time and Revelation in the Vision of Daniel from the St. Petersburg Collection*. Berlin/Boston: De Gruyter, 2026.

Volume 12
Sieroka, Norman. *Zeit-Hören: Erfahrungen, Taktungen, Musik*. Berlin/Boston: De Gruyter, 2024.

Volume 13
Birk, Ralph/Coulon, Laurent (eds.). *The Thebaid in Times of Crisis: Revolt and Response in Ptolemaic Egypt*. Berlin/Boston: De Gruyter, 2025.

Volume 14
Pallavidini, Marta. *(A)synchronic (Re)actions: Crises and Their Perception in Hittite History*. Berlin/Boston: De Gruyter, 2025.

Volume 15
Nosch, Marie-Louise Bech. *Time and Textiles in Ancient Greece*. Berlin/Boston: De Gruyter, 2025.

Volume 16
Klinger, Jörg. *Das Erfassen von Zeit im Kontext der Vergangenheit*. Berlin/Boston: De Gruyter, 2026.

Volume 17
Zachhuber, Johannes. *Time and History in Denis Pétau. Philosophy, Science, and Religion in Early Modern France*. Berlin/Boston: De Gruyter, 2026.

Volume 18
Ossendrijver, Mathieu. *Conceptions of Cyclicity in Babylonian and Greco-Roman Scholarship*. Berlin/Boston: De Gruyter, 2025.

Volume 19
Schumacher, Lydia. *From Eternal to Everlasting: God and Time in Franciscan Thought*. Berlin/Boston: De Gruyter, 2026.

Volume 20
Wiedemann, Felix. *The Modern Hammurapi: An Old Babylonian King in Imperial Germany*. Berlin/Boston: De Gruyter, 2026.

Volume 21
Niehoff, Maren R./Markschies, Christoph (eds.). *Aspects of Time in Jewish and Christian Exegesis*. Berlin/Boston: De Gruyter, 2026.

Volume 22

Korobili, Giouli/Miller, Kassandra/van der Eijk, Philip (eds.). *Synchronizing the Body in Ancient Medicine and Philosophy*. Berlin/Boston: De Gruyter, 2026.

Volume 23

Kraft, András. *Time in Byzantine Apocalyptica*. Berlin/Boston: De Gruyter, 2026.

www.ingramcontent.com/pod-product-compliance
Lightning Source LLC
LaVergne TN
LVHW020055110826
845155LV00022B/84

* 9 7 8 3 1 1 2 2 4 0 0 2 1 *